Studies in German Jewish History

Peter D. G. Brown, SUNY New Paltz
General Editor

Vol. 7

PETER LANG

Oxford · Bern · Berlin · Bruxelles · Frankfurt am Main · New York · Wien

Bram Mertens

Dark Images, Secret Hints

Benjamin, Scholem, Molitor and the
Jewish Tradition

PETER LANG

Oxford · Bern · Berlin · Bruxelles · Frankfurt am Main · New York · Wien

Bibliographic information published by Die Deutsche Bibliothek
Die Deutsche Bibliothek lists this publication in the Deutsche Nationalbibliografie;
detailed bibliographic data is available on the Internet at ‹http://dnb.ddb.de›.

British Library and Library of Congress Cataloguing-in-Publication Data:
A catalogue record for this book is available from *The British Library,* Great Britain,
and from *The Library of Congress,* USA

Cover photo by Henry Maitek, Cologne, of eruve matzo plate (1770),
Alsatian Museum, Strasbourg
Cover design: Thomas Jaberg, Peter Lang AG

ISSN 1079-2384
ISBN 978-3-03-910293-8
US-ISBN 978-0-8204-7219-5

© Peter Lang AG, European Academic Publishers, Bern 2007
Hochfeldstrasse 32, Postfach 746, CH-3000 Bern 9, Switzerland
info@peterlang.com, www.peterlang.com, www.peterlang.net

Printed in Germany

Preamble

Es ist dem philosophischen Schrifttum eigen, mit jeder Wendung von neuem vor der Frage der Darstellung zu stehen. Zwar wird es in seiner abgeschlossenen Gestalt Lehre sein, solche Abgeschlossenheit ihm zu leihen aber liegt nicht in der Gewalt des bloßen Denkens.

————— W. Benjamin, Ursprung des deutschen Trauerspiels.

Eine Erklärung, wie sie einer Schrift in einer Vorrede nach der Gewohnheit vorausgeschickt wird – über den Zweck, den der Verfasser sich in ihr vorgesetzt, sowie über die Veranlassungen und das Verhältnis, worin er sie zu anderen früheren oder gleichzeitigen Behandlungen desselben Gegenstandes zu stehen glaubt –, scheint bei einer philosophischen Schrift nicht nur überflüssig, sondern um der Natur der Sache willen sogar unpassend und zweckwidrig zu sein. Denn wie und was von Philosophie in einer Vorrede zu sagen schicklich wäre – etwa eine historische Angabe der Tendenz und des Standpunkts, des allgemeinen Inhalts und der Resultate, eine Verbindung von hin und her sprechenden Behauptungen und Versicherungen über das Wahre –, kann nicht für die Art und Weise gelten, in der die philosophische Wahrheit darzustellen sei.

————— G.W.F. Hegel, Phänomenologie des Geistes.

Deux infinis. Milieu.
Quand on lit trop vite ou trop doucement, on n'entend rien.

————— B. Pascal, *Pensées*.

Scripta, qua fragmenta s[ive] non extantes, cogitationibus in statu nascendi similes sunt […]. Quod in imaginibus, est in lingua.

————— P. Atticus, *Rhetorica*.

Contents

Acknowledgements

This book has been a fair while in the making, and most of the people on the list of 'those without whom' can all consider themselves adoptive parents of this little volume, in some way or another. It was conceived, quite illicitly, during a few beautifully grey and rainy evenings in Brussels with Lieven De Cauter, with the words 'somebody ought to…' The book has had its fair share of midwives, all of whom have been so kind as to grant me the benefit of their wisdom and the pleasure of their company. I am indebted to Steve Giles and Josephine Guy for their endless patience and support in guiding this volume all the way from conception to fruition, and of course to Seth Kunin for his expert advice, his time and his invaluable help in bringing this book to a general readership. I also gratefully acknowledge the generous assistance of the Conference of University Teachers of German and the German Department at Nottingham University in the publication of this book.

Thanks to J. Manuel Alonso, Jeroen Eggermont, Ben Everitt, Wim Maris and Karl Wilds, I was able to keep a little bit of sanity tucked away somewhere during all these years. More fundamental than instrumental is my gratitude to Flor and Marleen, who have supported me unconditionally in everything I have undertaken, no matter how hare-brained and ill-advised. Finally, I could not even begin to describe the debt or gratitude I owe to Eleanor, who has gracefully put up with my affair with Walter over the past five years. I promise I will stop seeing him, for a while…

——— B.M., Nottingham 2006.

Abbreviations

Briefe   Walter Benjamin, *Briefe*, 2 vols., edited by Gershom Scholem and Theodor W. Adorno, second edition (Frankfurt am Main: Suhrkamp, 1973).

GB   Walter Benjamin, *Gesammelte Briefe*, 6 vols., edited by Christoph Gödde and Henri Lonitz, (Frankfurt am Main: Suhrkamp, 1995–2000).

GF   Gershom Scholem, *Walter Benjamin: die Geschichte einer Freundschaft* (Frankfurt am Main: Suhrkamp, 1975).

M   Franz Joseph Molitor, *Philosophie der Geschichte oder über die Tradition in dem alten Bunde und ihre Beziehung zur Kirche des Neuen Bundes. Mit vorzüglicher Rücksicht auf die Kabbalah*, first edition, 4 vols. (Frankfurt am Main/Münster: Hermann/Theissing, 1827–1853).

SB   Gerschom Scholem, *Briefe*, edited by Itta Shedletzky, 3 vols. (München: Beck, 1994–1999).

TB   Gerschom Scholem, *Tagebücher nebst Aufsätzen und Entwürfen bis 1923*, edited by Karlfried Gründer und Friedrich Niewöhner, 2 vols. (Frankfurt am Main: Jüdischer Verlag, 1995–2000).

VBJ   Gershom Scholem, *Von Berlin nach Jerusalem: Jugenderinnerungen*, translated by Michael Brocke and Andrea Schatz (Frankfurt am Main: Suhrkamp, 1997).

Introduction

Trauernder, nah mir und doch stets verborgen
Nur die Berufung dich am Leben hält,
Doch Schweigst du. Auf dein Schweigen ist die Welt
Gebaut. Die Trauer ist der ewige Morgen,

In dem du stehst. Daß du noch nicht gestorben,
das ist das Wunder, das mich überfällt.
Du bist. Aus deiner tiefen Stille quellt
Die Frage, die dich mir, mich dir geworben.

Du warst bei mir in all den schweren Tagen
und bist doch fern bei dem, der dich besaß.
Was mich bewegt, muß stumm ich in mir tragen.

Denn was an dir geschieht, hat solches Maß
der Größe, daß die Worte, die ich finde,
nicht rein genug sind. Drum ist Sprechen Sünde.

This poem was written by Gershom Scholem in July 1918 on the occasion of Benjamin's twenty-sixth birthday.[1] It bears witness to a maturity and a complexity of critical insight into Benjamin, both as a person and as a writer, the like of which would not often be seen again. With the notable exception, perhaps, of Theodor Wiesengrund Adorno, who opened his preface of the first edition of Benjamin's correspondence with the words: 'Walter Benjamins Person war von Anbeginn derart Medium des Werkes, sein Glück hatte er so sehr an seinem Geist, daß, was immer sonst Unmittelbarkeit des Lebens heißt, gebrochen wurde.'[2] Both Scholem and Adorno paint a picture of a man they knew intimately for many years, but who never ceased to give the impression that the real Walter Benjamin was perpetually hidden behind the almost invisible mask of his meticulous prose. It is therefore hardly surprising that critics and scholars today continue to be fascinated by Benjamin's extraordinary biography and that his persona looms large over most explorations of his work. It is not surprising, but nevertheless acutely paradoxical, since Benjamin as an author quite consciously sought to conceal his personality *in* his writing, in the double sense of the word. Thus he did indeed become the medium of a work, which was both intensely personal and fundamentally disembodied. To put it in a simple formula, without him his texts would obviously not exist, yet he wrote them in such a way as to suggest that he himself never existed. This paradox pervades Benjamin's work in many different guises, from the themes and the content of his texts to their style and composition and even the graphology of their author's handwriting, which Benjamin claimed 'sei vor allem darauf angelegt, nichts merken zu lassen' (*Briefe*, 14).

In his personal life, Benjamin was by all accounts a quiet, reserved and exceptionally courteous man who maintained a 'natürliche Distanz' even from people he had known for years.[3] Throughout his work, too, Benjamin made a virtue out of this distance, which appears to have been his second nature. As the accomplished stylist that he unquestionably was, Benjamin even – modestly – attributed the superior aesthetic quality of his writing to the fact that he never used the word 'I':

> Wenn ich ein besseres Deutsch schreibe als die meisten Schriftsteller meiner Generation, so verdanke ich das zum guten Teil der zwanzigjährigen Beobachtung einer einzigen Regel. Sie lautet: das Wort 'Ich' nie zu gebrauchen, außer in den Briefen. Die Ausnahmen, die ich mir von dieser Vorschrift gestattet habe, ließen sich zählen.[4]

This passage from *Berliner Chronik* is also an excellent illustration of the composition of Benjamin's *Gesammelte Schriften*, which most scholars take as their source text. Thanks to this magnificent edition of Rolf Tiedemann and Hermann Schweppenhäuser, we have before us not only all of Benjamin's published works, but also a formidable collection of drafts, fragments, notes and letters. *Berliner Chronik*, for instance, is one of Benjamin's many 'esoteric' texts, manuscripts that remained unpublished during Benjamin's lifetime and were known only by a small circle of friends, invariably including Gershom Scholem and later also Theodor Adorno and Gretel Karplus. As was often the case, these esoteric texts formed the basis of his exoteric writings which, from 1910 to 1940, were published in books, journals, newspapers or even as radio talks, and which actually constitute the minor part of the 7,854 pages that comprise the *Gesammelte Schriften*. Composed in 1932, the fragmentary and abortive *Berliner Chronik* thus lay at the origin of the series of vignettes known as *Berliner Kindheit um Neunzehnhundert*, which was published in newspapers, feuilletons and periodicals between 1932 and 1938. Typically, Benjamin's unpublished notes and manuscripts are significantly more open and direct than his published work, and it is not a rare occurrence to find certain passages rephrased, bowdlerised or even excised to mask their initial candour. The passage from *Berliner Chronik* is no different. This rare moment when Benjamin the author allows himself to become visible through the text is also a brief one, as, true to his own 'only rule', this confessional passage is left out entirely from the published version, *Berliner Kindheit*. The 'I' who narrates its apparently private stories is not Benjamin's innermost, personal voice, but rather that of pre-pubescent Berliner bourgeois everyman, and the stories are perfect examples of the highly-crafted, literary style which make their author the imperceptible medium of his work.

It was clearly not just in his private life that Benjamin found the very idea of directness problematic, his thought, too, frequently revolves around the problem of immediacy, and it soon becomes clear that this is primarily a question of epistemology and methodology to him. In this context, he thematises the concepts of immediacy, language, meaning, experience and the image in several of his texts, from early efforts such as *Über Sprache überhaupt und über die Sprache des Menschen* to his very last, *Über den Begriff der Geschichte*, and we will have ample opportunity to discuss these in the following pages. Yet as Benjamin addresses these questions, the form and structure of his writing itself becomes affected by the often paradoxical structure of his thought. To Benjamin, the direct and categorical statement was as problematic as the concept of immediacy itself, an insight derived from his understanding of the concept of truth, which we will discuss extensively in chapters four and five. He was profoundly aware that a certain kind of directness in language was not only unfruitful, he was convinced that it was also impossible, even, in a theological sense, sinful. This is why his work abounds with excursions, parables, delaying strategies and detours. Benjamin's prose is *verführerisch* in the purest sense of the word, it tempts the reader on a journey with an unknown destination, along winding roads and ancient yet familiar-looking paths, perpetually promising that the point is just around the corner. As he wrote in *Zentralpark*: 'Das Labyrinth ist der richtige Weg für den, der noch immer früh genug am Ziel ankommt.' (I, 668).

Scholem's suggestion that Benjamin's silence had its own eloquence forms the perfect counterpoint to his labyrinthine style and his eternal procrastinations. In all of his published works, and even in some of his unpublished texts, his notes and his letters, Benjamin appears to be holding something back, no doubt finding the idea of revealing his innermost thoughts slightly vulgar. Even though we now have a substantial and well-edited corpus of texts at our disposition, we are still frequently struck by the impression that there is more behind it all. Even in his personal correspondence, it is certainly often the case that Benjamin refuses to write about his thoughts and instead promises to reveal them in the immediacy of conversations: 'Von meiner Arbeit wäre zur Zeit vielleicht mehr zu sagen denn je aber freilich desto weniger zu schreiben.'[5] There are only sparse records of these conversations in which Benjamin promised to say so much more, if indeed he ever did. What remains for us is silence, on which, according to Scholem, his world his built. One such 'silence' in Benjamin's work is the Jewish tradition, and the question as to the sources of his knowledge regarding this tradition. Commentators are only rarely loath to admit that there is more than just an element of the Jewish tradition concealed within the work of Walter Benjamin, and indeed to deny it would be unforgiveably myopic. Even Adorno, of all people, felt compelled to write that 'ein theologisches Modell, die Tradition der jüdischen, zumal mystischen Bibelauslegung [in seiner Methode] nicht zu verkennen [ist]'.[6] But for all these concessions, a serious study of the sources of Benjamin's Judaism still remains to be written: the question of the existence and the nature of Benjamin's Jewish Q has never really been asked.[7]

And yet it has already been answered, albeit tentatively and implicitly, by Gershom Scholem. This very prolific author once found himself, next to Dora Benjamin, in the most privileged position to comment on the development of Benjamin's interest in the Jewish tradition, namely at its very inception. Over the past ten years, a large number of new documents have been published from the archives of both Benjamin and Scholem, including a new, six-volume edition of the former's correspondence, replacing the old two-volume edition of 1966, a three-volume edition of Scholem's correspondence as well as a two-volume edition of his diaries and short texts from the crucial years 1913–1923, and a translation of his last completed work, the autobiographical *Von Berlin nach Jerusalem*. These documents contain a wealth of new information, which in itself already demands a reassessment of certain aspects of Benjamin's work, but in some cases, the voices they contain actually seem to ask us explicitly to look into the forgotten corners of the past. The most vocal, unsurprisingly, is Scholem. In an essay published in *Neue Rundschau* as early as 1965, he writes:

> Als ich [Benjamin] 1916 erzählte, daß das sechzig bis achtzig Jahre vorher erschienene große vierbändige Werk des Baaderschülers Molitor über die Kabbala, *Philosophie der Geschichte oder über die Tradition*, überraschenderweise noch beim Verlag zu haben sei, gehörte es zu den ersten Werken über das Judentum, die er sich anschaffte, und behauptete viele Jahre einen Ehrenplatz in seiner Bibliothek.[8]

The name Molitor appears on a reliably regular basis in Scholem's writings and correspondence, either with reference to Benjamin's exploration of the Jewish tradition, as in the quotation above, or with reference to his own interests in Kabbalah studies, as he writes to Jürgen von Kempski in April 1960: 'Ich sammle prinzipiell alles, was über Kabbala geschrieben wurde. Die Auslassungen Molitors und seiner Verehrer sind da von nicht geringem Interesse.'[9] The fewer responses Scholem seemed to elicit with his references to Molitor – *Molitorschüler*, then and now, are few and far between – the more insistent they seemed to become. In his book *Von der mystischen Gestalt der Gottheit*, he wrote: 'Es ist heute fast vergessen, daß Molitor der einzige ernst zu nehmende christliche Kenner der Kabbala im Zeitalter des deutschen Idealismus und wohl im ganzen 19. Jahrhundert war.'[10] Whether the question seemed too obvious to him, or whether his work both as an author and as a lecturer at the Hebrew University in Jerusalem forbade him to do so, Scholem never wrote a comprehensive account of the importance and the sources of the Jewish tradition in the work of Walter Benjamin. What he did instead, perhaps taking a cue from his friend, was insinuate, hint, suggest and even point towards those places from which he suspected, or knew, that a fruitful investigation could take root. Reading Scholem's correspondence, it is hard to rid onself of the impression that he wanted someone to write a book about Benjamin, Molitor and the Jewish tradition. Here, more than twenty years after Scholem's death, and more than sixty years after Benjamin's, I offer my answer to his call.

However, such an undertaking calls for a caveat. Traditionally, critics have been divided into two opposing camps, favouring either a marxist-materialist reading or a theological-metaphysical interpretation of Benjamin's work. Before Benjamin's star rose so dramatically in the last quarter of the previous century, these two conflicting visions were represented in broad terms by Adorno and Scholem, respectively, both of whom had their more or less loyal following. Now there is such a creature as the 'Benjamin scholar', ironically, and the second and even third generation of them is making its mark, such a reductive reading is becoming less popular. If the explosion of Benjamin scholarship over the last ten to fifteen years – some of it good, some of it bad, most of it eminently forgettable – has taught us anything, it is that the sweep of his work is too vast and varied to be classified simply as a form of marxism or a form of mysticism. Benjamin's writings, some more obviously than others but all of them to a certain extent, do indeed seem constantly to tap into the most diverse strands of human experience and history, from the intellectual and the spiritual to the quotidian and even the banal, from pathos to bathos, from the sublime to the ridiculous. As a commentator, there was very little Benjamin did not consider worthy of his critical attention, and the sheer breadth of his interests constantly compels his readers to reassess their own image of him. According to Lieven De Cauter, for instance, Benjamin's texts inscribe themselves into the 'nameless tradition' of language mysticism which includes the Biblical narratives of the Fall and the Tower of Babel in Genesis, the Kabbalah and Early German Romanticism, as well as some less anonymous – but no less mystical – figures such as Jakob Böhme, Franz von Baader, Johann Georg Hamann, Wilhelm von Humboldt and Franz Joseph Molitor.[11] It would not be difficult to construct a different family tree for other aspects of Benjamin's thought which would include Bachofen, Blanqui, Baudelaire and Bakunin, for instance, or possibly Kant, Nietzsche, Cohen, Bergson and Proust. With this in mind, it cannot be the aim of this book to present Walter Benjamin as a Jewish philosopher or theologian in the traditional sense of the word, much less as a philosopher or theologian of Judaism. There is nothing in either his life or in his work to suggest that this was ever the case. Nor can it be the aim to read all of Benjamin's texts exclusively in the context of his Judaism, scouring them for references or forcing them into a rigid and preconceived Jewish framework, which would neither be very scholarly, nor very productive. Nevertheless, Benjamin was of course Jewish, and if it is legitimate to describe him as a critic or a thinker, it is equally legitimate to describe him as a Jewish thinker. As he wrote himself:

> Von Wickersdorf aus, nicht spekulativ, nicht schlechthin gefühlsmäßig, sondern aus äußerer und innerer Erfahrung habe ich mein Judentum gefunden. Ich habe das was mir in Ideen und Menschen das höchste war, als jüdisch entdeckt. – Und um all das was ich erkannte auf eine Formel zu bringen[:] Ich bin Jude und wenn ich als bewußter Mensch lebe, lebe ich als bewußter Jude. (*GB*, 71)

Even though Benjamin was the first to confess that his knowledge of Judaism was somewhat limited, and even though Scholem is usually close at hand to say that this was indeed often the case, he appears to feel that the influence of his Jewishness, for all its ambiguity and elusiveness, is somehow more pervasive and more fundamental than the influence of directly traceable individual authors such as Cohen, Korsch and Rosenzweig. Addressing the philological question of the exact sources of Benjamin's language mysticism, Lieven De Cauter states: '[...] the question of sources is not as important as it seems. Tradition is nameless, it is something which is passed on, something which one has received because it was there, somewhere.'[12]

Rather than being influenced by the work of a clearly identifiable Jewish theologian or by a particular brand of Jewish mysticism, it is our contention that much of Benjamin's work can be read in the fluid, nebulous and often nameless context of the Jewish tradition. In this respect, it is paradoxically the vaguest hypothesis which carries the greatest weight, as this influence should not necessarily be sought in the presence of certain doctrines or *theologoumena*, although these do manifest themselves on occasion, but rather in the methodology and epistemology underlying some of Benjamin's most important writings. The thought patterns of the Jewish tradition, 'das Denken der Lehre' as he call it himself, inform Benjamin's work on a very fundamental and also on a very literal level. They affect its style, its strategy and its composition, its appearance, split between a public and a private side, with its parables and its hidden doctrines. To use one of his own terms from the essay *Über Sprache überhaupt und über die Sprache des Menschen*, tradition is the *medium*, the 'middle', in which his texts exist, consciously and unconsciously, intentionally and unintentionally, but in many ways inevitably.

These are the ideas which we will discuss over the following five chapters, in as systematic a way as the subject will allow. In the first chapter, we will give a brief overview of the Jewish tradition and its history, its theology and philosophy, its epistemology and its various methodologies. That it is all but impossible to do justice to such a complex and colossal phenomenon in such a short space goes without saying. We have therefore sought to discuss in some detail those elements which make the Jewish tradition so unique: its dynamics, its open-endedness, its focus on language and history, and its conception of the text, to name but a few. Much as tradition itself often moves in unexpected ways as well as sideways, heaping proof upon proof in an endless cycle of interpretation, it was not always easy to strike a balance between the brevity and order of the academic statement and the joy of the extended detour through tradition itself. We hope to have steered as straight a course as the subject would permit, and when the temptation simply became too hard to resist, we have reverted to that most eminently Jewish of all academic conventions: the commentary in a footnote.

The second and third chapters deal with the life and work of Franz Joseph Molitor, one of the three protagonists of our book. The second chapter provides a biographical background to this unique and often mystifying figure, which may go some way towards explaining the obvious fascination he held for Benjamin and Scholem. It also gives a detailed account of how and when Molitor's magnum opus, *Philosophie der Geschichte oder über die Tradition* fell into the hands of our two other protagonists, what they thought of it and which of Benjamin's texts mght have been influenced by his reading of it. In the third chapter, we address the book itself, making the case for the importance of *Philosophie der Geschichte* as one of the first systematic studies of the Jewish tradition ever to be published in Germany and indeed in Europe, recognised by writers, philosophers and scholars in his own day as well as by some of the foremost scholars of Judaism in the twentieth century. This chapter also explores the not inconsiderable merit of Molitor's book as an original work of philosophy in its own right, fusing German idealism, Romanticism, philology and mysticism. Molitor's concepts of tradition, language and education, and especially his conviction that Judaism and Christianity constitute different aspects of the same tradition, are of particular interest to our argument and are therefore treated in greater detail.

The fourth and the fifth chapters, finally, discuss the importance both of the Jewish tradition and of Franz Joseph Molitor to the work of Walter Benjamin. Having established beyond doubt the possibility and even likelihood of a direct influence on Benjamin of the book and the ideas and themes it brings to the fore, the fourth chapter addresses what are arguably two of his most seminal and challenging texts, *Über Sprache überhaupt und über die Sprache des Menschen* and the *Erkenntniskritische Vorrede*, the preface to *Ursprung des deutschen Trauerspiels*. Taking these texts as a starting point, we analyse the form and content of what we could call Benjamin's language theory and ask whether a recourse to theological and specifically Jewish patterns of thought might not shed on what are usually considered esoteric and even hermetic texts. The chapter also discusses the significance of Benjamin's language theory for the rest of his work, arguing that it provides him with an epistemological and methodological base which supports the majority of his writings. In the fifth chapter, this hypothesis is examined with reference to some of Benjamin's most interesting and most infamous texts, including *Zur Programm der kommenden Philosophie, Zur Begriff der Geschichte,* the *Passagen-Werk* and the *Protokolle zu Drogenversuchen.* The chapter addresses the consequences of Benjamin's use of tradition as an epistemological and methodological model for his views on truth, knowledge and history, which are explained and interpreted in the context of the nebulous but crucial concept of *Medium.* The chapter concludes with a brief discussion of the idea and the Name of God, the theological concept *par excellence,* both in the context of the Jewish tradition and with specific reference to Benjamin's work, and analyses its importance to the latter particularly in terms of its absence.

In many ways, the structure, style and form of this book is a good illustration of what it hopes to convey. At times, its self-imposed task has looked daunting and even forbidding, particularly in the face of the almost infinite number of texts and the sheer enormity of the concepts that are our subjects, so much so that no amount of interpretation and exposition seems able to do justice to them. But then, at other, more felicitous times, it seems that a single, well-placed phrase can have the eloquence of a thousand volumes. Of course, the one does not exist without the other. When Hillel taught that the phrase 'that which is hateful to you, do not to your neighbour' summarised the whole of the Torah, he supplemented this with the equally meaningful phrase 'go and study it'. Benjamin too was aware of the fact that the sudden flash of insight and the infinite task of study and interpretation were two sides of the same coin. Nowhere is this more clear than in the very first and apodictic *Lehrsatz* of the famous epistemological and methodological chapter of the *Passagen-Werk,* known as *Konvolut N,* which we gratefully take as the miniature, the model and the motto for this book:

In den Gebieten, mit denen wir es zu tun haben, gibt es Erkenntnis nur blitzhaft. Der Text ist der langnachrollende Donner. (V, 570)

Chapter One: The Jewish Tradition

Judaism in History, Text and Tradition

In spite of the progressive secularisation taking place since the Haskalah, the Jewish Enlightenment heralded by Baruch de Spinoza and inaugurated by Moses Mendelssohn, tradition remained and can still be considered a very real and almost tangible omnipresence in the Jewish experience. In fact, to Mendelssohn, Haskalah and tradition did not appear as opposites at all, as he considered his own enterprise to be still very much part of tradition, although admittedly he was not unchallenged in that conviction. This deference to tradition, continuing up to this day, may be partly due to the fact that, predictably, a process that only started about three hundred years ago could not conceivably have succeeded in eradicating all traces of a tradition that goes back almost 3,000 years – or as tradition itself would have it, 5,760 years in the year 2000. It may also be because reactions to the perceived crisis of Judaism after the Middle Ages were very diverse. As the accumulative process of interpretation of the law yielded ever more expansive textual corpora of increasing dialectic and theological complexity, segments of the Jewish community, especially those in Eastern Europe and Russia, felt themselves more and more isolated from the perceived legalism of their rabbis. The programme of rationalisation announced by Spinoza and continued by a host of authors from the second half of the eighteenth century onwards rebelled against what they saw as a blind subservience to an increasingly obscure and outdated authority.

An alternative reaction, taking place around the same time, was the return to a personal, intimate and anti-intellectualist experience of the faith propagated by Hasidism and its founding father Yisrael Ba'al Shem Tov.[1] Both Haskalah and Hasidism represent a movement away from the orthodoxy of their day, albeit in opposite directions, and the dynamics behind these movements continued to underlie subsequent developments in Judaism, from atheism, assimilation, liberalism and a sweeping secularisation to the Reform movements on the one hand and from the conservative and reconstructionist movements to orthodoxy, Zionism, Hasidism and fundamentalism on the other hand. Of course, not every modern Jewish movement allows itself to be subsumed quite as rigidly under one of these categories, and this tends to be even less the case with individual thinkers or authors. Individual confrontations with tradition tend to yield idiosyncratic responses and creative reinterpretations, merging elements from both mystical and rationalist traditions.

One such reinterpretation, or series of reinterpretations, is the movement that became known as the 'Christian Kabbalah', which originated in Germany towards the end of the fifteenth century and whose influence extended into the middle of the nineteenth century. Authors associated with the Christian Kabbalah include Johannes Reuchlin, Paracelsus, Christian Knorr von Rosenroth, Jakob Böhme, Franz von Baader and his pupil Franz Joseph Molitor, whose *Philosophie der Geschichte oder über die Tradition* (1827–1851) will be the subject of the next chapters. The Christian Kabbalists, whose influence extended to the early German Romantics, are a good example of the somewhat contrived nature of the above distinction between rationality and mysticism. However, as a basic framework the above outline may suffice. That it corresponded, at least in part, to the experience of European Jews at the turn of the century is in fact corroborated by a statement by Benjamin himself, describing the experience of growing up in a liberal environment:

> Ich bin, wie ich Ihnen kaum zu sagen brauche, liberal erzogen worden. Mein entscheidendes geistiges Erlebnis hatte ich, bevor jemal das Judentum mir wichtig oder problematisch geworden war. Was ich von ihm kannte war wirklich nur der Antisemitismus und eine unbestimmte Pietät. Als Religion war es fern, als Nationales unbekannt.[2]

This statement is very eloquent about experience of the average assimilated Jew, but also about the fact that, as it did for Benjamin, Judaism often 'resurfaced', as if it had maintained a dormant but pervasive presence all the time. Benjamin seemed to have believed this quite firmly himself, as he said to Scholem in August 1916: 'Wenn ich einmal meine Philosophie haben werde, so wird es irgend-wie eine Philosophie des Judentums sein.' (*TB* I, 391).

Clearly, this historical background alone cannot explain the persistent and pervasive role of tradition in modern Judaism. If anything, it makes the fact that tradition is still very much alive today even more mysterious, although it does illustrate what was at stake in the conflicts between tradition, the cultic practice of religion and the Enlightenment. Not dissimilar to its gentile variant, the Jewish Enlightenment disputed the authority of a tradition it saw as opaque and unintelligible, but, and this is Benjamin's position in the early essay *Über das Programm der kommenden Philosophie*, the Enlightenment failed to provide an adequate alternative to this authority, as it failed fully to understand its nature. So if we want to explain the elusive omnipresence of tradition, we need to turn to its most fundamental structures and characteristics, and one of its most fundamental characteristics is in fact its omnipresence. Tradition is the Aristotelian first ground of Judaism as a religion, of the Jews as a people, of either as a phenomenon, even. But it is also a process that enables Judaism to relate to Revelation in a dynamic way, resulting in a constant, yet very fruitful tension between conservation and innovation, between receptivity and spontaneity, in the words of Gershom Scholem.[3]

It should be emphasised here that the concept of tradition we are discussing in this chapter is largely limited to the law and its satellites, the *Halakhah* and the *Aggadah*, and that it excludes the notion of 'custom' or *Minhag*, which is considered to be neither universally binding nor divine. Next to a whole host of eclectic customs, the *minhagim* also include the various and diverse liturgical rites in Jewish communities across the world, which are an integral and essential part of day-to-day life for the observant Jew. As such, they are arguably as much a part of the Jewish tradition as the written law, and our only justification in excluding them from our discussion are the practical constraints of page length and readers' patience. This very impossibility of maintaining a rigid separation between the spheres of law and custom, and even of *Halakhah* and *Aggadah*, may serve as as a textbook example not only of the multi-faceted complexity of tradition, but also of its sheer reach.

The people of Israel, the Jews, were elected by God and entered into a *brit* or a covenant with him, a covenant which was tested and renewed several times, by Abraham and Moses, but which is ultimately sealed by Israel's promise to keep to God's law. The offer, the promise, the law itself as well as its transgressions and reaffirmations are all recorded in the Torah, or the Pentateuch. Or rather, they all *are* Torah. The history of the very term *torah*, meaning instruction, teaching or guidance, is fairly complex, and in trying to unravel this complexity, we will perform a movement of thought – a *Gedankenbewegung*, as Benjamin often calls it – which will be repeated many times throughout our argument. This movement can be best characterised as an unfolding and refolding, a development and 'envelopment', so to speak, of meaning upon meaning. It is a strategy of subtle and accumulative, yet paradoxically never exhaustive, overdetermination that typifies the Jewish tradition and the interpretative processes that underlie it. It is the same strategy, with a thoroughly different stake, which underlies Benjamin's work as much as it informs his writing style.

Originally, the term *torah* was used to designate individual instructions or laws, in the singular form *torah* or plural *torot*, next to a variety of similar terms. Only later, presumably during the Second Temple period, did it come to mean the Law or Teaching of Moses, and it is mentioned as such in one of the last verses of the Torah itself, Malachi 3:22, 'Remember the Torah of Moses my servant'. From the singular *torah*, Torah came to mean not only the precepts of the Law which God gave to Moses on Mount Sinai, and which are listed throughout Leviticus, Numbers and Deuteronomy, but also the genesis of the covenant and the history of the people of Israel up to the end of the Babylonian exile (late fifth century BCE). So strictly speaking, the term Torah refers only to the first five books of the Bible, which, as tradition has it, were dictated by God to Moses, including the accounts of the latter's birth and death. As Franz Joseph Molitor described it in the first book of *Philosophie der Geschichte*:

Die kanonischen Schriften der Juden bestehen aus vier und zwanzig Büchern, nämlich: fünf Büchern der Thorah, oder (Ch'mischah Chum'schee Thorah d.h. fünf Fünftheil der Thorah genannt); acht Büchern der Propheten, נביאים (N'biim); eilf Büchern verschiedener anderer heiligen Schriften, כתובים (Ch'thubim). Der Inbegriff der gesammten heiligen Schriften wird תנך (Th(e)n(a)ch) genannt, welches Wort blos eine Abbreviatur der drei Wörter Thorah, N-'biim, Ch'thubim ist. [4]

The entire collection of texts named above is considered divine, or at least divinely inspired, in the case of *Nevi'im* and *Ketubim*. In spite of the fact that they are blatantly the work of several generations of editors and that they actually include a whole variety of genres, tradition considers the Torah as a whole to be the word of God. This topos is what David Stern calls the 'rabbinic ideology of the canonical Torah – Pentateuch, Prophets and Writings – as the inspired word of God, a timeless unity'.[5] Or as James Kugel so poignantly formulated it: 'For still later ages [i.e., the Second Temple period], all Torah came "from Sinai", and that one primal divine revelation came to infuse all Jewish belief and practice: Torah is the entire fabric of Judaism.'[6] Torah indeed comes to infuse, define and flesh out Judaism, and as we will see later, the choice of the word 'fabric' is not at all arbitrary. Indeed, the Torah comes to be seen as the basic texture upon which the entire Jewish tradition is woven, so much so that the Aramaic term for rabbinic tractates is in fact *masekhta*, or 'woven fabric'. The Torah represents the dual covenant that defines the Jews as a people, it contains the Law Israel has undertaken to obey, it tells the story of God delivering his elected people from bondage, leading them to the promised land, and it tells of the second exile, of despair, but also of a renewed promise and a continuing (if not unproblematic) trust in the Lord. Specifically from rabbinic times onwards, the Jews come to owe their genesis, their existence and their history to Torah, and in that sense they truly became the People of the Book.

The fact that the canon of this book included superfluous repetitions, discontinuities, stylistic and theological variations, and even contradictions was not deemed to detract from the its eloquence or authority. The Torah, after all, was the word of God, written in a divine language, and could therefore not possibly be read or treated in the same way as human language. In Schwartz's words, the language of the Torah was deemed 'omnisignificant',[7] the divine revelation of the Torah was contained in all its aspects, and required careful and mindful interpretation. This notion, which has elicted many post-modern readings and 'applications' of the Jewish tradition, is not actually a new one. In *Philosophie der Geschichte*, Molitor already waxes lyrical about the Torah as an inexhaustible source of wisdom and knowledge: 'Denn die heilige Schrift, als das große Mysterium der Offenbarung Gottes, in welchem Alles in Allem enthalten, ist ein Hieroglyph von unendlichen Hieroglyphen, eine ewige Quelle von Geheimnissen, die nie zu erschöpfen, die unaufhörlich neu und herrlich quillt.' (*M* I, 49). David Stern goes even further in his de-scription of the divinity of the Torah, stating that it is 'a trope for God [...] in a metonymic fashion, whereby the Torah's being is treated as a kind of figurative extension of God's: just as he is timeless, so the Torah is beyond all temporality; just as all his deeds are meaningful, so every word in the Torah is full of significance.'[8]

It is indeed hard to overestimate the reverence the Jews had and continue to have for the Torah, both as a concept and as a physical object, and any discussion of the Jewish tradition must bear in mind this all-infusing sense of the divine that emanates from this notion. The very fact that the language of the Torah, and by extension the Hebrew language as such (and by an even further extension, language as such), was considered divine of course has far-reaching conse-quences. Whenever central issues of Judaism are addressed, whether they are the nature of God, theology, ethics or art, to name but a few, the question of language is never very far away. It is thus as good as inevitable that we will come to cover the same ground over and over again, only approaching it from different angles as we go along. One particular phenomenon that appears to unite all those topics, however, is study. One of the commandments contained in the Law in fact states that it is the duty of every Jew to study and interpret the Torah. This commandment of *Talmud Torah* is repeated several times, but it first appears in Deuteronomy 6:6–7, a very important place in the Bible, as the lines are preceded by yet another central text in Judaism, the *Shema*, or the Jewish *Credo* which is recited at various points through-out the day: 'Hear, O Israel: The Lord is our God, the Lord is One. [...] Keep these words that I am commanding you today in your heart.

28

Recite them to your children and talk about them when you are at home and when you are away, when you lie down and when you rise.' (Deut. 6:4–7).

The obligation of *Talmud Torah*, stating that the Torah had to be interpreted and completed, in its turn made study a divine activity, and the results of these interpretations were also considered to partake of this divinity. The rationale behind this was that because the Torah already contained everything, there was nothing man could read into it that was not already there in the first place. This characteristically Jewish *theologoumenon* inevitably leads to the equally Jewish notion that no detail is too small so as not to demand interpretation. That this way of thinking was not alien to Benjamin, is pointed out by Gershom Scholem in his essay *Walter Benjamin*: 'Daß im Kleinsten sich das Größte aufschließt, daß "der liebe Gott im Detail wohnt", wie Aby Warburg zu sagen pflegte, das waren in den verschiedensten Bezügen für ihn grundlegende Einsichten.'[9] What makes it appear all the more salient is that we find the same idea expressed very clearly in the first chapter of *Philosophie der Geschichte*:

> In der ganzen Darstellungsweise der Bibel findet sich nichts Zufälliges, sondern alles hat tiefe Bedeutung, selbst das Geringfügigste, namentlich jede scheinbar nicht zur Sache gehörige Episode, jede Erzählung von scheinbar kleinlichen unbedeutenden Neben-Umständen, jede Wiederholung von Dingen und Reden, jeder Pleonasmus in Worten, ja sogar in den Partikeln bis auf den Bindepartikel, alles ist durchaus bedeutungsvoll. Es ist daher auch gar nicht einerlei, ob dieses oder jenes Synonim, dieser oder jener göttliche name gewählt wird, sondern jegliches Wort, jeglicher göttliche Name, hat an der Stelle, wo er gebraucht wird, stets seinen besonderen eigenthümlichen Grund. (*M* I, 49–50)

Or as one saying from the Mishnah-tractate *Avot* has it: 'Turn it over and turn it over for all is in it.' [10] At the same time, however, great emphasis is placed on man's responsibility in uncovering those multiple meanings of the Torah through relentless study. In the words of Harvey Goldberg: 'As new meanings of text and rituals are discovered, through continuous interpretation, the attitude is maintained that one is simply uncovering further depths which always had been implicit in the divinely revealed or inspired writings.'[11] It is after all of little use to be reassured of the presence of hidden meanings when you are not obliged to look for them. In a curious way, this is a fascinating pre-emptive inversion of Nietzsche's as yet unmade remark that there is little to praise in a search for something you have hidden yourself.[12] Yet again it brings us back to a rival concept of meaning and, inevitably, language. Suffice to say at this point that a perspective which intimately links meaning to the very physicality of language, to the point of investing meaning in the ornamental crowns on individual letters, will differ from a perspective that perceives language as a(n arbitrary) carrier of a meaning which is in some way extrinsic to it.

The commandment of *Talmud Torah*, however, resulted in yet another extension of Torah, this time into the dual concept of *torah she-bi-khetav*, or written law, and *torah she-be-'al-peh*, or oral law, both considered equally divine. The books of the Torah, or the written law, had become a fairly stable corpus of texts by the end of the second century CE, determined by Yochanan ben Zakkai's legendary 'synod' at Yabneh, but the composition of the oral law was an entirely different matter. In fact, the compilation of the oral law has always been an ongoing process, which continues up to this day. Again, as was largely the case with the idiosyncratic sanctity of Torah, the oral law as such was a rabbinic construct, instituting rabbinic activity as the central focus of Judaism after the destruction of the Temple and the subsequent disappearance of the priestly cult. In the light of our hypothesis, it is interesting to note that the rabbinic tradition replaced a cult very much bound to a particular place by one that could survive a permanent disjunction. After the destruction of the Temple and the Holiest of Holies as the dwelling place of God, the text appears to have shifted into focus as the locus of the divine, with the ineffable Name of God as the immediate analogy to the Temple's inner sanctum. This may in part explain the tendency in Judaism to conceive of the text and of tradition itself as a physical space, exemplified, for instance, by the kabbalist notion of words as containers of wisdom or divinity. This notion is thoroughly different from one that sees words as signs or representations of a meaning that can be seen as external to them, and it is with this notion in mind that Benjamin's writings on language allow themselves to be read in a rather less perplexing light than they have usually been.

As the whole of the Torah, the written law, was meant to come from Sinai, so the whole of the oral law was said to have been revealed to Moses, even though there was sometimes no explicit mention of said laws in Scripture. This particular doctrine ensured that both written and oral law could be traced back to a single revelation, thereby imbuing the latter with the authority of the former. In *Philosophie der Geschichte*, Molitor actually echoes this traditional view of written and oral law:

> Deshalb wird dieses allgemeine Gesetz, nebst dem Buche der Schöpfung, תורה שבכהב (Thorah Schebich'thab, die geschriebene Lehre) genannt, im Gegensatze von jener Anweisung, welche Moscheh noch besonders als Aufschluß und Auslegung über den Inhalt des Gesetzes von Gott empfangen, welche שבעלפה תורה (Thorah Scheb'al Peh, die mündliche Lehre) heißt. (*M* I, 16)

In the Talmud, this belief was expressed in the formula *Halakhah Le-Mosheh Mi-Sinai*, meaning 'a law (given) to Moses from Sinai'. The first paragraph of the Mishnah-tractate *Avot* states this lineage in as many words: 'Moses received the Torah at Sinai and transmitted it to Joshua, Joshua to the Elders, and the Elders to the Prophets, and the Prophets to the men of the Great Synagogue.' (M. *Avot*, I, 1. It is customary to preface references to the tractates of the Mishnah and the Babylonian Talmud with a capital 'M' and 'B' respectively, and we will use this method of referencing throughout the book). From a historical perspective, the concept of the oral law is of course a retrospective rabbinic construct, as is the Hebrew Bible for that matter, designed to clothe rabbinism in the same aura of ancient authority as the priestly tradition. As such we can say, with Scholem, that 'die Tradition als ein besondrer Aspekt der Offenbarung historisch ein Produkt des Prozesses [ist], in dem sich das rabbinische Judentum zwischen dem vierten oder dritten vorchristlichen Jahrhundert und dem zweiten nachchristlichen Jahrhundert gebildet hat',[13] which may in its turn serve to justify our very limited selection of material to characterise the Jewish tradition as a whole. Yet in a way, the discrepancy which there so obviously is between the story a tradition tells of its own origins and the actual historical genesis of its texts and facts is neither here nor there. Perhaps surprisingly, Benjamin himself had understood this very clearly: 'Mag sein, daß die Kontinuität der Tradition Schein ist. Aber dann stiftet eben die Beständigkeit dieses Scheins der Beständigkeit die Kontinuität in ihr.' (V, 609).

Throughout the history of Judaism, this centrifugal movement causing the expansion of tradition is countered on by a recurring desire to condense and compile the ever-increasing body of the law. The first and still most important compilation exercise ended in the early third century CE with the completion of the *Mishnah*, an attempt by early rabbis to give an overview of the oral law thus far. Ironically, the *Mishnah* itself swiftly became the object of study, and over the next few centuries the rulings included in the *Mishnah* were discussed, explained and expanded, resulting in the Palestinian Talmud or *Yerushalmi*, compiled during the first half of the fifth century CE, and the Babylonian Talmud or *Bavli*, which was regarded as a closed work around 700 CE.[14] In the end, only the Babylonian Talmud was considered authoritative, and up to this day, it remains the foundation of most modern forms of the Jewish religion. Its afterlife is a matter of some complexity: whereas there was certainly no question of revising or tampering with the mishnaic or talmudic texts, they continued to be the subject of discussion and commentary, and true to the 'accumulative tendency' of the Jewish tradition, the most important of these commentaries were added in the margins of the Talmud. Since the first printed editions of the Talmud started to appear in the fifteenth century, for instance, the famous commentaries of Rashi (1040–1105) have appeared right next to the central text. Over the following centuries, Rashi's commentaries provoked still more commentaries, resulting in the compilation of the *Tosafot* or 'supplements'. These *Tosafot*, which continue to be printed on the outside columns of the Talmud pages, soon developed into a vast network of interconnecting questions, often referring to a completely different subject matter from that discussed on those pages. These hyperlinks *avant-la-lettre* give the Talmud its uniquely Jewish character as, in the words of Robert Goldenberg, 'numerous voices enter the discussion: cross-references to other Talmudic sources, a key to quotations from the Bible and another to the great codes of Jewish law, additional briefer commentaries from medieval and even recent centuries'.[15]

'Gewebe' im vollen Sinne des Wortes

The Mishnah is divided into six orders, or *Sedarim*, each encompassing a variable number of separate tractates or *Masekhtot*, a structure which is mirrored by the Talmud. As we mentioned before, *Masekhtah* literally means 'webbing' or 'fabric', analogous, in fact, to the Latin *textus*, and the Jewish tradition can be considered as a continuous weaving and interweaving of these fabrics, culminating in the creation of a hypercomplex whole with the addition of the *Tosafot*. Thus, the choice of the word 'fabric' to describe the Jewish tradition is not at all arbitrary. On the contrary, it is how tradition itself defines and understands its own form and appearance, and it is the logical structure of the most fundamental 'genre' of tradition, namely commentary. Benjamin himself was particularly fond of commentary as a genre, and not just because he saw himself as a (literary) critic. The *Wahlverwandtschaft* between Benjamin and commentary was based on exactly these textural qualities, which make particularly the talmudic commentary a very dense and intricate pattern, requiring the patience of a saint to follow its threads but promising holy rewards to those who do.

In *Berliner Kindheit um Neunzehnhundert*, Benjamin describes his fascination with such convoluted, baroque structures by referring quite literally to an embroidery pattern: 'Und während das Papier mit leisem Knacken der Nadel ihre Bahn freimachte, gab ich hin und wieder der Versuchung nach, mich in das Netzwerk auf der Hinterseite zu vergaffen, das mit jedem Stich, mit dem ich vorn dem Ziele näherkam, verworrener wurde.' (IV, 291). Benjamin's own work abounds with examples of these scholastic and labyrinthine structures, whose method appears to be the desire to delay their own outcome and prolong the enjoyment of the text. That Benjamin sees this quite literally as the unravelling of an intricately wound thread is clear from his description of the joy and desire of writing in *Haschisch in Marseille*, which he compares to unwinding Ariadne's thread in the Minotaur's labyrinth:

> Wir gehen vorwärts; wir entdecken dabei aber nicht nur die Windungen der
> Höhle, in die wir uns vorwagen, sondern genießen dieses Entdeckerglück nur
> auf dem Grunde jener anderen rhythmischen Seligkeit, die da im Abspulen
> eines Knäuels besteht. Eine solche Gewißheit vom kunstreich gewundenen
> Knäuel, das wir abspulen – ist das nicht das Glück jeder, zumindest prosa-
> förmigen, Produktivität? (IV, 414)

Moreover, Benjamin understood that the commentary form of the
theological tractate, such as the talmudic *massekhtah*, was determined
by constant digressions introducing new evidence or even new arguments, combining all of its different threads into a dense, multi-
layered texture. He also understood that this retracing and delaying
method was not incidental, but fundamental to the tractate. As he
wrote in *Ursprung des deutschen Trauerspiels*: 'Darstellung ist der
Inbegriff ihrer Methode. Methode ist Umweg. Darstellung als Umweg
– das ist denn der methodische Charakter des Traktats.' (I, 208). Benjamin was fully aware that this writing method would result in a text
which incorporated different layers and levels into one apparently
seamless whole, and this is reflected in his description of the tractate
in *Einbahnstraße*: 'So ist auch die gegliederte Struktur des Traktats
von außen nicht wahrnehmbar, sondern eröffnet sich nur von innen.
[…] In der ornamentalen Dichtigkeit dieser Darstellung entfällt der
Unterschied von thematischen und exkursiven Ausführungen.' (IV,
111).

This combination of different genres into a single text is not only
mirrored by the talmudic corpus, it is also reflected in the Jewish
tradition as a whole. The Talmud was itself already a mixture of legal
texts and a variety of commentaries, but around the turn of the first
millenium, 'the rabbinic writings themselves became the object of
commentaries and compendia, i.e. they became primary texts.'[16] Yet
the ever-expanding corpus of commentary was not restricted to what
we might call the talmudic literature. Alongside the commentaries on
the (commentaries on the) Mishnah and Talmud, a vast corpus of
rabbinic *midrashim*, or interpretations, was growing steadily and was
at least in part collected in the *Midrash Rabbah*. Although in essence
also commentaries, these midrashim went even further in blurring the
boundaries between the thematic and the excursive.

The rabbinic midrashim usually refer to the individual books of the Bible. The collection containing interpretations of Genesis, for instance, is called *Bereshith Rabbah* or *Genesis Rabbah*, sections of which at least were known to Benjamin, and indeed part of the cultural baggage of most Jews. These midrashim are generally divided into two different types, halakhic and aggadic, concerning themselves with either the statutes of the law, the *Halakhah*, or with the incidental stories, parables and illustrations accompanying and clarifying the law, the *Aggadah*. This elementary division also applies to the Talmud, which, even though its emphasis lies primarily on *Halakhah*, still includes a massive amount of *Aggadah*, with printed editions of the Talmud usually numbering around thirty volumes. Yet, as we suggested above, the distinction of *Halakhah* and *Aggadah* is not always as clear as their definitions may suggest. *Halakhah* frequently flows over into *Aggadah*, and vice versa: stories and parables may sometimes culminate in the formulation of a halakhic precept or gradually and almost clandestinely develop it. Even though the distinction is recognised as such, *Halakhah* and *Aggadah* are so thoroughly interwoven in the Jewish tradition that it would be perfectly impossible to extricate either one of them from it without ripping the texture apart. The phenomenon of *midrash* manifested itself very early in the Rabbinic period as an exegetical or homiletical method or technique, and continued well into the late Middle Ages, with the *Zohar* as an immense mystical *midrash* on the Torah. We could go even further and say with Barry Holtz that in a sense 'almost all Jewish writing, at least until the nineteenth century', can be seen as 'a kind of Midrash'.[17]

Both midrashim and the Talmud are indeed major constituents of the textual corpus of what we have called the Jewish tradition, but it goes without saying that this is far from an exhaustive picture. As mentioned before, we have already quite arbitrarily excluded the day-to-day experience of Judaism of the *mitzvot* from our discussion, and the same applies to other classes of written sources of the tradition. One such class is the large collection of legal compendia compiled in post-talmudic times from the Middle Ages to the present day. These compilations and their authors were held in very high esteem, illustrated by the fact that the great Maimonides himself tried his hand at one, the *Mishneh Torah*. Arguably these compendia have also had a greater influence on the everyday practice of Judaism than the often very specialised talmudic discussions, as evidenced by the *Shulhan Arukh*, a sixteenth-century compendium still in use today – with commentaries, of course. We have excluded the so-called *Responsa* literature, a kind of Jewish case law produced by halakhic scholars in reply to inquiries addressed to them.[18] We have also excluded the whole area of medieval and renaissance Jewish philosophy, whose practitioners were often also halakhic scholars, and finally we have omitted from our discussion the entire field, if that is the right word, of Jewish mysticism, which includes the Kabbalah. This latter omission is rather less arbitrary than the former, as this book seeks to deal with the influence of what we have called, for want of a better term, the 'mainstream' Jewish tradition. After all, the Kabbalah was and still is a highly specialised area about which people at the time, including Benjamin, knew very little indeed, despite all efforts to prove the contrary. This is not to say that we will not be able to find certain kabbalistic elements or concepts in Benjamin's work – it was after all one of his closest friends who introduced the study of Jewish mysticism into the curriculum – but it does mean that any substantial and structural Jewish influence on the work of Walter Benjamin will have to be found within the apparently less spectacular 'mainstream' tradition.

Yet appearances may deceive, as is so often the case. Even without the application of mystical hermeneutics, the Jewish tradition remains an inexhaustible source of inspiration, as it is open-ended in three different ways. Firstly because the process of interpretation in no way limits the number of interpretations that can be retrieved from Torah, but rather encourages renewed engagement with the text and attempts to reaffirm the relevance of the Torah to the present. Thus the Torah, although it remains 'supreme in authority', is by no means a rigid entity, the meaning of which was fixed at one point in the past and has not changed since. Most often, these changes of meaning do not so much challenge the orthodoxy directly as find unexpected ways in which the Torah heaps proof upon proof of its own divine message. The open-ended approach to interpretation, traditionally at any rate, does not often result in a meaning that is the mirror opposite of what orthodoxy has assumed until then, although the Jewish tradition does know such radically wayward figures as Shabbetai Tsevi, in whose theology redemption would come about through sin.[19] Yet when the community finds itself confronted with a commandment it no longer finds acceptable to enforce, the midrashic imagination will be called upon to reinterpret the orthodoxy. This is exactly what happened with the infamous *lex talionis* of Ex. 21:24 ('An eye for an eye'), when the word *mammash*, 'the removal of an eye of the perpetrator', was read as *mammon*, 'financial compensation' (B. *Baba Kamma*, 84a).

Secondly, and in the most obvious sense, tradition is open-ended because interpretation, halakhic and aggadic activity, continues up to this day, and will do so until the Last Day. Codifications and commentaries continue to be written and added one to the other, with Rashi's commentaries and the commentaries to his commentary being printed in the margins of the Talmud, which in its turn includes the whole of the Mishnah, to name but one such accumulative sequence. From this perspective, the Jewish tradition is not only an accumulative process, it also creates what we could call a single, homogeneous space. Later additions and supplements actually become part of the original work, creating an entirely new work while at the same time establishing a firm continuity between past and present. Thread upon thread is woven into and onto the original fabric, gradually turning it into a dense, multi-dimensional space in which every verse, every term and every concept never refers to one thing only, but rather forms a knot uniting and dispersing innumerable threads. This is intimately intertwined with the rabbinic methods of interpretation, which, as we shall explain later, showed a tendency towards the atomisation of Scripture, taking it apart into its most minute building blocks only to reconstruct an entire – moral and religious – conceptual universe from them. As we will also show later, this strategy has a remarkable structural parallel in Walter Benjamin's micrological readings.

The spatial metaphors we used in describing the Jewish tradition are crucial, so much so that they even determine the very layout of the Talmud. On a typical Talmudic page, which is traditionally in folio format, the original Mishnaic ruling is set high up in the centre, usually preceded by the formula 'it is taught'. In the column straight

37

underneath and set in the same type is the Gemara, abbreviated with the letters gimel-mem (גמ) immediately preceding it. Additions of lesser importance or of later origin are set in a smaller font than the central passages, so that, in fact, adding to the law becomes physically easier as time passes, so to speak, although the labour of deciphering the latest additions becomes more cumbersome. The commentary of Rashi is set in a single column next to the Mishnah and *Gemara* in the inner margin, and the commentary of the *Tosafot* is set at the other side of the central block of text. In the outer margins are cross-references to medieval codes of law, including amongst others the *Mishneh Torah* and the *Shulhan Arukh*. Further notes and commentaries, as well as cross-references to the Torah, textual emendations and printer's notes, set in ever decreasing type, crowd the page up to its very edges. The effect of this layout is to create a sense of space and depth, both by foregrounding the central Mishnaic passage and by framing it with subsequent commentaries. This actually mirrors a precept found in the Mishnah itself, which admonishes the aforementioned Men of the Great Assembly to erect a fence around the law (the so-called *Seyag la-Torah*) in order to protect the original commandment from losing its strength.[20] As it is stated in the first paragraph of the Mishnah-tractate *Avot*: 'The latter [i.e., the Men of the Great Assembly] used to say three things: be patient in [the administration of] justice, rear many disciples and make a fence around the Torah.' (M. *Avot*: I, 1). Thus the text of the Talmud can be seen to contain divine wisdom in a double sense of the word: rather than signifying it or referring to it, the text physically contains divinity, circumscribing it and by this act of circumscription cupping it, so to speak, as you would cup water in your hands.

In this accumulative process, the internal hierarchy between the Mishnaic or Talmudic texts and later additions is not always uniform. Whereas the older works are sometimes given precedence and are considered to have greater authority than the later works, deference is generally shown to the accrued knowledge of later authors, true to the principle that the Law must also be relevant to the present rather than merely reverential to the past. As Feldman says: 'the hierarchy is one of learning, rather than of authority'.[21] This principle of *halakhah k'batra'ei*, 'the law follows the latest ruling,' has been embedded in

38

the canon of rabbinic decision-making from as early as geonic times, and it brings us to the third way in which the Jewish tradition resists closure. As difficult as the distinction between what is *halakhic* and what is *aggadic* may be, most of the works cited in our overview are part of the legal tradition, or *Halakhah* proper. Collections of rabbinic *midrashim* like the *Midrash Rabbah* are considered to be *baraitot*, literally meaning 'outside', and not part of the law as such. These works were not included in the Mishnah, either by editorial decision or simply because they had not yet been written. They are, however, paid due attention in the Talmud, standing alongside *mishnayyot* and *Gemara*. Similarly, the mystical writings of the kabbalists were not originally part of the legal tradition, but elements of the Lurianic Kabbalah, for instance, have been incorporated into halakhic compendia (the nineteenth-century *Kaf ha-Hayyim* of Ya'aqov Hayyim Sofer, to be precise). If one were to plot tradition on a graph, it would be come clear that this all-important principle of accumulation is not merely at work on the horizontal axis, continuing over time an adding new material to an existing corpus, but also on the vertical axis, in the revision and reinterpretation of that very corpus, thickening its very fabric. Tradition in the Jewish sense is as close as one can get to a transitive noun, or a substantive verb, as it represents the process of interpretation as well as the fluctuating collective of these interpretations at the same time, embedded, as they are, in 'the Jewish mind'. As David Feldman writes: 'Philosophic works of the Middle Ages partake of the same status [as the non-halakhic Bible commentaries]: they are extralegal and, as elements in the "Jewish mind", help shape the picture, but are only auxiliary to the legal process.'[22] Tradition, then, is the act and shaping of the Law in the widest possible sense.

In a discussion of the study of Talmud, Adin Steinsalz writes:

> In the opinion of virtually every modern scholar 'the Talmud was never closed' – not only in the historical-factual sense, but also with regard to the manner of its understanding and study. The method of Talmud study was an extension of Talmud itself; its interpretation and analysis required the student continually to involve himself in the discussion, to evaluate its questions and argumentation. As a result, abstract reasoning and the dialectical method became an integral part of the Jewish culture.[23]

This echoes the *mitzvah* of *Talmud Torah*, seeing study as a divine occupation, as well as the idea of an open-ended tradition, but it also gives an impression of the 'transcendental' nature of study. The text of the Torah is very much seen as a living entity, 'a trope for God', and by a similar metonymic movement, those engaged in the study of Torah are considered to be sharing, as equals, in its divine emanation. Their interpretations, whether they were considered authoritative or not, are considered to contain aspects of the divine, which they do not forfeit even when replaced by a new ruling. There is no sense of an older interpretation being somehow antiquarian, redundant, or, heaven forbid, disposable. Accumulation, creative conservation and mindful remembrance are the keywords. In this respect, the preoccupations of the Jewish tradition show a remarkable similarity to the methodology of Benjamin's unfinished *Passagen-Werk*, which now exists as a huge collection of fragments and quotations. In one of the *Konvolute*, Benjamin reveals his main focus to have been exactly these discarded fragments of past writing: 'die Lumpen, den Abfall: die will ich nicht inventarisieren sondern sie auf die einzig mögliche Weise zu ihrem Rechte kommen lassen: sie verwenden.' (V, 574). And, as we have seen, this principle works both ways: older texts are not automatically considered more authoritative than younger interpretations.

Throughout the Jewish tradition, there has in fact never been the same sense of dogmatic exclusivity which has so often been a feature of Christian theology. This may not be unconnected with the disappearance of the central Jewish authority after the destruction of the Second Temple in 70 CE, when religious authority shifted to the rabbinic academies elsewhere in Israel and in Babylonia. Judaism now no longer had a single centre of authority, or at least not a physical one. As we suggested above, the locus of the divine shifted from the actual Temple to the text of Torah, which then became heir to some of the spatial and physical metaphors used to describe the Temple as a 'container' of God on earth. In the first volume of *Philosophie der Geschichte oder über die Tradition*, Molitor uses a similar analogy between the physical Temple and the spiritual Temple (i.e., the Torah), yet, most significantly, his analogy is based on the physical appearance of the original Torah scrolls. These scrolls lack both punctuation and spacing, resulting in an extremely dense consonantal text, which Molitor compares to the veil that conceals the holiest of holies in the Temple:

> Das ursprüngliche Sepher Thorah von Moscheh hatte, wie jetzt noch jeder Abschrift derselben in den Synagogen, weder Vokale noch irgend einige Unterscheidungs- oder Lesezeichen. Es sind darin weder Kapitel noch Verse unterschieden, selbst die Worte nicht sehr merklich von einander: es ist alles fast nur ein einziges fortlaufendes, blos [sic] hier und da durch einzelne leere Stellen (B'thuchoth und S'thumoth genannt) unterbrochenes, Ganzes, in welchem so geringe Zwischenräume sich finden, daß Buchstabe an Buchstabe, Wort an Wort so dicht zusammengedrängt sind, wodurch es dem Unkundigen durchaus unmöglich wird, sich ohne Anleitung darin zu finden, und den fortlaufenden Zusammenhang aufzufassen. Gleichwie nämlich alles innere Geistige nur dem geweihten innern Auge sich erschließt, das leibliche Auge aber blos das äußere Gewand der Innerlichkeit zu schauen vermag, und wenn es auch weiter eindringen wollte, doch nimmermehr das wahre innere erblicken, sondern nur in Unordnung geraten würde: also hat man auch in der alten Kirche, ehe der Vorhang zerrissen, nicht nur das Heilige und Allerheiligste des leiblichen Tempels, sondern auch das Heilige und Allerheiligste des geistigen Tempels, der Thorah, nämlich die Vokale und Accente dem äußern Auge entzogen, und blos den Vorhof des Tempels und den äußern Bau der Thorah, die Consonanten, zur ehrfurchtsvollen Verehrung öffentlich dargestellt. (*M* I, 21–22)

But even when the Jerusalem Temple was still standing, there were several smaller temples both inside *Eretz Yisrael* and outside, and despite the predictable rivalries between the Jerusalem Temple and the other temples, there was never an attempt to centralise the entire cultic and religious experience of Judaism. As was mentioned before, discussion and dissent have always been important factors within the Jewish tradition, finding their most radical expression in the antinomian and even anarchic streak of its messianic movements. But even within what we have called mainstream Judaism, the simultaneous presence of varying or sometimes dissenting practices and opinions has been tolerated. In the *Halakhah*, the entire discussion leading up to a decision (a discussion which, in its turn, can be re-opened at any moment), often encompassing several generations of scholars, was included in the text. Dissenting opinions were stated and acknowledged, and the decision, reached by a majority vote, was preceded by

41

the statement 'in this matter, the *Halakhah* is in accordance with such-and-such'. As the Mishnah-tractate *'Eduyyoth* states: 'And why do they record the opinions of Shammai and Hillel to set them aside? – To teach the following generations that a man should not [always] persist in his opinion, for behold, the fathers of the world did not persist in their opinion.' (M. *'Eduyyoth*: I, 4).

This form of mutual respect, equality and humility before the Law is not just prevalent in space, as is witnessed for instance by the courtesy shown in the famous discussions between the rival Houses of Hillel and Shammai, but also in time. Just as there is no perception of anomaly or anachronism in a third-century midrash appearing side by side with a ninth-century commentary, the present-day student of Talmud can see Yehuda ha-Nasi, Yohanan ben Zakkai or Rashi as his contemporaries, united in study, one in the quest for God through an understanding of his law. In this sense, tradition is much more than the linear accumulation of knowledge, and a far cry from the ideology of progress whereby every step forward is a 'transgression', quite literally passing by the past, leaving it lifeless in its wake. It is easy to see in which notion of tradition Benjamin's famous angel of history has its roots, or at least where its affinities lie. This specifically Jewish form of tradition is an organic rather than a logical entity. It is a construction, but it is not constructed. On a micrological level, this pattern is mimicked by the nature of the texts within the tradition:

> Since the Talmudic discussion of any subject within the tractates, however, follows not a logical but an organic sequence, and since all of Jewish law is interconnected, with analogies adduced from one sphere to the other, references from the whole of the Talmud are brought to bear on the subject at hand in the relevant literature.[24]

This way, the *Mishnah Avot*'s statement on the Torah quoted above can be extended towards Jewish tradition as a whole: 'Turn it over and turn it over for all is in it.' There is a dominating, and sometimes imposing, feeling that tradition encompasses everything, past, present and future. This can result in a not unambiguous or even negative feeling of powerlessness, as it is voiced most famously in the

42

work of, Micha Joseph Berdyczewski, who writes about this problem: 'Our eyes are not our own, our dreams and our thoughts are not our own, our will is not the one implanted in us; everything we were taught long ago, everything has been handed down to us.'[25] But it also results in a real desire for a learning, a doctrine that can incorporate and explain everything. And it is in this sense that Benjamin's comment should be read, stating that no doctrine is worth studying which would be incapable of explaining the art of reading coffee-grounds.[26]

History and Language

At this point, it may be useful to dwell a bit more extensively on one of the strands that have been underlying our argument up to now, and to which we will come in a subsequent paragraph. As we mentioned before, the concept of history used in a tradition like the Jewish one is diametrically opposed to the historicist notion of history, in which the past no longer has any real existence in the present and can only be reconstructed as another 'virtual present', with which the 'real' present in its turn has very little to do other than in the form of causal links or logical connections, if the past in question is not too distant. In a traditional perspective, however, the past is seen to exist as a function of the present, and the present exists (or ought to exist) in function of the (possibly utopian) future.[27] One consequence of this notion is that, in the traditional perspective, nothing is ever perceived as 'past', 'over' or 'irrevocably lost'.[28] Nor is the past seen as an irreducible difference, the establishment of which is the basis of historicist criticism. On the contrary, tradition exhibits a deep-seated, thoroughly religious sense of solidarity between past, present and future. A good example of this is the annual Passover or *Pesach* festival, commemorating the Exodus of Israel from Egypt. The rituals and the language used in the act of remembrance, the *Pesach Haggadah*, are explicitly focused on the actuality of this event for all Jews, stating that '*we* were slaves of Pharaoh in Egypt'. This actuality – which is not the sentimental *Einfühlung* or identification of the petty bourgeois with the past lambasted by Benjamin, but rather a pre-emptive *Einfühlung* of the past with the present, its future – is what Neusner termed the 'vivid contemporaneity of tradition', and it comes to the fore even more explicitly at the end of the *Pesach Haggadah*:

> Forever after, in every generation, everyone must think of himself as having gone forth from Egypt, for we read in the Torah, 'In that day thou shalt teach thy son, saying, All this is because of what God did for me when I went forth from Egypt.' It was not only our forefathers that the Holy One... redeemed. Us too, the living, he redeemed together with them.[29]

It is this view of history which provides Judaism with its most elementary *religio*, linking the present to the past and both to a future redemption promised in revelation, a *religio* which is thus eminently theological in kind. Benjamin's *Geschichtsphilosophie* or philosophy of history appears to have taken its inspiration from this Jewish concept of remembrance, as he interprets the literally religious attention to the past as an inversed messianic hope for the future:

> Bekanntlich war es den Juden untersagt, der Zukunft nachzuforschen. Die Thora und das Gebet unterweisen sie dagegen im Eingedenken. Dieses entzauberte ihnen die Zukunft, der die verfallen sind, die sich bei den Wahrsagern Auskunft holen. Den Juden wurde die Zukunft aber darum doch nicht zur homogenen und leeren Zeit. Denn in ihr war jede Sekunde die kleine Pforte, durch die der Messias treten konnte. (I, 704)[30]

But whereas in Judaism, the so-called contemporaneity of the past is enacted in language, symbols and rituals such as the eating of the paschal lamb, Benjamin's philosophy eradicates the radical separation of the past from the present, imposed by the ideology of historicism, in his '*Archäologie des Jüngstvergangenen*' or 'archaeology of the recent past'. The ultimate avatar of this archaeology is the figure of the collector, who collects the so-called refuse of history ('*Abfall der Geschichte*'), the immense diversity of bits and bobs discarded in the process of progress, to which fragments of the utopian hopes and expectations held by the past still adhere. This obviously requires an extensive discussion, and we will have the opportunity to come back to this topic in the final chapter, but with the foregoing in mind, even this short description will suffice to highlight the crystal-clear correspondences between this image and the kabbalist metaphor of the *Klipot* and kicking up the sparks. Benjamin's collector, who clearly refers to the kind of philosopher of history Benjamin considered himself to be, comes together with the Jewish tradition in one single aspect, both approaching it from a slightly different angle but ending up in exactly the same spot: the physical and spatial metaphors of history and tradition. The Mishnaic admonition to 'turn it over and over' applies perfectly to the image of the collector turning over a children's toy from twenty years ago, and reading from it the utopian hopes that the recent past invested in the future, the obligation which the present has towards the past. But before we attempt to paint the whole picture of Benjamin's philosophy of history, its correspondences to and elective affinities with elements in the Jewish tradition, it is best to first complete our very brief picture of the Jewish tradition itself. This way, we will be able to see that these apparently tangential correspondences are actually symptoms of an underlying structural resemblance, or rather mimesis, as we are convinced that the affinity was consciously elected by Benjamin to provide him with the authoritative theoretical foundation upon which to erect his alternative to the then dominant, and according to him catastrophic, ideologies of progress and historicism.[31]

The aforementioned dynamism of Jewish tradition is probably best exemplified by the emphasis of the process of interpretation rather than just the results of it, as important and authoritative as the latter may be. In the words of Aaron Lichtenstein: 'The *mitzvah* of *Talmud Torah* charges the Jew to acquire knowledge of Torah, insofar as he is able; but it addresses itself primarily to the process rather than the result.'[32] With such an emphasis, it is easy to see why not even an 'overruled' interpretation could legitimately be considered disposable. A rabbinic interpretation is revered as much for its authority as for its bearing witness to the divine act that gave birth to it, study. It cannot be stressed enough that study, the process of interpretation and the search for knowledge, is considered to be an act of devotion, competing only with prayer as the fundamental religious duty of the

Jew. Janet Aviad summarises this very neatly: '*Talmud Torah* became a distinct and powerful form of religious experience for the Jews. Study was more than a search for knowledge – it was an act of devotion and a form of prayer.'[33] This is of course not to say that *Talmud Torah* took precedence over the love of God or the love of one's neighbour: on the contrary, it was considered not only to be a prime expression of this, but also to be the shortest and most direct path to a life in accordance with all of God's commands. Communion and communication with the divine, study and prayer, must lead to a participation in the divine. And in Judaism, communication *with* the divine automatically meant communication *in* the divine, in language. Exactly how inextricably the process of tradition, study, is related to language, is borne out by the Hebrew word for tradition, *masorah* or *masoret*. 'Franz Molitor', Nathan Rotenstreich writes, 'observed that *masorah* is implicit in the biblical text because of the nature of the Hebrew language: it is written only in consonants. To read Hebrew texts aloud requires a combination of vowels and consonants and involves in this very fact the establishment of textual vocalisation which facilitates the transmission of an oral rendition of the written word.'[34]

In the narrow, technical sense of the word, the *Masorah* refers to an apparatus for the writing and reading of a biblical text. Biblical Hebrew, as well as most texts in contemporary Hebrew, contains no vowels, and originally did not even contain spacing, so it had to be vocalised in the most radical sense, literally by being voiced, by being read aloud. The reading of the Torah was traditionally a communal matter, with members of the community reading passages from it in public to celebrate special occasions, such as their coming of age or their wedding. Torah passages are cantillated, or chanted, rather than read, but as the text contains no vowels, no spacing or no accents, the correct pronunciation and cantillation had to be learned in advance of the public reading in the synagogue. By using vowel letters initially, and later through an entire system of punctuation, the Masoretic text provides the traditional vocalisation of the Torah, as it was handed down for centuries by schools of Masoretes. The composition of the Masoretic text is thought to have begun as early as the time of Ezra (fifth century BCE). Similar to the page composition of the Talmud,

46

the Masoretic text is written around the consonantal framework of the Biblical text, and like the Talmud, again, its redaction has taken many centuries. The Masoretes not only vocalised the biblical text, but also compiled extensive notes on it. Working on what we could call a sub-textual and increasingly micrological level, the Masorah not only focuses on the division of the text into paragraphs, sentences and words, but also on the different vocalizations, spellings and accents within each word, determining which letters must be written large, small, suspended, inverted, or dotted. The Masoretes counted the letters, words, and verses in the individual books and in the Bible as a whole and pointed out differences between pronunciation (*qeri* [what is read]) and spelling (*ketiv* [what is written]). True to the doctrine of inclusiveness, a special category existed for possible but unacceptable alternatives, called *sevirin*, which were highlighted but left un-changed.[35] There are three sets of progressively longer masoretic notes: the Minor Masorah, written in the side margins, the Major Masorah, placed on the tops and bottoms of the page, and the Final Masorah, the most extensive annotations, which are included at the end of the Bible. Again, the drive towards accumulation is notable, even going so far as to include traditionally unacceptable alternatives, the aforementioned *sevirin*, on the very pages of the Torah. It is this commanding desire for accumulation, extending even to unofficial, apocryphal or possibly subversive elements, which parallels the tense but constant presence of a (messianic) antinomianism under the skin of tradition, and which also must account for much of its dynamism.

It has been suggested that this necessity to vocalise the con-sonantal Hebrew text might be the origin of the mystery of the Tetragrammaton, the holiest and also unpronounceable name of God. Simply based on the position of the mouth and the tongue during the pronunciation of the sequence of semivowels and aspirants that is the Tetragrammaton, the vocalisation of YHWH automatically becomes (Y)aou(HW)ei(H), in other words, the entire sequence of vowels necessary to vocalise language as such. This would firmly root the divinity of God in language, or the divinity of language in God, and would explain the strict prohibition against pronouncing the Tetra-grammaton, as it would reveal the linguistic essence or being of God. The origin of this *aggadah*, if *aggadah* it is, cannot be traced. It is mentioned in a footnote by Lieven De Cauter, and, as tradition has it when faced with an untraceable interpretation, he received the tradition from Yohanan ben Zakkai, who heard it from his teacher, and his teacher from his teacher, as a Halakhah given to Moses on Sinai.[36] The analogy between the Tetragrammaton and the Holiest of Holies in the Jerusalem Temple we have pointed out before hints at an almost physically direct experience of language in the Jewish tradition, whereby the notion of the divinity of language does not derive from an intricate metaphorical displacement, but is experienced directly as the dwelling place of God, or even more literally, as actually *containing* God. The very notion of language as a 'container' of the divine is intimately linked with physical and spatial conceptions of the text, and indeed of language as such, as they are reflected in the layout of the Talmud. The concept itself, however, is a focal point of the Jewish tradition, in which the apparently divergent narratives on history, language and divinity intersect much like a Benjaminian *Begriff* unfolds into a Goethean *Ursprung*. This intersection is exemplified in the Talmudic legend explaining the origin and meaning of the so-called *tagin*, or decorative crowns, which are added onto certain letters without any apparent reason, on the *mezuzah* and *tefillin* scrolls as well as on the (handwritten) Torah scroll. The revealing way in which the rabbis read these ornamental curiosities will finally link the foregoing with the last part of our discussion of the Jewish tradition, *midrash*, and it is worth quoting in its entirety.

> When Moses ascended on high, he found the Holy One, blessed be He, engaged in affixing coronets to the letters. Said Moses, 'Lord of the Universe, Who stays Thy hand? [i.e. is there anything wanting in the Torah that these additions are necessary?] He answered, 'There will arise a man, at the end of many generations, Akiba ben Joseph by name, who will expound upon each tittle heaps and heaps of laws'. 'Lord of the Universe', said Moses; 'permit me to see him'. He replied 'Turn thee round'. Moses went and sat down behind eight rows [of R. Akiba's disciples, and listened to the discourses upon the law]. Not being able to follow their arguments he was ill at ease, but when they came to a certain subject and the disciples said to the master 'Whence do you know it?' and the latter replied 'It is a law given unto Moses at Sinai' he was comforted. (B. *Berakhot*, 29b)

This peculiar *aggadah* is like a dense gordian knot in the texture, absorbing several strands of the fabric of the Jewish tradition as it was described above. For one, it ties in with the (retrospective) rabbinic concept that 'all Torah came from Sinai', here even stating fairly explicitly that a suspicion of the authorial intention or original meaning need not, indeed should not, arrest the process of interpretation. That is to say, the fact that previous generations, standing closer to the original revelation and exemplified by the scribe or author by proxy of the law that bears his name, understood a particular *mishnah* in a given sense does not absolve future generations from the duty of *Talmud Torah* and from questioning the relevance of that sense to their own age. Of course, using the terms of 'authorial intention' or 'original meaning' can be very deceptive here, as the author of the Torah obviously intended it to mean everything it ever meant, can and will mean. It is quite interesting to note that Molitor refers to the same Talmudic legend very early on in the first volume of *Philosophie der Geschichte*, in order to suggest that the concept of secret or hidden meanings of the Torah was deeply ingrained within the Jewish tradition:

> Im Thalmud wird bei allen Gelegenheiten der Glaube an die verborgenen Geheimnisse der Schrift als eine ganz unbestrittene Thatsache vorausgesetzt. So heißt es z.B. im Traktat M'nachoth: 'Als Moscheh auf den Berg Sinai stieg, sah er, wie der höchstgebenedeite Kronen um die Buchstaben wand' (wodurch auf die Geheimnisse gedeutet wird, welche in den Buchstaben und ihren Kronen verborgen liegen). (*M* I, 15)

The story also emphasises the radically different concept of history inherent in the Jewish tradition. As Robert Gordis wrote: 'It is often maintained that the ancients did not have a sense of history. Hence it was possible for the rabbis to conceive of Jacob studying the Torah with his ancestor Shem, or of David and his warriors being members of a Sanhedrin and arguing points of Jewish law, or of the sinful King Menasseh disputing with God on theological doctrine.'[37] Yet rather than not having a sense of history, the Jewish tradition has a rivalling sense of history, which does not necessarily follow the 'laws' of a linear chronology that isolates historical events into autonomous experiential compartments.[38] As the legend illustrates in a very direct way, the abovementioned solidarity of past, present and future is not even unidirectional, but takes place within a continuum of shared experience. The past is not an abstract construct, revived only by the detached scholarly effort of the present, it has its own claims on and promises for the present and the future.[39] Nor is the past dead, fossilised, and the present the only living reality: that is what Benjamin called the vision of the victorious, the current hegemony whose victory completely eradicates the hopes and dreams of the conquered, thus denying them even the consolation of admitting that they once *did* exist. The Jewish vision of history places a far greater ethical demand on the present, namely to recognise the past as its neighbour, as real and tangible as the next person. What makes the legend even more salient is that it physically transposes Moses into the academy of Akiba, thus emphasising the sense of tangibility in this view. It is tempting to draw the analogy between the prophet Moses turning himself around to find that he is surrounded and enveloped by the word of God, from the supreme divine revelation in direct conversation with God to the very modest but no less worthy derivation of this revelation from the most minute fragments of Scripture, and the Torah that needs to be turned over and over to find that it envelops and surrounds the student, that all is in it.

The thread of this hermeneutical credo is closely linked to the story of the *tagin*, which can be read as one of the many blueprints of *midrash*. Just as the rabbis believed that all was in it, so they were convinced that, because of the nature of the Torah, all was in its everything. Because it was the word of God in its entirety, nothing in and around the biblical text could possibly be considered incidental, accidental, coincidental. Even those elements that are, strictly speaking, *hors-texte*, such as the essentially meaningless *tagin*, must be presumed to have a certain meaning, perhaps as yet uncovered, simply because they are there. In the words of David Stern: 'Since every verse, indeed, every word in the Torah is divine, it follows that nothing in it, not even a letter or enclitic, is without meaning or purely ornamental. Instead, every word and letter is susceptible to interpretation [...]'[40] By way of a preliminary definition, we can thus say that midrash is the interpretative labour of showing the truth of Torah even where people did not suspect it to be. As is the case with the words *Talmud (Torah)*, the word *Midrash* also refers both to the activity of inquiry and interpretation as well as to its results, to the individual *midrashim* as well as to the anthologies. In fact, insofar as the redaction of these anthologies frequently spanned several generations or even several centuries, again as in the case of the Talmud, the ambiguity inherent in their very name seems quite apt. Deceptively simple on the surface, midrash it has been suggested, 'cannot be precisely defined, but only described'.[41] And this is for this precise reason that we have circumambulated the matter for such a long time.

Midrash: How to Work with a Holy Language

As William Scott Green remarked: 'The Talmud has fallen on easy times. No longer a theological menace to be censored and defaced or an abstruse and trivial sophistry to be deprecated and ignored, the Talmud and its interpretive discourse are now in vogue, suddenly legitimate and mainstream.'[42] During the past two or three decades, much has indeed been made of 'rabbinic hermeneutics', with midrash as its flagship, as a forgotten precursor of (post)modern literary theory. Perhaps the most famous exponent of this is the work of Susan Handelman, whose controversial book *The Slayers of Moses* jumped straight in at the deep end, reviving the age-old Hebrew–Greek dichotomy, and declaring rabbinic Judaism as the advocate of a rivalling concept of time (opposed to the Western, linear view), a rivalling concept of meaning (in which a word and its referent seem all but interchangeable) and hence a rivalling concept of reading (in which midrash is said to produce an infinity of meanings from a single verse from the Torah, thus launching the whole enterprise into a semiotic free-fall). Whereas some of Handelman's parallels and analogies are certainly thought-provoking, her conclusions are rarely borne out by her rather scanty evidence, and the fact that she professes to follow the example of midrash herself by merely (gratuitously?)

pointing out structural analogies indicates that she has neither properly understood midrash nor the structure of the Jewish tradition that underlies it. Scholars like Jacob Neusner, David Stern and William Scott Green have rightly cautioned against making such sweeping statements. As Stern wrote in the introduction to one of his studies on midrash:

> As paradoxical as it may appear, the first duty of a literary approach to midrash, therefore, must be to suspend temporarily more immediate concerns with literature proper and to go over, as it were, to the other side in order to describe the specific language of midrash and the special conditions which created its literary forms and modes of expression.[43]

Midrash is in fact at the furthest possible remove from being an informal, non-committal play on multiple meanings, and the fact that it is not would at least in part explain its fascination to a writer like Benjamin. As we mentioned before, midrashim follow the main distinction in the Jewish tradition between *Halakhah* and *Aggadah*, and tend to be either exegetical or homiletical in their basic thrust, although these divisions are typically not quite as rigid on the ground. The halakhic midrashim are predictably exegetical, as their aim, amongst other things, is the derivation of *Halakhah* from the Bible, supplying details which are missing in the Bible, resolving contradictions or providing instructions for the application of a biblical rule. Yet since they are conceived as continuous *catena*-like commentaries on the individual books of the Bible, the halakhic midrashim do not exclude its narrative passages and frequently include a great deal of *Aggadah*. The sheer volume of midrashim produced over the centuries as well as their prominent position in the Jewish tradition indicates that the midrashic literature is in no way second to the Talmudic literature discussed above. Not only do they frequently have the same authors, they also often address the same issues, and fragments and even citations of one frequently find their way into the other. The principles of accumulation, interweaving and exponential complexity in the Jewish tradition clearly transcend the precarious boundary of genre; indeed, they appear to be what makes this boundary so precarious.

The structure of the individual midrash is illustrated quite well by the composition of a typical homiletical midrash, a dense constellation which, in a sense, mirrors the methodology and perspectival lines of the Jewish tradition as such. The homiletical midrash opens with a preamble, typically beginning with a verse from *Ketubim*, or in any case not usually a verse from the book from which the lectionary verse of the Torah reading is taken. The preacher or *darshan*, a word derived from the same root as *midrash* and *darash*, then proceeds to explain the meaning of this verse with the aid of other verses from the Bible, which, other than perhaps having one word or name in common, are not necessarily related to the opening verse in any way. We have emphasised before, with reference to the Talmudic literature, that the Jewish tradition can be seen as an almost spatial, homogeneous and simultaneous whole, and this is certainly the most tangible micrological manifestation of that. To the *darshan* and his audience, be they the community at large or students in a rabbinic academy, there is no hierarchical difference between any two verses in the Bible. They are both infused with equal divinity, and whatever their individual historical, legal or narrative import, it necessarily comes second to this fact. As Stemberger phrased it: 'The context [...] is the entire Bible; any of its verses can be related to any other, while the specific intention of an individual book is rarely of interest. One encounters the Bible as an integral whole, which accordingly carries a uniform divine message.'[44]

Paradoxically, perhaps, it is this characteristic which lends midrashic hermeneutics their greatest freedom as well as their greatest restraint. The fact that any verse, any word, any root or even any sequence of letters from anywhere in the Bible can be used to back up an argument, encourages students to move freely within the confines of the text, to swim in the Book, so to speak, and let chance correspondences take them to unexpected revelations.[45] But whereas, on the one hand, the most minute similarity is enough to justify a connection, the conclusion drawn from that connection, on the other hand, will predictably be in line with the main tenets of orthodoxy. This is not so much because midrashic hermeneutics cannot beget unorthodox conclusions, but because these conclusions are usually pre-emptively policed. The fascination of midrash, however, as with any other form of theological hermeneutics, lies in the very fact that unorthodox conclusions are indeed possible, as is witnessed by the rich, colourful and sometimes dramatic history of heresy in both the Jewish and the Christian tradition. As Jorge Luis Borges wrote so memorably in his short story 'The Library of Babel', it is enough for a book to be possible to ensure that it will exist.

Midrash, as Stemberger points out, is indeed a literature of compilation and quotation.[46] In both exegetical and homiletical midrashim, it is not unusual to find several different interpretations of the same verse, phrase or even word chained one after the other, separated by the phrase *dabar aher*, 'another interpretation'. This accumulation of interpretations not only serves to pile proof upon proof, or simply to provide alternative readings, their juxtaposition sometimes creates a constellation in which a carefully edited meaning appears to emerge. It is the same desire to create a constellation that animates the preamble to the homiletical midrash, which, in a final turn, always links up with the lectionary verse of the sermon proper. This turn is both expected and unexpected, as the congregation knows what is going to happen, but does not know how. The rhetorical and dialectical strategies of some of these preambles indeed suggest that the *darshanim* themselves derived great pleasure from leading their audience away from anything resembling a straight line to a conclusion and towards tortuous by-roads and detours, almost consciously delaying their final arrival at the lectionary verse which, when it finally came, must have seemed an intellectual *(dé)tour de force* indeed. One particular strategy the rabbis used in order to create their constellations was the atomisation of the opening verse into smaller units, a strategy which in its turn had a delaying effect, as the full meaning of the verse would only emerge after the several meanings that the *darshan* elicited from its constituent parts had all been woven together. The first midrash of *Bereshith Rabbah* is a fine example of this, as it not only picks apart the opening verse, but quotes the most disparate verses from the rest of the Bible to expand and enrich its meaning:

> R. Oshaya commenced: *Then I was by Him, as a nursling* (amon); *and I was daily all delight* (Prov. 8:30). '*Amon*' means tutor; '*amon*' means covered;

'*amon*' means hidden; and some say '*amon*' means great. '*Amon*' is a tutor, as you read, *As an* omen (*nurse*) *carrieth the sucking child* (Num. 11:12). '*Amon*' means covered, as in the verse, Ha'emunim (*they that were clad* – i.e. covered) *in scarlet* (Lam. 4:5). '*Amon*' means hidden, as in the verse, *And he concealed* (omen) *Hadassah* (Est. 2:7). '*Amon*' means great, as in the verse, *Art thou better than No-amon* (Nah. 3:8)? which is rendered, Art thou better than Alexandria the Great, that is situate among the rivers? Another interpretation [*dabar aher*]: '*amon*' is workman (*uman*). The Torah declares: 'I was the working tool of the Holy One, blessed be He.' In human practice, when a mortal king builds a palace, he builds it not with his own skill but with the skill of an architect. The architect moreover does not build it out of his head, but employs plans and diagrams to know how to arrange the chambers and the wicket doors. Thus God consulted the Torah and created the world, while the Torah declares, IN THE BEGINNING GOD CREATED (1:1), BEGINNING referring to the Torah, as in the verse, *The Lord made me as the beginning of His way* (Prov. 8:22). (*Bereshith Rabbah*, I.1)[47]

The opening verse is selected from a section of Proverbs in which Wisdom, speaking in the first person, tells of its role in Creation (8:22–31). Halfway through the preamble, Oshaya states explicitly what a perceptive reader or hearer may well have suspected already, namely that the speaker here is the Torah itself. The speaker of the verse that is the actual subject of the midrash, set here in capitals, is of course the Torah, and this self-referentiality is exploited by the *darshan*, saying that (IN THE) BEGINNING refers to the Torah. In fact, it refers to the Torah *à coups redoublés*. By uttering the words *Be-Reshith*, IN THE BEGINNING, the Torah not only invokes the beginning, but also brings it about, both in a mystical and in a very real sense. In the mystical sense, the analogy is voiced by the kaballist doctrine according to which God created the world by uttering his own name, composed of all the letters of the alphabet and all the words of the Torah. In a real sense, the word *Bereshith* invokes and articulates the beginning quite simply by actually beginning the text. There is another analogy lurking under the surface which is not made explicit in this midrash, or indeed any other we are aware of, and that is the fact that all five books of the Bible are named after their first word or words, which would make *Bereshith* metonymical not only for Genesis, but also for the entire Torah.

Given the importance attached to this beginning, it may seem odd that the great midrash on Genesis should open with what to all intents and purposes seems to be a random verse from Proverbs, *in medias res* rather than 'in the beginning.' Yet the standard beginning of the preamble, 'R. Oshaya commenced', takes us even further forward, somehow suggesting that a humble third-century rabbi was allowed to pre-empt the beginning – as his text commences before the BEGINNING – and the in itself apparently secondary opening verse, taken from *Ketubim* and not from the Torah, in its turn takes a second place. This could be seen as an exemplary instance of the methodological detour, but there is a good deal more to it. The rabbi's emphatic presence can be read as an affirmation of the authority of the oral law, almost on a par with the written Torah itself, and a confession to the holy duty of *Talmud Torah*, its recognition as the breath of life of the Torah.[48] The verses from Proverbs, Lamentations, Numbers, Esther and Nahum can come to explain the opening words of the Bible – their own origin, so to speak – because they are already inherent in its very first word. Stern wrote about this phenomenon:

> a fundamental tendency of midrash [is] the urge to unite the diverse parts of Scripture into a single and seamless whole reflecting the unity of God's will. This tendency derives directly from the rabbinic ideology of the canonical Torah – Pentateuch, Prophets and Writings – as the inspired word of God, a timeless unity in which *each and every verse is simultaneous with every other, temporally and semantically*; as a result, every verse, no matter how remote, can be seen as a possible source for illuminating the meaning of any other verse.[49]

Echoing a conclusion about the structure of the Talmud, we can again say that the effect of this tendency towards temporal and semantic simultaneity, of which the prolific quotations and cross-reference in midrash are but symptoms, is to create an almost tangible, homogeneous space. It could perhaps be compared to a cumulative hypertext, whereby links do not substitute one another but are superimposed, the first still visible through the second. With another favourite metaphor in modern literary theory, the space of tradition could also be compared to an infinite regress or a *mise-en-abyme*, without the connotation of gradual decline or the hierarchy of superior original and inferior copy. In the terminology borrowed from what seems a radically different system, we might say that the second law of thermodynamics does not apply to theology.

But, taking our cue from Stemberger, we will turn to description rather than definition in order to illustrate these fairly awkward analogies. Rabbi Oshaya opens by quoting a verse from Proverbs and highlighting a single word from it, *amon*, which, as the Hebrew Bible is not vocalised, in fact appears as a typical trisyllabic root, אמן or *'mn*. Oshaya then gives four other meanings which this root can take, 'tutor', 'hidden', 'covered' and 'great', and quotes the verses from which he culled these variants, which, by dint of sharing a single root with his opening verse, are taken to shed light on it. By describing itself as God's nursling, *amon*, the Torah thus also becomes the tutor, *omen*, of the Jewish people, having remained hidden, *(ha)'emun(im)*, and covered, *omen*, once before Creation and once before Revelation, and it is also great, *(No-)amon*, the Hebrew name for Thebes or Alexandria, outshining the earthly glory of the latter and all the books in its legendary library. Another interpretation: *amon*, the 'great, hidden, covered nursling tutor', is also *uman*, a workman, God's tool in creation. The Torah is all these things at the same time, because all these meanings appear through the root *'mn*. This root is the central focus of the midrash, its Archimedean point so to speak, and Oshaya fits the relevant verses around it, allowing these verses to shed light upon the Torah as much as he lets the light to shine through the root from different angles, thereby allowing it to assume different meanings. Oshaya's tool is in fact this trisyllabic root, which he wields to perfection, weaving a dense, layered texture through it. The *darshan* turns the root around and around, and at every turn it accumulates another meaning. Only the necessity of eventually commencing the midrash proper brings this exercise to a halt, but if the movement were to be endlessly repeated, the ultimate *Umweg*, it would in fact unfold the whole of tradition. This very belief, this very desire is the vanishing point of the Jewish concept of study, and thus, in a sense, the afterlife of tradition is already contained in the beginning, in its first word, *Be-Reshith*. It is in this sense that midrash can be seen as a micrological version of the entire Jewish tradition, a compact monad which, however minute, contains the whole development of tradition tucked away into its folds.

Midrash, as we said above, tends to atomise Scripture into ever smaller units. The starting point is usually the verse, which is cut up into phrases or words. These words are reduced to their root, and these roots in turn are often divided into their constituent letters and recombined into different words. The fact that the scrolls of the Torah contained no vowel points or spaces before the composition of the *Masorah* made this exercise less anomalous than it may seem at first. With a technique known as *notarikon*, a word is often divided into two or more, or read as an acronym, using each of its letters as the first letter of another word. A fine example of this is God's reassurance to Moses that he will enjoy divine protection from his critics and detractors if he but holds on to the Throne of Glory, 'as it is said *He maketh him to hold on to the face of his throne, And spreadeth* [PaRSHeZ] *his cloud over him* (*Job* 26:9), whereon R. Nahman observed: This teaches that the Almighty [*Shaddai*] spread [*PiRash*] the lustre [*Ziw*] of His *Shekhinah* and cast it as a protection over him.' (B. *Shabbath*, 88b). One word is thus expanded into an entire sentence, individual letters unfold into new words, forming a new constellation which typically weaves yet another layer of meaning into the already dense texture.

At another point in the Talmud, the same technique is applied to the entire Hebrew alphabet, with a kind of religious primer as its result: '*Alef Beth* [means] learn wisdom [*alef Binah*]; *Gimel Daleth*, show kindness to the poor [*Gemol Dallim*]; [...]' (B. *Shabbath*, 104a). This passage is in turn a perfect example of what we have constantly referred to as a constellation. Leaving out all the editorial additions that make the Talmud legible to a lay audience, the previous example simply reads as '*Alef Beth alef Binah; Gimel Daleth Gemol Dallim*'. The interpretation acquires its full effect exactly because of the immediate juxtaposition of the letters and the words they are taken to represent. The rabbi, so to speak, does not need to step out of the sphere of language, because all is in it. The almost deceptive simplicity that makes these interpretations very *literally* literally self-evident points towards a tendency that is inherent in rabbinic or midrashic interpretation as such, from this simple *notarikon* as a

58

midrash stripped to the bare essentials to the elaborate detours of a preamble on its way to the midrash. The same tendency is also borne out by the very appearance and the immensity of the corpus of the Jewish tradition, rich as it is in discussions and elaborations, commentaries and commentaries on commentaries, which it accumulates and weaves into its texture, one on top of the other. This tendency is a marked aversion towards the bare, dogmatic statement, balanced by a predilection towards demonstration, discussion, reasoning, and the construction of arguments. As the fate of Maimonides's *Mishneh Torah* so eminently illustrates, even the greatest authority brushes this tendency against the grain at his own peril. Only when the evidence and discussion for the halakhic decisions in the *Mishneh Torah* was shown to exist and conscientiously provided could it be assumed into a position of authority. And, as we have seen from the examples from Talmud and Midrash, the ultimate evidence in the Jewish tradition is always textual, in its first and most basic meaning, that is, scriptural. In rabbinic interpretation, the quotation of a verse from the Torah that can be shown to be relevant to the matter at hand will never fail to carry infinitely more weight than any argument brought to it from the outside, however logical, expedient or desirable it may seem. In fact, the best way to illustrate this complex tendency may well be to simply juxtapose it to another quotation, akin to the rabbis' in orientation and sparseness of diction:

> Methode dieser Arbeit: literarische Montage. Ich habe nichts zu sagen. Nur zu zeigen. Ich werde nichts Wertvolles entwenden und mir keine geistvollen Formulierungen aneignen. Aber die Lumpen, den Abfall: die will ich nicht inventarisieren sondern sie auf die einzig mögliche Weise zu ihrem Rechte kommen lassen: sie verwenden. (V, 574)[50]

Both as a method and in its results, as a *Gedankenbewegung* and as a medium, the basic thrust of midrash is metonymical and mimetic. One verse is taken to reveal a truth about another verse because they share a phrase or a word. A point is made through proximity, but also through repetition and the revelation of a likeness. Midrash constructs a constellation, with superimpositions and juxtapositions, which hinges on proximity, repetition and likeness. And recalling Barry

Holtz's statement that 'almost all Jewish writing is a kind of midrash', we can say that by extension, just like the structure of an individual molecule mimics the structure of the snow crystal to which it belongs, what is true for midrash is also true for the Jewish tradition as a whole. Its blueprint, too, is metonymical and mimetic. The very first word of the Torah creates a chain which links its every single word. Yet this chain does not end with the Bible's last word, as the thread of the written law is picked up and continued by the oral law, exercising authority by proxy and by proximity. And even within the sphere of the Torah itself, the chain not only folds back on itself but also creates a dense network in which every single word is linked to every other word, every single letter to every other letter. The immense corpus of *Halakhah* and *Aggadah* that is attached to this Torah echoes, mimics, repeats and rehearses both its origin and itself.

Oshaya's midrash described the Torah as the architectural plan according to which the world was formed, and just as the Torah thus already traces the structure of everything in this world, every word in the tradition is in some way linked to a word in the Torah. These links, both 'inside' and 'outside' the Torah, defy space and time. By metonymy, they create a space of simultaneity which is meaningful by mimesis, and ultimately, recalling David Stern's metaphor, this metonymy is 'a trope for God'. Because of the divine nature of this continuous metonymy, which was described by the mystics in terms of divine emanations, the mimesis in question is anything but a chance correspondence. One consequence of this credo is that the accumulation of interpretations and meanings we have spoken of should not strictly speaking be seen as a mere addition, but rather a belated revelation of what was already there, an ongoing accomplishment and completion of Revelation. As James Kugel has it: 'Some students of midrash would argue – correctly, I think – that in the midrashic view divine words have an existence independent of circumstance and immediate intention, that, in short, a text is a text, and whatever hidden meaning one is able to reveal in it through "searching" simply *is there*, part of the divine plan.'[51] The accumulation does not so much move outwards as dig inwards. The texture of tradition does not so much stretch and extend as contract and condense. Tradition is in fact at its most inclusive and accumulative where it concentrates on and into its most minute components and unfolds their full potential. Tradition uses its own 'rags and rubbish' and does justice to them in the only possible way: by using them, by hallowing them. The rabbinic tendency towards the atomisation of Scripture does not stop at the triconsonantal root, the individual letter, nor even at the individual pen strokes of which a letter is composed, it goes right down to the single *ziyyun* or downward stroke of the apparently a-textual *tagin*:

R. Ashi said, I have observed that scribes who are most particular add a vertical stroke to the roof of the letter *heth* [note: normally ח, the form of this letter in Scrolls to the present day is ﬨ, and suspend the [inner] leg of the letter *he* [ה]. They add a vertical stroke to the roof of the letter *heth*, signifying thereby that He lives in the heights of the wor[l]d[52] [note: the letter *heth* is the initial letter of the word חי, 'He lives', and the stroke or tower above indicates that the abode of the living God is on high.]. And they suspend the [inner] leg of the letter *he* for the reason given in the following discussion. For R. Judah the Patriarch asked R. Ammi, What is the meaning of the verse, *Trust ye in the Lord for ever; for in Yah the Lord is an everlasting rock* (*Isa.* 26:4)? He replied, It implies that if one puts his trust in the Holy One, blessed be He, behold He is unto him as a refuge in this world and in the world to come. This, retorted the other, was my difficulty: why does the verse say *in Yah* and not *Yah*? The reason is as was expounded by R. Judah b. R. Ila'i. [*Yah*, he said,] refers to the two worlds which the Holy One, blessed be He, created, one with the letter *he* and the other with the letter *yod* [י]. Yet I do not know whether the future world was created with the *yod* and this world with the *he*; but since it is written, *These are the generations of the heaven and of the earth when they were created* (Gen, 2:4) [note: the latter half of the verse reads: כי ביה ה' צור עולמים, and this is interpreted as meaning 'for with Yah (i.e. with the letters *yod* and *he*) the Lord formed the worlds.']: read not *be-hibare'am*, when they were created, but *be-he bera'am*, He created them with the *he*; hence I may say that this world was created with the *he* and the future world with the *yod*. And wherefore was this world created with the *he*? – Because it is like an *exedra* [i.e. closed on three sides and open on the fourth, as is the letter *he* (cfr. B. *Baba Batra*, 25a–b)] and whosoever wishes to go astray may do so. And wherefore is the [left] leg of the *he* suspended? – To indicate that whosoever repents is permitted to re-enter [through the small opening at the side]. And why should he not re-enter by the same [way as he went out]? – Such an opportunity would not arise [note: the repentant sinner requires encouragement and support, so that an additional entrance is made ready for him]; ... (B. *Menahoth*, 29b)

As we have mentioned time and again, the differences between Talmudic and Midrashic literature, as well as those between *Halakhah* and *Aggadah*, especially as far as their textual practice is concerned, should never be overstated: the Jewish tradition is fairly consistent and homogeneous in its approach to language and interpretation. However, this does not so much stem from a rabbinic theory of language, the precursor of poststructuralism as Handelman *cum suis* would have it, but rather from a more profound belief – and this word is important, as the eminently *theological* nature of the matter is all too often forgotten – in a certain narrative of creation, election and revelation. Rather than a consciously constructed and explicitly formulated hermeneutic theory, the logic of midrash could be said to derive from a specific view of the Torah, which we have discussed in this chapter, and which David Stern describes as the 'virtual ideology of rabbinic thought'. 'According to this ideology,' says Stern,

> the Torah is not so much a text – it is certainly unlike any other text in human reality – as it is a trope for God, not in the later kabbalist sense in which the very words of the Torah are said to constitute the names of God and to embody his attributes, but in a metonymic fashion, whereby the Torah's being is treated as a kind of figurative extension of God's: just as he is timeless, so the Torah is beyond all temporality; just as his deeds are meaningful, so every word in the Torah is full of significance; and so on.[53]

It is thus the ineffa(cea)ble underlying doctrine of the pervasive and literally 'contagious' sanctity of the Torah and the concomitant concepts of its identity with the Divine that results in the above-mentioned consistency of the rabbinic approach to language and inter-pretation. The passage from the Talmudic tractate *Menahoth* quoted above is symptomatic of this doctrine. Although taken from the Tal-mud, it exhibits practically all of the characteristics that are generally attributed to midrash. There is the element of discussion, taking place here between three different rabbis of three different generations, with questions and answers transcending time and space; there is the cross-reference between verses from different parts of the Bible, as a verse from Genesis (2:4) is used to solve what at first sight – or to all intents and purposes, depending on one's perspective – is a textual anomaly in Isaiah (26:4); there is the alternative spacing and vocalisation, as *be-hibare'am* is read as *be-he bera'am*; there is the constellation, in this case a constellation of letters, created by reading ביה as *with YH* rather than *in Yah*, which is in its turn used as the pivot of the entire passage. And then there is the atomisation, not only of verse and word, but also of individual letters. The contrast between the big gap in the underside of the letter *he* and the small gap between its horizontal stroke and its left leg is read as the proof that it is easy to be lead into temptation, but hard to repent. This interpretation is linked to Scripture only insofar that Yehudah bar Il'ai has proven, with an alternative reading of the verse, that the letter *he* refers to the present world (thereby implying that the letter *yod*, the other letter in the constellation, must needs refer to the future world). From there, the actual conclusion is reached independently of scriptural 'evidence', as the verses in question say nothing about temptation or redemption. Yet, the point is that there is a clearly substantiated reason for every single step of the argument, however slowly it progresses and whatever winding ways it may take.

The methodical care with which the rabbis establish a discernible, motivated link between every single step of their argument brings us to the final articulation of our own argument. Just as the Jewish tradition sees the Torah as a trope for God, partaking of equal divinity by metonymy, the rabbis saw their own enterprise, expounding the oral law by expanding the written law, as sharing in the same divinity of the latter, by metonymy. For this reason, they took great care in their work never to lose touch, in the most literal sense of the word, with the written law, the Torah. Even though much of rabbinic law is said to be 'like a mountain hanging from a hair', the sense of a certain tangible connection to revelation, however minute it may seem, appears to be a constant preoccupation. The Talmud can in fact be seen as an attempt to provide these links for the Mishnah, to sew its texture to that of the Torah, so to speak, with an innumerable amount of different threads. This meticulous tracing of the divine genealogy of an argument or interpretation bears witness to a certain conception of language which makes such a notion possible in the first place. As the passage from *Menahoth* indicates, individual letters and even parts of letters are considered to be infused with meaning, to contain sparks of Revelation. This is because the world was created with language, because this language was then given to man, because man used it to name the creation that had been entrusted to him, and because God had used the same language – which is of course Hebrew in all four instances – to reveal the Commandments to Moses.

Exactly because there was considered to be such an intimate link between language, Creation and Revelation, it could simply not occur to the Jewish mind that this language would consist of mere signs, let alone arbitrary signs. The opposite was rather true, as language was endowed with elements of the reality which it had created. And as we have seen time and again, in midrashic and Talmudic literature, words and letters are handled and manipulated as if they are three-dimensional, as if they have a full, physical existence in the semiotic-ally pregnant sphere of the continuous Revelation that is tradition. Such a fullness, we have seen, is even attributed to the tiniest details, the epiphenomena of language. It is inconceivable that such a belief would not read and treat those words as a valuable, tangible reality. This sense of the tangibility of language and its intimate connection with the divine is voiced by Shalom Rosenberg:

> The symbolic essence of the Torah is expressed in the statement that the Torah is nothing but a tissue of the names of God. The words of the Torah are not only linguistic creations consisting of information about God and the world, but also concrete objects – 'names'. This identity of symbols and reality leads to an understanding of the sacredness of the Torah as well as to consciousness of its divine status.[54]

It is in fact the name, both with and without a capital *N*, which brings together the concepts of divinity, tangibility and a warranted, non-arbitrary meaning. 'Die Theorie des Eigennamens', Benjamin wrote, 'ist die Theorie von der Grenze der endlichen gegen die unendliche Sprache.' (II, 149). It is also the name as the vanishing point of the divine in Benjamin's philosophy which makes the latter a genuine heir of the Jewish tradition, if a slightly unorthodox one, who was able to state that Adam and not Plato should be seen as the father of philosophy, as he writes in *Ursprung des deutschen Trauerspiels*:

In solcher Haltung aber steht zuletzt nicht Platon, sondern Adam, der Vater der Menschen als Vater der Philosophie, da. Das Adamitische Namengeben ist so weit entfernt Spiel und Willkür zu sein, daß vielmehr gerade in ihm der paradiesische Stand sich als solcher bestätigt, der mit der mitteilenden Bedeutung der Worte noch nicht zu ringen hatte. (I, 217)

Chapter Two: Franz Joseph Molitor

Der Mann Molitor

Franz Joseph Molitor was born in Oberursel near Mainz in 1779 as the son of a local civil servant.[1] At the age of eighteen, his father persuaded him to study law at the university of Mainz and later at Marburg. Molitor appears to have lost interest in his law studies pretty swiftly, and turned instead to history and philosophy, encouraged by his friend and mentor, historian and statesman Nikolaus Vogt. Molitor immersed himself in the idealist philosophy of Kant, Reinhold, Fichte and particularly Schelling. In 1802, Molitor set up a journal with his friend Kollmann with the resounding title *Zeitschrift für eine künftig aufzustellende Rechtswissenschaft nach dem Princip eines transcendentalen Realismus*, but the enterprise proved to be quite short-lived. When, however, Friedrich Wilhelm Schelling published his book *Philosophie und Religion* in 1804, Molitor was profoundly impressed. He had clearly found his intellectual home in Schelling's idealism and read the book often and, in his own words, 'mit heiliger Andacht'.[2] Although it is *Philosophie und Religion* which inspires him, Molitor soon finds himself in disagreement with certain elements of Schelling's brand of idealism. In 1805, therefore, he publishes a short book, entitled *Ideen zu einer künftigen Dynamik der Geschichte*, in which he accuses Schelling's radical, 'postlapsarian' idealism of having retreated into the mind and given up on the divine as a unifying principle. Much like Benjamin more than a century later, Molitor did not believe in the idea of discrete historical epochs that either had the ability to be in touch with the divine or not at all, that were either an era of growth or an era of decay.[3] As he writes in the introduction to the book: 'Es gebricht allen bisherigen Versuchen gänzlich an objektiver Einheit eines allgemein durchgreifenden Beziehungspunktes; es gebricht ihnen allen an dem wahren innern Lebenskeime eines organisirenden Prinzips.'[4] In the same year, Molitor wrote another short book on the same theme, entitled *Der Wendepunkt des Antiken und Modernen*, with the subtitle *Versuch den Realismus mit dem Idealismus zu Versöhnen*. This preoccupation with a single organising principle that would nevertheless be able to draw in the whole array of human experience would continue to inform Molitor's work, and his later writings on the Jewish tradition can be read as an attempt to construct the one perspective from which the entire (theological) history of both Judaism and Christianity can be explained.

After his studies, Molitor moved to Frankfurt am Main and became a teacher. In 1804, he was involved in a project which, for the first time, would see Jewish and non-Jewish children being taught alongside each other by both Jewish and Christian teachers. In 1807, this school becomes the famous *Philanthropinum*, the Jewish secondary school in Frankfurt, and Molitor takes up a full-time post, teaching ethics, history, geography and physics. But even more than by the actual teaching, Molitor was driven by the desire to integrate the Jewish children into European culture, and it is here that his lifelong fascination with Judaism and the Jewish tradition really began. Through his work at the *Philanthropinum*, Molitor also came to the attention of Bettina Brentano von Arnim, the well-known author and herself a major benefactor of the Jewish community, with whom he shares a very keen interest in pedagogical matters. She grows very fond of him and is full of admiration for the idea of 'her Molitor' to educate Jewish and Christian children in the same classroom: 'und wenn ich sagen soll, so schien mir dies eine Alleinerziehung; nämlich: Kinder gleichen Alters, gleicher Fähigkeiten früh daran zu gewöhnen, daß sie auch gleich menschliche Rechte haben, sie mögen Juden oder Christen sein.'[5] The picture Bettine paints of Franz Joseph Molitor is, like all contemporary testimonies, that of a god-fearing, good-natured, selfless and self-effacing man, who works tirelessly for the Jews, but it also reveals another facet of his interests, apart from the teaching, which Bettina appears to find rather mystifying:

> dieser Edle ist der Meinung, daß, da er einen Leib für die Juden zu opfern habe und einen Geist ihnen zu widmen, beide auch recht nützlich anzuwenden; es geht ihm übrigens nicht sehr wohl, außer in seinem Vertrauen auf Gott, bei

welchem er jedoch fest glaubt, daß die Welt nur durch Schwarzkunst wieder ins Gleichgewicht zu bringen ist; [...] brav ist er und will ernstlich das Gute; bekümmert sich deswegen nicht um die Welt und um sein eigen Fortkommen; ist mit einem Stuhl, einem Bett, und mit fünf Büchern, die er im Vermögen hat, sehr wohl zufrieden.[6]

It is not immediately obvious what Bettina means by this *Schwarzkunst*, but when she says that Molitor is convinced that this 'black art' is the only thing capable of putting the world right again, we may safely assume that this refers to Molitor's interest in Jewish mysticism. Bettina von Arnim's evident bewilderment at this is a fairly typical reaction, from Jews and Gentiles alike, and although Molitor rarely had to deal with outright hostility, it is clear that he was venturing into thoroughly unfamiliar territory and that he was very much on his own. Still, thanks to Bettina's enthusiasm, even Goethe became interested in Molitor and his work, requested and read copies of his books, with which he appears to have been suitably impressed, as he wrote to Bettina: 'Wenn der Mann so vernünftig wirkt als er schreibt, so muß er viel Gutes erschaffen.'[7]

As a result of his experience in the *Philanthropinum*, Molitor wrote a short book on pedagogy, *Ueber Bürgerliche Erziehung mit Beziehung auf die Organisation des jüdischen Schulwesens in Frankfurt am Main* (1808), in which he argues passionately in favour of the integration and assimilation of especially the poorer sections of the Jewish community into civil society. His approach here is again holistic, focused on an overarching principle that would unite the perceived opposition of theory and praxis. At this point it is very interesting to note that Molitor's description of this unifying principle is beginning to resemble, at least in part, the epistemological definition of tradition, with the emphasis on continuity and inclusiveness:

Denn von der Entwicklung des allerersten sinnlichen Begriffs in der kindlichen Seele, bis hinauf zu dem höchsten Sichselbstbegreifen des Geistes, in der Philosophie, ist alles nur eine einzige fast [*sic*] zusammenhängende Kettenstufe von Begriffen. Nichts ist in dem menschlichen Geiste gesondert, und isolirt von einander, sondern jede Gedanke stehet mit allen andern in einer Verkettung.[8]

Molitor seems to have become interested in the Kabbalah through his friendship with Ephraim Joseph Hirschfeld, the renowned Jewish freemason and kabbalist, with whom he became acquainted as a member of the masonic lodge *Zur aufgehenden Morgenröthe*.[9] Yet Molitor's involvement with the masons is a curious episode, as it reveals an uncharacteristically intolerant side to the character of a man who had for many years been a passionate advocate of Jewish integration. Founded in Frankfurt in 1808, this lodge was unique in that it not only allowed Jews to become members, but also in that its membership was very probably predominantly Jewish, and Molitor appears to have joined this lodge with great enthusiasm. Unfortunately, this enlightened experiment proved to be rather shortlived, as the lodge excluded Jews from the higher degrees that became available in 1812 and was ordered to disband in 1816 by the Landgraf of Hessen-Kassel at the very moment that a Jew, Carl Leopold Goldschmidt, was elected Grand Master of the Chair. Molitor appears to have been quite seriously implicated in this sorry affair by personally posting the official notification of the closure to the temple door and by acquiring permission from the Landgraf to found – and head – an exclusively Christian lodge, *Carl zum aufgehenden Licht im Orient*.[10] Oddly enough for someone with his background, Molitor went even further down this path of discrimination during the 1830s and 1840s, when members of his lodge blocked attempts to remove the restrictions on Jewish membership of the freemasons in Frankfurt. He even wrote to George Kloss, then head of the Eclectic Covenant of Frankfurt (uniting all Frankfurt lodges), explicitly stating that 'no man could ever attain the excellence aspired to by the Masons through his own efforts, unless he was aided by Christian divine grace'.[11] This statement seems out of character for a man who spent more than thirty years of his life researching the Jewish tradition, wrote the most detailed study of the Jewish purity laws in his time and maintained throughout his *Philosophie der Geschichte* that 'das Christenthum daher in seiner wahren Tiefe gar nicht gründlich verstanden werden [kann], ohne die tiefste Erkenntnis des Judenthums, welches die Grundlage und Wurzel von ersterem ist' (*M* I, 312).[12] But then, as Scholem does not cease to remind us, Molitor is a most paradoxical and at times almost antinomian figure, which in turn would have done his standing in the eyes of Scholem and Benjamin no harm at all.

When Franz Joseph Molitor made the acquaintance of Ephraim Joseph Hirschfeld during the early, undisturbed years of the so-called *Frankfurter Judenloge*, the latter lived in Offenbach near Frankfurt. At that time Offenbach was still a major centre for the Frankist movement, with whom Hirschfeld maintained close contacts, and it is highly likely that Hirschfeld introduced Molitor to Frankists living there. In any case, it is true that the kabbalistically inspired, syncretist projects of both Hirschfeld and Molitor showed great affinity to the spirit of Frankism. What can be established with a greater degree of certainty is that, in 1813, Molitor was introduced to Rabbi Anschel Metz in Offenbach, with whom he started his studies of Hebrew, Aramaic, the Talmud and possibly also kabbalist works. These studies continued in later years with various, but always anonymous, liberally and theosophically minded rabbis and covered not only the Talmud and the Midrashim, but also the *Zohar*, the *Sefer Yetsirah* and the Lurianic Kabbalah. From that point onwards, Molitor devoted his entire life to the study of the Kabbalah, writing four volumes of his titanic *Philosophie der Geschichte oder über die Tradition* between 1827 and 1857.

Despite persistent ill-health, financial difficulties – he gave up his teaching positions in several schools to devote more time to the book – and often even hostility from both Jewish and Gentile quarters, he pursued his project single-mindedly, writing to Schelling in 1828: 'Der Wunsch, dieses angefangene Werk auszuführen, ist das einzige Ziel meiner ganzen Erdentätigkeit.'[13] In a way, it is hardly surprising that a book which interprets Christianity as a spiritualised form of Judaism, without claiming either that the former had replaced the latter or was even in any meaningful way superior to it, would have met with a hostile reception from most Christians at the time. But as Molitor himself says in his letters to Schelling, the reaction from the Jewish community was at times also decidely frosty: 'Bei den theologischen Juden hat meine Arbeit einen sehr üblen Eindruck gemacht, sie werfen mir vor, durch die Lobpreisung und Wiederauf-suchung des alten Obskurantismus der modernen Zivilisation des Judentums zu schaden.'[14] As a result of this disapproval, Molitor

published all four volumes of *Philosophie der Geschichte* anonym-
ously, so as to conceal the identity of the rabbis with whom he had
studied the Kabbalah because they feared 'sich den größten Verfol-
gungen ihrer orthodoxen Glaubensgenossen auszusetzen'.[15] This experience is particularly interesting in the light of Gershom Scholem's
analysis of the state of Jewish Studies in the nineteenth century, and
consequently of Franz Joseph Molitor's role in it, which we will discuss in the following paragraph.

Immer noch beachtenswert...

Molitor's exposition of the Jewish tradition and Jewish mysticism in
his masterpiece, *Philosophie der Geschichte oder über die Tradition*,
is nothing if not passionate, and this makes his illiberal obstinacy he
showed as a member of the masonic lodges even harder to understand.
Initially intended to cover two and later three volumes, Molitor finally
settled on the idea to write five volumes of the work, of which only
the first four were written. In the end, it was only the fifth volume
which was supposed to be specifically on the Kabbalah, whereas the
first four volumes were taken up with all the background information
Molitor thought necessary for a correct and in-depth understanding of
the tradition of Jewish mysticism. To him, this not only meant a high
level of familiarity with the nature and structure of the language in
which the books of the Jewish tradition were written, but also with
their expansive historical and religious context. He came to this
conclusion during his preparatory studies with a Talmud scholar and
Semitic philologist, which seemed to necessitate ever further excursions and contextualisations. As he wrote in a letter to Schelling in
1828:

> Denn das thalmudische und kabbalistische Studium ist mit außerordentlichen
> Schwierigkeiten verbunden, da das meiste noch ohne alle systematische
> Ordnung auseinander liegt, und um ein Buch gehörig zu verstehen, voraus-
> gesetzt wird, daß man die anderen auch gelesen hat. Daher nützt die bloße

syrochaldäische Sprachkenntnis noch keineswegs zum Verständnis der kabbalistischen Schriften, sondern man muß zugleich den Thalmud und die Midraschim ganz auswendig wissen, um in diesen Schriften fortzukommen.[16]

True to this method, the first volume of *Philosophie der Geschichte* opens with an eighty-page introduction of the Jewish tradition discussing the role of the Torah, the concepts of oral and written law, the Mishnah – with a complete list of all its *Sedarim* and *Massekhtot*[17] – the Talmud, the medieval compendia, the Midrashim and the Kabbalah, where he lists a catalogue of mystical works from the Zohar (which Molitor mistakenly dates back to 121 CE) up to the early eighteenth century. In the same introduction, he also addresses the concept of tradition from a Jewish perspective, explaining the obligation to study the Law and its aims, *Talmud Torah* and *Seyag la-Torah*, but also the importance of language, rabbinic and mystical hermeneutics, including *gematria* and *notarikon*. The nine chapters that follow provide further explanation and background to the texts and concepts from the introduction, and follow the same slow and meticulous method. The sheer detail and the measured pace of his method meant that even though Molitor had completed only four volumes of *Philosophie der Geschichte* by the time of his death in 1860, they still stretched to more than 2,000 pages, all by way of introduction to the fifth volume on the Kabbalah, which of course never materialised.

With its four volumes as they have come down to us today, *Philosophie der Geschichte* still constitutes a pretty comprehensive general introduction to the Jewish tradition and its mystical dimension that by and large has stood the test of time. As we mentioned in our introduction, Gershom Scholem himself was particularly fond of the book and its author, professing to collect everything he could find by and about him – not that this constituted an inordinate amount of material. But he was not just interested in Molitor as a kind of curiosum, a friendly aberration in an environment that was generally unsympathetic to Jews and Judaism, he also genuinely thought that Molitor knew what he was talking about. In his book *Von der Mystischen Gestalt der Gottheit*, first published in 1962, Scholem gives him an unambiguously glowing reference, stating: 'Es ist heute fast vergessen, daß Molitor der einzige ernst zu nehmende christliche Kenner der Kabbala im Zeitalter des deutschen Idealismus und wohl im ganzen 19. Jahrhundert war.'[18] And as far as *Philosophie der Geschichte* is concerned, Scholem is no less laudatory: 'Obwohl dieses Werk der Kabbala durchaus grundlos eine christologische Wendung zu geben suchte – der Autor gehörte zum liberalen Flügel der deutschen Katholiken–, ist das Buch noch immer beachtenswert.' (*GF*, 53).

In fact, Scholem quite often waxes lyrical about Molitor and his 'remarkable' book: from as early as 1916, in his diaries and letters, to as late as 1982, the year of his death, Molitor's name occurs with regular frequency in Scholem's writings. With almost identical frequency, of course, he reminds his readers that *Philosophie der Geschichte* was fundamentally flawed as an exploration of Jewish mysticism, as it sought to reinterpret the Kabbalah in the light of Christianity, but still his reasons for liking the book are quite enlightening. In his last book, the autobiographical *Von Berlin nach Jerusalem*, Scholem tells the familiar story of how he acquired a copy of *Philosophie der Geschichte* 'für einen Pappenstiel' directly from the publisher, and proceeds to say how it was crystal-clear to him 'daß die christologischen Umdeutungen dieses Autors, eines Schülers Schellings und Baaders, ganz verfehlt waren, aber er hatte doch mehr von der Sache verstanden als seine zeitgenössischen judaistischen Koryphäen' (*VBJ*, 132). In Scholem's work, the term '(judaistischen) Koryphäen' is shorthand for the main protagonists of what became known as the *Wissenschaft des Judentums*. This nineteenth-century phenomenon was not so much a movement as a loose collection of Jewish scholars who were united by a similar outlook and similar aims, namely to write a critical analysis and history of Jewish religion, literature and culture.[19] It all began when Leopold Zunz and Eduard Gans set up the *Verein für Cultur und Wissenschaft der Juden* in 1819, of which the poet Heinrich Heine was a one-time member, and some of its later representatives included such luminaries as Abraham Geiger, Zacharias Frankel, Moritz Steinschneider and of course Heinrich Graetz.[20] Although these authors are usually all subsumed under the single heading of *Wissenschaft des Judentums*, they all came to the project from a range of different backgrounds and with a range of different agendas, which means that they did not always see eye to eye.[21] However, for the sake of Scholem's argument as well as our own, it would be fair to say that these scholars, inspired to varying degrees by the Enlightenment on the one hand and German Romanticism on the other, not only aimed to avoid any (Jewish) religious bias in their work, but also to provide a counterbalance to the accounts of Judaism and Jewish history that had been and were being written from a Christian perspective.

In spite of the undeniable value of their achievements, which he also recognised, Scholem came to have mixed feelings towards the *Wissenschaft des Judentums* in general and Heinrich Graetz in particular. The movement was very much a product of its time, and as such, the writings of the *Wissenschaftler des Judentums* frequently became an exercise in apologetics, directed towards both a Jewish and a non-Jewish readership, as much as it was a genuine attempt to frame Judaism in a critical, scientific perspective. Scholars such as Geiger, Frankel and Zunz were very active in the various Jewish Reform movements of the nineteenth century, and Zunz's groundbreaking book *Die gottesdienstlichen Vorträge der Juden*, for instance, sought to prove to the Jewish community in Germany as much as to the German authorities that holding a sermon in the vernacular was historically justified.[22] Scholem acknowledges that in its apologetic role, the *Wissenschaft des Judentums* was responsible for great political and social progress, proving to be an invaluable tool, as it did, in making Judaism an acceptable subject for polite conversation, quite literally *salonfähig*. Yet in this its greatest achievement also lay its deepest flaw, as this apologetic role forced scholars to skirt around aspects of Judaism that did not sit comfortably with their readers, areas that proved to be 'recht widerhaarig', in Scholem's words:

Daß solche Gebiete von der jüdischen Wissenschaft dann mit größtem Mißtrauen, mit Abneigung, ja mit offener Feindschaft betrachtet wurden, versteht sich von selbst. Es gilt das für große Gebiete der jüdischen Literatur, des jüdischen Lebens, der Kultur, die unter den Gesichtspunkten eines aufklärerisch gesonnenen, eines geläutert rationalen Judentums des 19. Jahrhunderts nicht recht verwertbar schienen und daher als unjüdisch, allenfalls als halbheidnisch, herausgeworfen wurden, wie etwa alle Phänomene der jüdischen Mystik, deren Studium ich meine eigene Arbeit gewidmet habe [...].[23]

Scholem accuses the *Wissenschaft des Judentums* of seeking to reduce Judaism to a spiritualised religion, very much in line with the Enlightenment project of a universal, natural religion which has been stripped of historical peculiarities, henceforth derided as obscurantism or superstition. The very emphatically political and even worldly aspect of Jewish messianism, for instance, which Scholem discusses so eloquently in his essay 'Zum Verständnis der messianischen Idee im Judentum', was downplayed in order to make Judaism appear more like a respectable and safely bourgeois conversation partner. Similarly, the long-standing tradition of Jewish mysticism, from Hasidism and the Kabbalah to Shabbatai Tsevi, was swept under the carpet as it manifestly did not fit in with the notion of a humanist-rationalist religion.[24] Heinrich Graetz in particular interpreted mysticism as a hellenic and hence fundamentally non-Jewish phenomenon, and he was consistently and unequivocally dismissive of the Kabbalah, and extraordinarily rude about its authors. This is apparent in his 1846 book *Gnosticismus und Judenthum* and recurs in his expansive and enormously influential book *Geschichte der Juden von den ältesten Zeiten bis auf die Gegenwart* (1853–1875), as well as in its abridged version *Volkstümliche Geschichte der Juden* (1888), in which he writes about Abraham Abulafia and Moshe de Léon:

> Sie haben das Geisteslicht innerhalb des Judentums mit dem Düster eines wüsten Wirrwarrs verdunkelt und an die Stelle eines geläuterten Gottesglaubens pahantastische, ja gotteslästerliche Wahngebilde gesetzt. Die Verfinsterung der folgenden Jahrhunderte in der Judenheit ist zum großen Teil ihr Werk. Sie haben ihre Zeit und die Nachwelt durch geflissentliches oder unabsichtliches Gaukelwerk in die Irre geführt, und die Schaden, die sie dem Judentum beigebracht, sind noch bis auf den heutigen Tag fühlbar.[25]

Whereas Graetz's rejection of the Kabbalah is doubtless the most emphatic, the sentiment behind it was shared by the other authors. Thus the *Wissenschaft des Judentums* banished mysticism from the panorama of Jewish history and experience, seeing it as an unfortunate aberration at best, or quite simply ignoring it completely at worst. As Scholem summarises it: 'Man behandelte grundsätzlich nicht, was im Keller vorging; man betrachtete nur, worum es im Salon, zwischen der Bibel und Luther, zwischen Hermann Cohen und Kant, zwischen

Steinthal und Wilhelm von Humboldt handelte.'[26] What Scholem objected to most of all was that such a project excluded a perfectly valid and valuable expression of Jewishness, or *das Jüdische* as he frequently terms it, and this meant that the *Wissenschaft des Judentums* was fundamentally unable to grasp Judaism in its totality as a dynamic, living whole, which, to Scholem, means they had not understood it at all.[27] Another consequence of the exclusion of mysticism from scholarly attention was that a whole area of the Jewish tradition had remained uncharted and was gradually beginning to disappear in the mists of time. In this respect, Scholem shared the sense of urgency in Benjamin's hermeneutic and methodological conviction that the past can only be truly grasped 'als Bild, das auf Nimmerwiedersehen im Augenblick seiner Erkennbarkeit eben aufblitzt' (I, 695). The problem with the selective treatment of Jewish history and tradition by the Jewish scholars of the *Wissenschaft des Judentums* was that it was thus left to others to talk about those aspects of the Jewish experience which were considered dangerous or unsavoury. To Scholem, who was very much in favour of a warts-and-all approach to Jewish studies, this also literally included the Jewish underworld, with its rogues, thieves and robbers, a topic that was anxiously avoided by Jewish scholars, but freely addressed by non-Jewish authors, sometimes in a purely factual manner, but quite often with some kind of antisemitic agenda.[28]

Towards the end of his 1944 essay 'Überlegungen zur Wissenschaft vom Judentum', Scholem laments this missed opportunity, but suggests that not all the books written by non-Jewish scholars, however derided they might have been at the time, were without merit: 'Fremde die wir als Ignoranten verlachten, haben Gesamtdarstellungen geschrieben, die uns beschämen.'[29] We do not need to go very far to find out who Scholem was thinking of. In the introduction to *Die jüdische Mystik in ihren Hauptströmungen*, which appeared in English in 1941 and in Scholem's own German translation in 1957, he again comes to the regrettable conclusion that the *Wissenschaft des Judentums* showed no interest at all in the tradition of Jewish mysticism, and that a great deal of (Jewish) expertise around that time was lost forever as it was simply ignored.

Und so haben wir denn wenig Ursache, darauf stolz zu sein, daß die meisten der Ideen und Anschauungen, die wirkliche Einsicht in diese Welt verraten, von christlichen Gelehrten mit mystischen Neigungen stammen, wie etwa dem Engländer Arthur Edward Waite in der letzten Generation oder dem Deutschen Franz Josef Molitor vor hundert Jahren.[30]

The reasons why Scholem valued Molitor's contribution so much were twofold. First of all, Molitor saw the Kabbalah as an integral part of the Jewish tradition, rather than as an aberration or an exception, and as such his concept of *das Jüdische* comes far closer to the all-encompassing model proposed by Scholem. Yet Molitor goes even further in his commitment to mysticism inasmuch as he is convinced that the Kabbalah contains both the most secret doctrines and also the purest essence of Judaism, which is why Scholem refers to him as a 'theosophist', rather than a philologist or a theologian, although he still merited the description 'ein Mann von nicht zu verachtenden Einsichten'.[31] Whereas Scholem did not call himself a mystic, it is clear that he was quite receptive to the idea that the Kabbalah was the very place 'wo das geheime Leben des Judentums […] einmal ge-wohnt zu haben schien' (*SB*, 471). But apart from seeing the Kabbalah as the true heart of Judaism, Molitor also saw the gnostic philosophy of Jacob Böhme and Franz Xaver von Baader as the direct and true heir of this mystical tradition and, even more surprisingly and contro-versially, the 'germanische Völkerstamm' as its new guardians. After studying the Kabbalah, Molitor says he was 'freudig, erstaunt und überrascht'

eine unverkennbare Identität der grundwesentlichsten Ideen der ältesten Theosophie der Ebräer, mit der tiefsten Philosophie der deutschen Nation […] zu entdecken. Erwägt man nun, daß das israelitische Volk, der Träger der göttlichen Manifestationen in dem alten Bunde war, so wie der germanische Völkerstamm es gewissermaßen im neuen Bunde geworden; so muß jene Identität der ältesten Theosophie des Menschengeschlechts bei den Juden, mit der aus dem tiefsten Quell des deutschen Nationalgeistes hervorgegangenen Philosophie J. Böhm's [*sic*], welche der geniale Franz v. Baader in unsrer Zeit zur wissenschaftlichen Verständigung zu erheben berufen ist, jedem auf-richtigem Forscher von der höchsten Bedeutung erscheinen; […] (*M* II, 260)

As a 'catholic kabbalist' (*SB* I, 58), Molitor not only reads the Kabbalah as a precursor to the gnosticism and mystical idealism of his mentors, Baader and Schelling, he also reduces Judaism itself to a stage within a Christian *Heilsgeschichte*, albeit a crucial stage without which Christianity itself would make little sense. This is perhaps the most manifest and by far the most drastic of the 'christologischen Umdeutungen' to which Scholem obviously fundamentally objected, yet he did not allow this to cloud his judgement on what he considered to be Molitor's merits. Scholem's comments on a chapter from the second volume of *Philosophie der Geschichte*, entitled 'Versuch einer spekulativen Entwicklung der allgemeinen Grundbegriffe der Theosophie nach den Grundsätzen der Kabbala', summarises this perfectly: 'Wo Molitor nicht, wie ja auch die anderen Anhänger der sogenannten "christlichen Kabbala", von seinen christlichen Voraussetzungen zu oft verwegenen Umdeutungen geführt wird, ist gerade dies Kapitel noch immer wertvoll und eindrucksvoll.'[32] Throughout his life, Scholem continued to put great stock by Molitor's pretty encyclopaedic factual knowledge of the Kabbalah, but this was only part of the reason why *Philosophie der Geschichte* attracted him. Even more important to Scholem than the fact that Molitor recognised mysticism as an expression of Judaism worth studying, was the fact that he recognised language as the ground upon which the entire Jewish tradition is built and the key to unlocking the mystical meanings of the Torah. In the first book of *Philosophie der Geschichte* in particular, Molitor frequently refers to 'jenen tief verborgenen Sinn' within the Torah (*M* I, 127), which can only be read by meticulously paying attention to the phenomenology and physicality of the Hebrew language. But it is not just the language of the Torah which merits such close attention: to Molitor, as indeed to the Kabbalists, Talmudists and rabbis, Hebrew as such is a holy language, replete with meaning and, as we discussed in the previous chapter, omnisignificant. Thus all study of the theological content of the Torah is in a very real and primary sense the study of language. In November 1916, Scholem approvingly quotes Molitor's account of this doctrine in his diary:

Die Buchstaben, *welche der Ausdruck geistiger Kräfte sind* (könnte wörtlich Hirsch im Pentateuchkommentar geschrieben haben!), *haben ihre Wurzeln oben*' (Molitor I. [p. 59]), d.h. in der Wahrheit, es ist also im Sinne der Kabbalisten alle wahrhafte Wahrheitsforschung im Zentrum Sprachforschung, indem man nach den Wurzeln der Buchstaben, dem 'himmlischen Alphabet' (Sohar II 130b) zu forschen hat, und den geistigen Kräften, die darin abgebildet sind. (*TB* I, 422)[33]

Der Molitor ist gekommen

Perhaps more than any other, the name of Franz Joseph Molitor is a mysterious apparition in the work of Walter Benjamin. It appears very abruptly in a letter dated 23 May 1917 and crops up again some six weeks later in a letter dated June 1917. The next and last time the name Molitor is mentioned is on a postcard to Scholem dated 15 March 1919, only to disappear from Benjamin's correspondence as suddenly as it had flashed up less than two years before that. There is something profoundly odd about the desire to hang up a fully-fledged reappraisal of Benjamin's writings on three casual mentions of an obscure nineteenth-century writer, whose *magnum opus* has survived the onslaught of the twentieth century in only very few traceable copies. In fact, it is to the credit of Benjamin's keen collector's mind that he actually predicted the future rarity of the book in 1917, as he writes to Scholem: 'Ich habe mich mit dem Besitz des Buches sehr gefreut: übrigens wird es ja, wie der Baader, gemäß der Zeitströmung selten, geschätzt und auch teuer werden, wie ich glaube.' (*GB* I, 361). Nevertheless, on the basis of these three letters as well as ample corroboration from the letters, diaries and (auto)biographical writings of Gershom Scholem, a compelling case can be constructed which argues forcefully in favour of the profound influence Molitor's *Philosophie der Geschichte* had both on the younger and the older Benjamin.

The first letter which talks about Molitor, dated 23 May, reads as if it was written on a desk cluttered with papers and open books, as

Benjamin gives the impression that he is in the middle of intense and concentrated study. 'Lieber Herr Scholem,' he writes,

> kaum habe ich die Zeit und die äußere Möglichkeit Ihnen zu schreiben gefunden als ich auch sogleich deutlich an einen Anlaß erinnert wurde. Es kamen nämlich heute früh die lange gesuchten sämtlichen Schriften Baaders und weil ich jetzt doch mit einiger Intensität zu studieren hoffe, so will ich was zusammen gehört beieinander haben. Anders kann ich nicht lernen. Und Baader und Molitor gehören so sehr zusammen, daß gleich unter dem ersten was ich gelesen habe zwei wichtige Briefe von ihm an Molitor waren, die unter anderm Wesentliches und Schönes über die Schechinnah sagen. (*GB* I, 357)[34]

This does not at all sound like Benjamin had only just become acquainted with the man and his work. On the contrary, the statement that Baader and Molitor are inseparable suggests that Benjamin was already fairly familiar with the work of these two authors, and already knew something of its substance before he acquired either. The letters from Baader to Molitor of which Benjamin speaks can be found in the penultimate volume of the sixteen-volume edition of Baader's collected writings, and the fact that there are only three such letters in over seven hundred pages of correspondence rather suggests that Benjamin was expressly looking for them, and probably looked up the name Molitor in the index volume.[35] This suspicion is confirmed in a later letter, where Benjamin refers back to the passage about the Shekhinah, saying: 'Die Sache steht zerstreut da und es wäre mühsam sie zu exzerpieren.' (*GB* I, 364).[36] It is fascinating that it should be precisely these two topics, Molitor and the Shekinah, that Benjamin made a beeline for on the very first day that the books came into his possession. The collected writings of Baader arrived, as the letter tells us, in the early morning of 23 May 1917. We cannot be quite as exact about the date when Benjamin acquired Molitor's book. In the second letter, dated simply June 1917, he writes: 'Der Molitor ist gekommen und das Geld dafür geht heute an Sie ab.' (*GB* I, 361). There is a supplementary problem involved in the dating of the letters, in that they are, in both cases, Scholem's estimates. His meticulous and encyclopaedic scholarly accuracy may be the stuff of legends, but it is still no substitute for absolute certainty. As there is no further circumstantial evidence, however, we have little choice but to accept these datings and conclude that the *termini post quem* and *ante quem* are 23 May and 30 June respectively.

We can therefore presume that *Philosophie der Geschichte oder über die Tradition* was probably in Benjamin's possession by 30 June 1917. However, the same letter contains a sentence which complicates matters somewhat, as Benjamin writes: 'Nur um den Überblick über die Disposition zu haben frage ich Sie nach dem Thema des zweiten Bandes.' (*GB* I, 361). Scholem explains the import of this question in a note to this letter, stating that the second volume of the book was no longer available from the publisher at the time. He confirms this in one of his last autobiographical writings, *Von Berlin nach Jerusalem*, the second edition of which was finished in 1982 (which serves to illustrate that we are working with data that are, in the fullest sense of the expression, 'few and far between'). As it contains two other vital pieces of information on the elusive presence of Molitor's work in the intellectual biography of both Scholem and Benjamin, it is worth quoting the paragraph in question:

> Ich las die vier Bände von Franz Joseph Molitors Werk 'Philosophie der Geschichte oder über die Tradition', das in Wirklichkeit über die Kabbala handelte. Im Jahre 1916 stellte sich heraus, daß drei der Bände, die bis 1857 erschienen waren, noch beim Verlag für einen Pappenstiel zu kaufen waren, und ich erwarb sie so schnell wie möglich (den fehlenden Band kaufte ich sechs jahre später bei einer Auktion). Es war mir klar – und auch kaum zu übersehen –, daß die christologischen Umdeutungen diesen Autors, eines Schülers Schellings und Baaders, ganz verfehlt waren, aber er hatte doch mehr von der Sache verstanden als seiner zeitgenössischen judaistischen Koryphäen.[37]

Thus we are forced to conclude that Benjamin only had volumes one, three and four in his possession in 1917, and possibly might not have had direct access to a copy of the second volume before Scholem bought his at an auction in 1922. However, there does remain the possibility that Benjamin consulted the volume missing from his own collection in any of the municipal or university libraries in one of the many towns where he lived at the time. In the letter of 23 May 1917, he states his intention to do so in case Scholem fails to send him a copy of the book: 'Haben sie es nicht erhalten, so werde ich mich auf der münchener Universitätsbibliothek darum bemühen.' (*GB* I,

357). Said 'münchener Universitätsbibliothek' still has a copy of *Philosophie der Geschichte* to this day, so it is quite possible that Benjamin did indeed consult the book before acquiring a copy for himself. It is impossible to say exactly when he would have done so, but we do know from his correspondence that in November and December of 1916, when he was writing *Über Sprache* and sending excited letters to Scholem, Benjamin was in fact in München, of all places. Unfortunately, the loan records of the University Library of München do not date back as far as 1916, so the question as to whether Benjamin did indeed consult *Philosophie der Geschichte* there, as he obviously intended, must remain open.

Between 1917 and 1922, the most important stations of Benjamin's *Wanderzüge* were Munich, Bern and Berlin, amongst many towns of lesser renown. He might thus have consulted the missing volume in any of these cities, but we have no information either to confirm or to deny this. The fact that he returned to Berlin in 1920 is potentially very interesting, as we know that the Berliner Staatsbibliothek held a copy of the book at least up until 1933. On 10 May of that year, the first of the infamous book burnings took place, and it is quite conceivable that a book such as Molitor's might have fallen prey to this 'bibliocaust'. But if not that one, it may well have been another, as the catalogue of the Staatsbibliothek still adds a rather ominous 'Kriegsverlust möglich' to the entry for *Philosophie der Geschichte*.

Yet in the quotation from *Von Berlin nach Jerusalem*, Scholem also tells us that he had been reading all four volumes of *Philosophie der Geschichte* before he finally bought them in 1916 and 1922.[38] This is confirmed in Scholem's seminal biography of his friendship with Benjamin, entitled *Walter Benjamin: Die Geschichte einer Freundschaft*, which speaks in similarly respectful terms of Molitor's work. That in itself is striking, especially in view of Scholem's more than simply ambiguous attitudes towards Christianity and Christians, particularly after 1945.[39] In *Geschichte einer Freundschaft*, Scholem presents the same version of the facts of the book's availability as *Von Berlin nach Jerusalem* and the notes to both editions of Benjamin's collected correspondence, but, most crucially, he dates his own engagement with the book back to the beginning of 1915:

Damals begann auch sein [Benjamins] Interesse an Franz von Baader, auf den er in München durch Max Pulver gekommen war, und für Franz Joseph Molitor, einen Schüler Schellings und Baaders, der als einziger ernstzunehmender philosophischer Autor in deutscher Sprache fünfundvierzig Jahre an das Studium der Kabbala gewendet und zwischen 1827 und 1857 vier Bände als Einleitung einer von ihm geplanten Darstellung der Kabbala anonym veröffentlicht hatte, unter dem denkwürdigen Titel: *Philosophie der Geschichte oder über die Tradition.* Obwohl dieses Werk der Kabbala durchaus grundlos eine christologische Wendung zu geben suchte – der Autor gehörte zum liberalen Flügel der deutschen Katholiken –, ist das Buch noch immer beachtenswert. Ich hatte es Anfang 1915 zu lesen begonnen und kam in unseren Gesprächen mehrfach darauf zu sprechen, erzählte ihm auch, daß drei Bände des Werkes noch immer beim Verleger zu haben seien. Es waren dies unsere ersten Gespräche über Kabbala, von deren Quellenstudium ich damals noch weit entfernt war, mich aber doch schon von dieser Welt dunkel angezogen fühlte. (*GF*, 53)

In the same book, Scholem tells us that their first conversation took place on 21 July 1915, a conversation which Benjamin begun '*in medias res*', talking about the essence of the historical process, the philosophy of history, socialism and Zionism, amongst other things (*GF*, 13). This intense level of intellectual activity would continue to characterise their conversations and correspondence until Benjamin's death in 1940. It allows us to conclude not only that Benjamin could have known about Molitor's work as early as July 1915, from which date Scholem says they spoke about the book 'repeatedly', but also that it would have been highly unlikely, bearing in mind the sheer level of their conversations, that Benjamin would have remained unaware of the substance of the book before he decided to buy a copy in May 1917 (in fact, the reason why he bought the book was probably precisely because he was aware of its content to a certain extent). This suspicion is confirmed by the aforementioned letters written around that time, in which he speaks about Molitor in a very matter-of-fact way, suggesting that he was at least conversant with the gist of the author's work and his relationship to Baader and the Jewish tradition. The reason why it is so important to establish these dates is because it allows us to presuppose the possibility, or at least stops us from dismissing the possibility, of an actual and traceable Jewish influence on

Benjamin's crucial essay *Über Sprache überhaupt und über die Sprache des Menschen*, which he wrote in early November 1916. As we shall soon see, this is one of the moot points among Benjamin scholars.

Scholem's letters and diaries, which have been published in the course of the past five years, also provide us with valuable information of both his and Benjamin's intellectual preoccupations during these early years. As Benjamin wrote in a letter to Scholem of 11 November 1916, in which he mentions the language essay as a work in progress, their discussions and ensuing correspondence appear to have revolved around the issue of language and truth in relation to Judaism and mathematics. Benjamin says that he started writing a letter to his friend 'der bei achtzehn Seiten Länge abschloß' in an attempt to construct a coherent answer to a number questions put to him by Scholem. As the letter was becoming intolerably lenghty, Benjamin decided 'ihn zu einer kleinen Abhandlung umzuarbeiten', which became, of course, *Über Sprache* (*GB* I, 343). What is particularly interesting is that Benjamin confesses that he did not yet feel able to address the 'unendlich schwere Thema' of mathematics and Zionism, as his thoughts on the matter were not quite ready yet. instead, he sees his essay as an exploration of the essence of language 'und zwar – soweit ich es verstehe: in immanenter Beziehung auf das Judentum und mit Beziehung auf die ersten Kapitel der Genesis', adding 'Ihr Urteil über diese Gedanken werde ich in der sicheren Hoffnung durch dasselbe sehr gefördert zu werden erwarten.' (*GB* I, 343).

Unfortunately, apart from the ones written between 1933 and 1940, Scholem's letters to Benjamin have not been preserved, which means that we do not know exactly which questions Benjamin was attempting to answer. However, Scholem's diary entries around that time may give us a fairly clear notion as to what he and his friend were discussing, and it is clear from these diary entries that the questions of language, tradition, truth and totality were very much on both men's minds. Scholem's diary suggests that Benjamin's hope of being aided by his friend's judgement was not misguided, as the latter is thinking and writing about these matters with the greatest knowledge and eloquence. Moreover, it is exactly one month before Benjamin's letter that Molitor is mentioned for the first time in Scholem's diary, in an entry dated 11 October 1916. At the end of a discussion of the Kabbalist doctrine of the tripartite soul, consisting of *ruach, nefesh* and *neshama* – a subject to which Molitor devotes a great deal of attention in volumes II and III – Scholem simply adds: 'In der Gottheit als dem allerrealsten Sein gibt es keine Möglichkeit. Siehe Molitor II, § 94.' (*TB* I, 404). Five days later, another diary entry reads: 'Im Molitor Band III, § 620 finde ich endlich, daß die Stelle: Am Orte, wo die Umkehrenden stehen, die Gerechten nicht stehen können, in Berachot 34b steht [...]' (*TB* I, 408). These diary entries, and there are several others from around the same time, suggest that Scholem was now not just reading *Philosophie der Geschichte*, but actually scrutinizing it, searching for sources, quotations and passages. It is quite meaningful that he should have been doing this around the exact time when Benjamin's work took a 'Jewish turn', finally to use this dangerous term, and as we shall see in a subsequent chapter, Scholem's reports on their discussions mention the very same questions about language, tradition and totality, summarised in the concept of the *Lehre*, that we have addressed in the context of Judaism in the previous chapter.

Benjamin, Scholem and the Book

This fine-toothed philology is of course essential in determining the possible influence of Molitor's book on Benjamin's work, which has no doubt been underestimated by scholars up to this date, probably not because of any great prejudice against it, but because it is so very hard to trace, and, with its length approaching two thousand pages of the densest German, hardly an inviting read. The author of Molitor's entry in the 1885 edition of the *Allgemeine Deutsche Biographie* seems to have pre-empted this when he remarked laconically that *Philosophie der Geschichte* was written 'in einer nicht sehr genießbaren Darstellungsweise'.[40] But it is also important because it can lead us to suspect that those scholars who have dismissed the influence of Molitor as negligible or irrelevant have not actually read, consulted or even seen the work themselves. Thus, up to this date, the reasons given for this dismissal have been largely circumstantial. The question of the book's actual contents has never been critically addressed, all four volumes of it have always been dismissed as being merely 'about the Kabbalah'. It would amount to much the same if we were to refuse to read the *Passagen-Werk* because it is merely 'about Paris', just because the majority of its quotations are indeed linked to that city in some way.

Let us take for example Winfried Menninghaus's book *Walter Benjamins Theorie der Sprachmagie*. This influential book is an admirable achievement in many ways, if perhaps slightly outdated on certain topics now, some twenty years after it was first published. Menninghaus disregarded *Von Berlin nach Jerusalem*, for instance, and most of the documentary evidence we are using here was simply not available to him. The book is particularly eloquent on the influence of the early German Romantics on Benjamin (Schlegel, Humboldt and Hamann, amongst others), yet on the subject of the importance of the Jewish tradition to Benjamin's theory of language, Menninghaus's reasoning can hardly be accused of great subtlety. To begin with, he states that 'Versuche einer Annäherung an Benjamins Sprachphilosophie [...] darin [überein]stimmen, daß sie die Frage nach deren Traditionshorizont gleichsetzen mit der Frage nach Benjamins Kenntnis der jüdischen Kabbala',[41] thus essentially reducing the Jewish tradition to what we have shown in the previous chapter was actually only a historical and textual subdivision of a vast corpus of texts. The only reason he gives to justify this is the fact that Scholem would later become the leading light on Jewish mysticism in general and the Kabbalah in particular.

Interestingly enough, on the same page Menninghaus says that even Scholem's presence in 1915 and 1916 could not have guaranteed a Jewish influence on Benjamin's *Über Sprache überhaupt und über die Sprache des Menschen* (the aforementioned moot point of Benjamin studies), as 'noch nicht einmal Scholem mit der Erforschung der Kabbala begonnen hatte'.[42] To corroborate this point, Menninghaus refers to the passage from *Geschichte einer Freundschaft* which we quoted above. This passage, however, does not say that Scholem had not yet begun to study the Kabbalah as such (*Erforschung der Kabbala* are the exact words Menninghaus uses), it only states that he was still some way from studying the Kabbalah's sources (*deren Quellenstudium*). Scholem says in the same passage that he had begun to read Molitor's book, which he described in 1975 as '*noch immer beachtenswert*', as early as 1915. If, as Menninghaus himself writes, *Philosophie der Geschichte oder über die Tradition* is indeed a book about the Kabbalah, does that then not mean that Scholem had begun to study the Kabbalah, even though he did not instantly rocket to the lonely heights of the expert who wrote *Major Trends in Jewish Mysticism* in 1941? In fact, in a letter which he wrote in 1937 to the publisher of *Major Trends*, Salman Schocken, Scholem reveals how important Molitor's book had been to his intellectual development as a scholar of the Kabbalah:

> Damals aber war Molitors seltsame Buch 'Philosophie der Geschichte oder über die Tradition', das mir bei Poppelauer in die Hand gefallen war, von faszinierender Wirkung auf mich. So unfundiert es im Historischen auch sein mochte, es gab eine Adresse an wo das geheime Leben des Judentums, dem ich meinen Meditationen nachhing, einmal gewohnt zu haben schien. (*SB* I, 471)

It does seem that Menninghaus wants to have it both ways, denying the relevance of the book to Benjamin on the grounds that it is only about the Kabbalah, yet also denying that Scholem had studied this very Kabbalah despite the fact that he had, for the past two years, been reading a book which is supposedly only about the Kabbalah. Furthermore, in *Von Berlin nach Jerusalem*, Scholem writes that his interest in the Kabbalah was already awakened in 1915, when he read and annotated books about Hasidism and the Kabbalah, and started to fill 'nicht wenige Hefte mit Exzerpten, Übersetzungen und Betrachtungen zur Kabbalah', although he freely admits these were still 'noch weit von wissenschaftlicher Bemühung und Erkenntnis entfernt' (*VBJ*, 132). The secondary literature he could lay his hands on was very quickly exhausted, so Scholem started to turn to the original texts. Yet without any knowledge of the kabbalist style and symbolism, he soon found himself lost, so he turned to the teacher with whom he studied the Talmud, Anton Bleichrode, for assistance:

Ich versuchte einmal, Dr. Bleichrode zu veranlassen, mit einigen von uns R. Elia de Vidas' "*Reschith Chochma*", einen berühmten Traktat über kabbalistischen Ethik aus dem Safed des 16. Jahrhunderts zu lesen. Nach einigen Stunden sagte er: 'Kinderlach, wir müssen es aufgeben. Ich verstehe die Zitate aus dem Sohar [deren das Buch voll war] nicht und kann euch die Sache nicht richtig erklären.' (*VBJ*, 131)

At that point, Scholem decided to grasp the nettle, bought himself a copy of the *Zohar* in the original Aramaic, and with Molitor's *Philosophie der Geschichte* at hand, he started to decipher the most infamous kabbalist text. After all, if he could remain undaunted reading the German Romantics, there seemed to be no reason why the *Zohar* should be beyond him: 'Schließlich war ja der Sohar, wenn auch aramäisch geschrieben, nicht krauser als etwa die Schriften Hamanns, von denen mehrere Bände in meinem Zimmer standen.' (*VBJ*, 132). The only thing Scholem is saying is that his knowledge of the sources of the Kabbalah in these early years could not be called scientific, in other words, that he was not yet the great expert and innovator he would later become. Yet as these quotations show, it does not matter whether Scholem's knowledge of the Jewish tradition at the time was factually correct to present-day standards, the point is that he did have a more than decent knowledge of the state of the debate in Judaica at the time, and it is this knowledge which he would have communicated to Benjamin.

Yet there is another problem with Menninghaus's claim. By reducing the question of Jewish influences to a question of factual knowledge of the sources of the Kabbalah, which he subsequently denies to Scholem at that time, Menninghaus not only performs an objectionable reduction of the entire Jewish tradition, he also trivialises Scholem's already considerable conversancy with this tradition. It is not even necessary to be familiar with the biographical details surrounding Scholem's education to know that even the knowledge of the very existence of the Kabbalah at the time, let alone of its nature, cannot simply have emerged out of the blue in 1917. As Scholem tells us in both *Geschichte einer Freundschaft* and *Von Berlin nach Jerusalem*, he had been very vigorously engaged in the study of the Hebrew language and the biblical and post-biblical sources of Judaism from as early as 1913. Around that time, he started to attend advanced classes in a yeshivah close to his Berlin home on the Mishnah, the Talmud, and even Rashi's commentaries to them (*VBJ*, 52). Scholem proved to have been an extremely enthusiastic and avid learner, studying the language for ten to fifteen hours a week and studying the Talmud for another five to six hours a week, figures which impressed Benjamin when he told him (*GF*, 24). And even though the name Scholem has now become almost exclusively associated with the Kabbalah, it appears to have been his first confrontation with the source texts of 'mainstream' Judaism which made the most lasting impression on him:

> Wenn ich mich frage, ob ich eigentlich je das hatte, was man in meiner Beziehung zum und Erfahrung des Jüdischen ein Erlebnis nennen dürfte, so weiß ich nur eine Antwort. Das war die Erschütterung im Frühjahr 1913, als ich an einem Aprilsonntag bei Bleichrode die erste Seite des Talmud im Orginal lesen lernte ('Von wann an liest man das Schema' am Abend?' und Raschis Kommentar dazu), und später, am gleichen Tag, die Erklärung Raschis [des größten aller jüdischen Kommentatoren] zu den ersten Versen des Genesis. Es war meine erste traditionelle und direkte Begegnung nicht mit der Bibel, sondern mit jüdischer Substanz in der Tradition. Jedenfalls hat diese Begegnung meine Bewunderung für das Jüdische und meine Hinneigung dazu mehr als jede andere, die ich dann später auf diesem Gebiet gehabt habe, bestimmt. (*VBJ*, 53)

These were the things about which Benjamin and Scholem talked most at the time, not about the ultimately very specialist field of kabbalist language mysticism. After all, Scholem did not know he was going to become the foremost authority on Jewish mysticism of the twentieth century in 1915, so we can safely assume that at the time he felt no obligation towards future scholars to talk only about the Kabbalah. Yet this is the gist of Menninghaus's argument when he says that any Jewish influence on Benjamin's work must have come from the Kabbalah, because Scholem was to become an expert in this field some ten years after they met.[43] Instead, Scholem told Benjamin about his Talmud studies, and Benjamin wanted to know what they studied and how this form of study went about itself, as the former witnesses in *Geschichte einer Freundschaft*: 'Er wollte wissen, wie das vor sich geht, und ich bemühte mich, ihm zu erklären, was mich an dieser Lektüre talmudischer Diskussionen so faszinierte.' (*GF*, 24). During these years, Scholem appears to have become Benjamin's sounding board for all things Jewish. In fact, the self-confessedly assimilated and secularised Benjamin did not attempt to perform a similar operation on Scholem, but actually encouraged him to venture further into the realms of Judaism and deepen their mutual understanding of it:

> Benjamin hat diese Bindung, so paradox das bei seiner ziemlich totalen Unwissenheit in jüdischen Dingen scheinen möchte, niemals in Frage gestellt. Er war weit davon entfernt, mich von diesen Neigungen abbringen zu wollen, fand sie im Gegenteil sehr interessant, ja tendierte dazu, mich darin noch, wenn man so sagen dürfte, zu bestärken, da ich seine Adresse für alle Fragen auf diesem Gebiet würde. [...] Philosophische und literarische Interessen verbanden uns, aber die Fragen, die er, wenn ich – gleich bei unseren ersten Begegnungen – von Jüdischen erzählte, in seinen gänzlich originellen und unerwarteten Variierungen und Formulierungen an mich stellte, regten mich außerordentlich an und erzwangen bei mir eine viel intensivere Konzentration, als ich sie im Kreise meiner zionistischen Jugendfreunde aufzubringen hatte. (*VBJ*, 75)

This passage again indicates, as we have pointed out above, that the level of their conversations was considered by both to be quite intensive, with the (relative) amateur posing questions to the (relative) expert which not only excited the latter, but also demanded a more intensive level of concentration from him. This in itself, as we mentioned in the first chapter, is a characteristic of the traditional Jewish way of studying Torah and Talmud, whereby the distinction between teacher and pupil, between *Lehrer* and *Lehrende*, gradually dissolves into the sphere of learning, into the 'continuum of the *Lehre*' (*VBJ*, 53–55), a concept of which Benjamin became particularly fond.[44] At a very early stage of their friendship, when they had only known each other for a couple of weeks, Benjamin already seemed to have become fascinated by the study of Talmudic discussions and about the nature and the dynamics of the Jewish tradition. Scholem told him how halakhic discussions take shape and how teachers tended to approach any given matter from a number of different angles, as we discussed in the previous chapter. He also praised his aforementioned teacher, Dr

Bleichrode, 'einen sehr frommen und ganz zurückgezogen lebenden und bescheidenen Rabbiner [...], der sich großartig darauf verstand, eine Seite Talmud zu erklären und überhaupt Jüdisches zu tradieren'. Whereupon Benjamin sighed and said: 'Ach, wenn es das doch in der Philosophie gäbe.' (*GF*, 24). We pointed out before that Scholem's interest lay in 'das Jüdische,' encompassing the Jewish essence and experience in all its facets. Here, however, he uses the adjectival noun without the article, 'Jüdisches', a structure which is unavailable in English and which, if at all possible, is even less specific than 'das Jüdische'. Literally, it would translate as 'to hand down Jewish(ness)'. This not only suggests an almost physical reality of Jewishness in (the German) language, but also conveys the notion that the Jewishness Scholem is referring to can be found in the most diverse and disparate manifestations. This kind of 'meta-semantic' content, something which is communicated *in* language but not *by* language is quite similar to Benjamin's preoccupation in his 1916 essay *Über Sprache überhaupt und über die Sprache des Menschen*. Some three years later, between November 1917 and March 1918, he would reiterate his wish to have a philosophy cast in such a 'traditional' mould in a more systematised form, in the essay *Über das Programm der kommenden Philosophie*.

We will analyse these crucial texts further in a subsequent chapter. Here, however, this conversation may serve to illustrate the fact that Benjamin's interest in the Jewish tradition was not a mere passing fad. Nor was his reliance on Molitor in this respect either incidental or negligible. In fact, in March 1919, a year after completing the *Programm* and two years after buying the book, Benjamin writes a letter to Scholem in which he asks when he will return the copy of the Molitor, which, according to the editors, Benjamin had lent to him.[45] This is the last time Molitor was mentioned in any of Benjamin's surviving letters. Lonitz and Gödde, the editors of the new six-volume edition of Benjamin's correspondence, point out that the new edition, replacing the old two-volume edition of 1966, was more than justified in view of the many letters that have been discovered since then and also in order to restore some of the passages in the already available letters which Scholem and Adorno had censored in their edition. The first edition was culled from 'etwa 600 Briefe', the second edition presents about 1270 letters, more than double the amount, none of them censored or abridged (*GB* I, 518–519). They also admit that more letters are being discovered regularly, mostly from private collections, so the possibility that Benjamin wrote about Molitor to other people than Scholem (to whom he presumably primarily talked about Molitor, as suggested by the tone of the letters and confirmed in *Geschichte einer Freundschaft*) cannot be excluded.

The final mention of Molitor in the letter dated 15 March 1919, asking Scholem when he will return the book, can hardly be used to indicate that the book was performing a mere *acte de présence* in Benjamin's collection. On the contrary, if we contrast this to the titles of other books on Judaism which Scholem lent him, including Samson Rafael Hirsch's *Neunzehn Briefe über das Judentum, Rom und Jerusalem* by Moses Hess and a number of essays by Achad Ha'am (the pen name of Asher Ginzberg, the founding father of cultural Zionism), Molitor's name stands out through its sheer longevity in Benjamin's correspondence. The final mention of Molitor comes in April 1934, when Scholem, in one of his many attempts to provide Benjamin with a means of subsistence, suggests that he should edit selections from *Philosophie der Geschichte* for Schocken: 'Ich hatte den Vorschlag gemacht, Dich eine Auswahl aus Molitor besorgen zu lassen.'[46] Even though neither the publisher nor Benjamin seemed to be brimming with enthusiasm for the idea at the time, the very fact that Molitor seems to be at the forefront of both Scholem's and Benjamin's professional minds after more than fifteen years is itself testament to the author's importance. It sounds as if Benjamin had actually been fulfilling the intention he stated in the first letter of studying the material thoroughly, and that he not only felt the need to return to the book two years after buying it, but might even have been prevailed upon, had circumstances been different, to deliver a scholarly edition of the work.

Even if any *direct* influence of *Philosophie der Geschichte oder über die Tradition* on the language essay of 1916 is denied, the possible bearing of this very book on the essays Benjamin wrote since then, including *Über das Programm der kommenden Philosophie, Aufgabe des Übersetzers, Theologisch-politisches Fragment, Zur Kritik der Gewalt, Über das Mimetische Vermögen* and *Lehre vom*

Ähnlichen, to name but six striking titles, cannot be justifiably discounted without at least knowing the content of what is being discounted.[47] And there is in fact sufficient reason to suspect that Menninghaus not only failed to read or consult *Philosophie der Geschichte oder über die Tradition*, but that he probably never even saw an actual copy of the book, instead relying entirely on information provided by Scholem in *Geschichte einer Freundschaft* and in the notes to the first edition of the letters. The fact that Menninghaus mentions the book in his '*Verzeichnis der Zitierten Schriften*' without ever actually quoting *from* it is in itself enough to arouse suspicion, a suspicion that is only reinforced by a thorough reading of the book itself, which contains quite a large number of passages which bear a striking resemblance to certain elements in Benjamin's language philosophy, as we will see later.

Yet if we again revert to fine-toothed philology, although some might call it pedantry, we are confronted with certain elements that may confirm these suspicions. There is the fact that Menninghaus does not quote the full title of the book, which is the rather cumbersome, but to his argument quite relevant, *Philosophie der Geschichte oder über die Tradition in dem alten Bunde und ihre Beziehung zur Kirche des neuen Bundes mit vorzüglicher Rücksicht auf die Kabbalah*. But, although very arbitrary, this in itself could still easily be attributed to a sense of bibliographical economy. The one fact that truly hypothecates the credibility of Menninghaus's argument is that the bibliographical details are not only incomplete, but also wrong. The dates of publication he mentions are 1827 to 1857, which are the dates of *five* volumes instead of four: volume one was published in 1827, volume two in 1834, volume three in 1839, volume four in 1853 and the second edition of volume one in 1857. In *Geschichte einer Freundschaft*, Scholem gives the same dates (1827–1857) without, however, making any mention of the second edition of volume four (*GF*, 53). Oddly enough, in the notes to the first edition of the correspondence, he gives the dates of the first editions of all volumes, 1827–1853 (*Briefe*, 136).

What Scholem fails to mention in both cases is the publisher or the place of publication. Menninghaus gives the place of publication as 'Münster', which is, however, only correct when referring to the first edition of volumes two, three and four and the second edition of volume one, which were indeed published in Münster by Theissing from 1834 to 1857. The date of the first edition of the first volume is indeed 1827, but the place of publication is not Münster, and the publisher is not Theissing. The first edition of volume one was in fact published in Frankfurt am Main by Hermann. If Menninghaus had consulted the book, he would have known this, and the entry in his bibliography would have read either *Frankfurt and Münster, 1827–1857 (or 1853)* or *Münster, 1834–1857*. Admittedly a pedantic point, but this is not a mistake one makes when one writes down the details from the actual copy of the book rather than from a secondary source. We may therefore conclude that Menninghaus's objection to Molitor ought to have been overruled twenty years ago, on the grounds that it was based entirely on hearsay, and that the sentence should hence be reviewed. Actually, if we would call for the Molitor case merely to be re-opened, we would already fail to do it justice, as all the evidence points to the fact that it was never really opened in the first place.

En lieu of a lengthy literature review, suffice it here to say that, until the recent publication of Eric Jacobson's book which we discussed in the introduction, Menninghaus was the only author who even mentioned Molitor in connection with Benjamin, which means that the literature review is essentially complete once we have dealt with Menninghaus's claim. None of the authors named in the bibliography, including Alter, Buck-Morss, De Vries, Handelman, Konersmann, Menke, Meschonnic, Mosès, Nägele, Opitz, Rabinbach, Rochlitz, Rose, Schmidt, Schöne, Schweppenhäuser, Smith and Weber address the role of Molitor in Benjamin's *Auseinandersetzung* with the Jewish tradition. In his biographical study *Walter Benjamin: Der Intellektuelle als Kritiker*, Bernd Witte mentions the possible influence of Molitor in a footnote, but he relates it only, and very briefly, to Benjamin's theory of allegory in *Ursprung des deutschen Trauerspiels*, quoting as his source an MA dissertation by Reiner Dieckhoff, *Mythos und Moderne: Über die verborgene Mystik in den Schriften Walter Benjamins*.[48] Although he has read *Philosophie der Geschichte* and even provides the odd quotation from it, Dieckhoff's study is neither very informative nor very rewarding, concerned, as it is, with Baader's influence more than with Molitor's. It thus remains somewhat of a mystery why Witte should have singled Dieckhoff out for such praise. Some authors, however, such as John McCole, have actually managed to write an entire book about Benjamin and tradition without devoting even so much as a subsection to Judaism. McCole's 1993 book, *Walter Benjamin and the Antinomies of Tradition* does at least mention Molitor, if only very much in passing, but he essentially culls all his information about him from Menninghaus. Oddly enough, *Walter Benjamin and the Antinomies of Tradition* is almost exclusively concerned with Benjamin's well-known theories of experience, with a few token references to the concepts of messianism and Kabbalah, which makes the title somewhat misleading, to say the least. A thorough reading of Molitor's book nevertheless shows not only that the Jewish tradition is of considerable importance to Benjamin's thought, but also that *Philosophie der Geschichte* is an extremely likely source of his knowledge of this tradition. We will therefore embark on such a detailed reading in our next chapter.

Chapter Three: Philosophie der Geschichte

Despite all the circumstantial evidence which we discussed in the previous chapter, the strongest argument in favour of the relevance of Molitor to Benjamin's work, direct as well as indirect, first-hand as well as second-hand, is still the actual content of the book. As we suggested above, *Philosophie der Geschichte oder über die Tradition* is an extremely wide-ranging and truly encyclopaedic book. Very broadly speaking, the book has three basic aims, although even this very elementary level of inner organisation sometimes appears to lose itself in the most unexpected, but utterly fascinating, digressions. And in a way, as we suggested in the previous chapter, these digressions and circumambulations of the main topic become the point, and the actual 'topic' then becomes a dark and hidden presence surrounded by the halo of ideas. This peculiar *Gedankenbewegung* is the elusive conceptual intersection where Molitor's and Benjamin's thought meet, as this chapter and the next will seek to illustrate, gradually and peripatetically, as is meet for traditional wisdom.

Die wahre innere Seele des Judenthums

The first aim of *Philosophie der Geschichte* is to prepare the ground for an in-depth discussion of the metaphysics of the Kabbalah: 'Die Aufmerksamkeit auf diese wichtige, seit so langher vernachlässigte, Untersuchung der alten jüdischen Urtradition aus ihren Quellen, von neuem wieder zu wecken, ist der Zweck gegenwärtiger Schrift.' (*M* I, 9). Molitor never arrived at this discussion, but in his preparations for it, he frequently quotes from various mystical traditions next to the more conventional Talmudic sources. He thus effectively presents a picture of the Jewish tradition that lacks the strict separation of mystical and theosophical writings from the more 'mainstream' legal, ethical and philosophical texts. The hypothesis that there is a strict division between 'mystical' and 'mainstream' Judaism was put forward during the Haskalah with the aim of presenting Judaism as a *Vernunftreligion*, and it was later contested in several ways by Gershom Scholem. This tendency to relegate everything that sounded faintly mystical to the realms of irrationality and obscurantism, and thus outside the scope of rational inquiry and explanation, explains the near total lack of serious inquiry into the Kabbalah, which persisted until Scholem embarked on his lifelong study of the subject. Molitor, however, does not believe that the division was as radical as even 'einige jüdische Theologen behaupten':

> Im Judenthum aber war das Esoterische vom Exoterischen nur leise geschieden, und von dem einen zum andern ein leichter stufenmäßiger Uebergang eröffnet. Die Juden kannten keine abgeschlossenen Mysterien im Sinne der heidnischen Völker. Alles war auf Erziehung des Ganzen, als eines heiligen göttlichen Volkes und priesterlichen Reiches angelegt. (*M* I, 201)

Molitor claims that most of the knowledge of what is now termed the Jewish mystical tradition actually trickled down to the ordinary people, the *Am Ha'aretz*, through the oral teaching of priests and rabbis. According to Molitor, in other words, the mystical teachings that were later written down in such books as the *Zohar* and the *Ra'ja Mehemna* were already contained in the *Torah She-be'al-peh* or the oral Torah. Molitor's hypothesis is that these mystical teachings were far less esoteric in early Mishnaic and Talmudic times, and that their essence was therefore part and parcel of the religious experience of most Jews. The terms 'mysticism' or 'mystical teachings', although Molitor does not provide us with a straightforward definition of them, are predominantly used in the context of hidden, secret or allegorical meanings of Scripture. With reference to these hidden meanings of the Torah, he writes:

> Obwohl nun zwar in der Thorah nirgends mit ausdrücklichen Worten gelehrt, noch auch, in der jüdischen Glaubenslehre, geradezu zu glauben geboten wird, daß die heilige Schrift noch einen innern verborgenen Sinn in sich schließe, der dem Moscheh auf dem Berge Sinai eröffnet worden; so gehöret doch der

Glaube an diesen geheimen tiefern Sinn der Schrift keineswegs, wie einige jüdische Theologen behaupten, zu den blos [sic] subjektiven, theologischen Meinungen, sondern er macht einen wesentlichen Bestandtheil, – er macht die wahre innere Seele – des Judenthums selbst aus. (*M* I, 12)

Although he admits that a full and intimate knowledge of the mystical tradition was granted only to the wisest of the Jews, and that the study of secret, mystical meanings of the Torah was not actively encouraged (the active study of 'higher mysticism' was discouraged, even, to protect the 'weak and unprepared characters' from its potentially dangerous effects[1]), Molitor insists that the mystical tradition was not only an integral part of the Jewish tradition as a whole, but that there was no fundamental opposition between them, as they were both based on the same age-old principles and have grown out of the same seed. The description of these mystical teachings as the 'wahre innere Seele des Judenthums' is quite crucial, suggesting, as it does, a hidden, inner continuity which survived even the most drastic of outward changes, even, up to a certain extent, the advent of Christianity, as we will see later. Describing the gradual expansion of the Jewish tradition throughout the centuries, he writes:

Diese immer größere Erweiterung der Tradition ist aber nicht etwa eine Folge fremdartiger Zuthaten gewesen, die man von außen in dieselbe hineingeschwärzt, sondern es war in der That ein wirkliches Wachsen und Entfalten von innen heraus; denn alle spätere Satzungen und Institutionen, sammt dem ganzen Lehrgebäude der Kirche, sind alle gewissermaßen auf die uralten Prinzipien basirt, und liegen in denselben gleichsam wie in ihrem Keime verschlossen da. *Die gesammte jüdische Tradition, ein dogmatisches, fortschreitendes Ganzes bildend, gleicht also einem Baume, dessen mannigfaltige Auszweigungen doch alle aus einem Stamme hervorgesproßt sind.* (*M* I, 19; Molitor's emphasis)

The botanical metaphor Molitor uses to describe the fundamental unity of the Jewish tradition, which recurs several times throughout the four volumes, is reminiscent of Goethe's concept of the *Urpflanze*, of which Benjamin himself was also quite fond. The idea that the whole development of a plant, from the budding shoot to the fully-grown plant, is contained within its seed is taken up in the *Erkenntniskritische Vorrede* to *Ursprung des deutschen Trauerspiels*, where it is applied to the realm of ideas and used in conjunction with Leibniz's concept of the monad to form an extraordinarily complex doctrine of ideas.[2] Applied to the Jewish tradition, however, the effect of this metaphor is to create not only a sense of unity and integrity, but also a sense of simultaneity. It means that the ultimate doctrinal complexities of Judaism are already present within its origin in a very real sense, which is exemplified both by the formal structure of the Talmud, as a twin process of continuous accumulation and conservation, and by the conceptual structure of rabbinic literature, which allows the appearance of figures from different historical eras within one and the same sphere. The metaphor in question thus suggests that the Jewish understanding of the sphere of temporality is essentially characterised by a sense of simultaneity. Tradition, in other words, is seen as a viscous, multi-dimensional whole, in spatial rather than in temporal or linear terms, brought together in the concept of the *Lehre*. Significantly, this is also the conclusion which Scholem drew from his reading of *Philosophie der Geschichte*, as he states quite emphatically in a long letter to Siegfried Lehmann dated 9 October 1916, a month before Benjamin wrote *Über Sprache überhaupt und über die Sprache des Menschen*:

> [...] das ist der Begriff und die Wirklichkeit der 'Thora', das ist der jüdische Begriff der Lehre, das ist der unerhört tiefe, wahre und von uns in Wahrheit zu verwirklichende jüdische Begriff der 'Tradition'. Nicht mit Leichtsinn hat Franz Molitor, der große christliche Kabbalist, sein außerordentliches Buch über die Kabbala – mit dem die ganze Größe des Mannes tatsächlich in einem Worte kennzeichnenden Titel versehen: Philosophie der Geschichte oder über Tradition!!! Herr Lehmann, ein Buch über die jüdische Mystik von einem Mystiker mit dem Titel über Tradition! Jawohl, wer das 'Wort' hat, hat das Judentum, aber dieses Wort begreift man nicht, wenn man nicht das Werk kennt, das Wesen der Thora begreift man nicht, wenn man sie nicht kennt, und den jüdischen Gottesbegriff begreift man nicht, 'erlebt' man nicht, wenn man nicht Gottes Werk kennt, Gottes Tat. Thora ist nicht Pentateuch allein, Thora ist der Inbegriff, das Integral der religiösen Überlieferungen der Judenheit von Mosche Rabbenu bis auf Israel Hildesheimer, bis auf Sie, Herr Lehmann, wenn Sie ein Jude sind, und die Thora – nach dem wahren Worte der Mystiker – vollkommen sein in den Tagen des Messias. (*SB* I, 47–48; Scholem's emphasis)

This quotation, proclaiming the integrity and inclusiveness of the Jewish tradition, could serve as a concise summary of the argument Molitor stretches across nearly two thousand pages, and, in fact, as an abstract of our previous chapter. But what makes it even more noteworthy, apart from its temporal proximity to that fateful 11 November 1916, is the fact that Scholem actually read out this letter to Benjamin a week after it was written and that Benjamin 'congratulated him' on it, asking for a transcript and stating 'es sei das erste Mal, daß jemand diese Ansichten wie er habe' (*TB* I, 409). This means that less than three weeks before Benjamin was to start writing *Über Sprache*, he actually confessed to having the same thoughts on tradition and the *Lehre* as Scholem, who was, as we have seen, not only thoroughly impressed by Molitor's work, but was at that very time engaged in an in-depth study of *Philosophie der Geschichte*, which helped him to order and focus his thoughts on tradition in Judaism. With this knowledge, we can comfortably and definitively reject Menninghaus's argument that Benjamin could not possibly have picked up that much information about the Jewish tradition from his conversations with Scholem at the time. In fact, the sheer intelligence and authority even of Scholem's private writings during these years is so remarkable that, if Benjamin only retained half of what Scholem told him, he would have been well-informed on matters Jewish by any standard.

Molitor's insistence on the unity of tradition is probably reinforced by his (mistaken) conviction that the mystical tradition is a good deal older than nineteenth-century scholarship thought. He believes that the mystical doctrine of Judaism, which constituted the 'soul' of the religion in Biblical times, was kept alive primarily in an oral form and gradually found its way into writing as early as patriarchal times, when its essential doctrinal statements were set down in esoteric documents (which did not survive, or remain hidden to this day):

> Diese mystische Lehre, die einst im Alterthum die wahre Seele des ganzen Lebens ausmachte, wurde meistens blos mündlich fortgepflanzt; doch sollen schon die frühern Weisen, ja sogar die Patriarchen, die wesentlichsten Lehrsätze derselben in besondern geheimen Schriften niedergelegt haben. (*M* I, 64)

But Molitor also dates surviving mystical documents further back in time than other scholars of his (and our) age. The *Sefer Yetsirah* or the *Book of Creation*, for instance, a very complex document from the third or fourth century CE expounding the famous doctrine of the *Sefirot* or numbers, which the kabbalist tradition attributes to Abraham, is said by Molitor to bear the marks 'eines hohen Altherthums' (*M* I, 65). Similarly, the *Ra'ja Mehemna*, a book which is traditionally attributed to Moses and which is part of the *Sefer ha-Zohar* (better known simply as the *Zohar*), is said by Molitor to stem from Biblical times. It is Molitor's dating of the *Zohar* itself, however, which has the most far-reaching consequences for his view of Jewish mysticism. Essentially, he accepts the kabbalist attribution of this most famous and influential book in the Jewish mystical canon to Rabbi Shimon ben Yochai, a pupil of Rabbi Akibah, who lived in the second century CE. Gershom Scholem has since confirmed the hypothesis that the actual author was the Spanish kabbalist Moshe Shem Tov of León, who died in 1305 and probably wrote the work in the latter quarter of the thirteenth century.[3] Oddly enough, Molitor is actually aware of this hypothesis, but he rejects it outright in favour of the traditional kabbalist attribution, arguing against post-Amoraic times as the *terminus ad quem* on the grounds that the mystical hermeneutics of the *Zohar* were already known, in a primarily oral form, during Mishnaic times.[4]

This is basically the same argument he used to hint at the intimate relationship between the mystical tradition and the oral Torah, and its effect is to produce a more homogeneous picture of the different strands of the Jewish tradition than modern scholarship has indicated. In this sense, in fact, Molitor's book is closer to the letter of the Jewish tradition itself, however unorthodox it may seem in other places. One of these unorthodox connections made by Molitor is directly related to his backdating of the main writings of the mystical tradition to early Tannaitic times, i.e., the second century CE. These were the times, immediately after the destruction of the Second Temple, when a small messianic-apocalyptic sect produced its primary texts, later canonised as the four (Christian) Gospels. And Molitor does indeed appear eager to suggest a connection between the *Zohar* and the Gospels, however vague it remains here. In a discussion of the dialogical and peripatetic teaching methods of Rabbi Shimon ben Yochai, Molitor adds a footnote saying: 'Daher hat der Sohar *in dieser Hinsicht* auch mit der Form der Erzählung des neuen Testamentes große Aehnlichkeit.' (*M* I, 70n; Molitor's emphasis).

This brings us to the second intention of *Philosophie der Geschichte*, conveyed by the subtitle *über die Tradition in dem alten Bunde und ihre Beziehung zur Kirche des neuen Bundes*. In a not entirely systematic way, *radikal* rather than *konsistent*, Molitor seeks to bring Judaism and Christianity closer to one another, and in some ways even to construct a more or less unified *JudaeoChristianity*, in which both religions enter into infinitely complex relationships with one another, ultimately becoming mutually inclusive. It is a movement similar to the one he performed with regard to the twin traditions of Judaism itself, and he reverts to the same metaphor to describe it: 'Judenthum und Christenthum verhalten sich wie Knospe und Blüthe, was in dem einen noch verschlossen liegt, ist in dem andern durch die Sonne des Lebens in reicher herrlicher Fülle aufgegangen.' (*M* I, 313). Of course, by intertwining Judaism and Christianity so intimately, the conclusion that neither can exist without the other becomes inevitable. It is needless to say that this unorthodoxy *à coup redoublé* failed to charm a large number of people in Molitor's day. In fact, the three hundred supplementary pages in the second edition of the first volume are almost exclusively concerned with polemics against both Jewish and Christian scholars who disagreed with Molitor.

Of course, Molitor remains a Christian author, which means that he fundamentally disagrees with Judaism's rejection of Jesus as the Messiah (he is always very careful to say that this is a doctrinal error of Judaism, not of the Jews). Yet these statements, which he does not make frequently, are more than balanced by Molitor's reverent and respectful attitude towards Jews and Judaism, convinced that in spite of its 'error', for want of a milder term, Judaism has been promised 'eine Dauer bis zum letzten Ende'.[5] On the one hand, he is in favour of assimilation, saying that it should not under any circumstances be discouraged, yet on the other hand, he firmly opposes attempts of any kind to threaten the existence of Rabbinic Judaism. But for all his tolerance, which is extremely broad for its day and age, Molitor does indeed seek to give Judaism a christological turn by importing the persons of the Holy Trinity into the Kabbalah and equating them with the first three Sefirot, *Keter Elyon*, *Hokhmah* and *Binah*, which together form the *Ein Soph* or the unfathomable Godhead (*M* II, 52 ff.). Of course, as Molitor himself says as well, it is an equally valid perspective to see this as a kabbalist interpretation of the Holy Trinity.

If Molitor's version of Judaism is academically idiosyncratic – because it is, in its own paradoxical ways, closer to a traditional *Überarbeitung* of the Jewish tradition than it is to a scientific interpretation of it, as even Gershom Scholem admitted – his version of Christianity is no less thought-provoking, or even provocative. Rather than seeing the filial relationship between the two religions as it is traditionally interpreted by Christians in terms of a revolution, a break, an overturning, a sublation or an abrogation, Molitor is trying to think the relationship between Judaism and Christianity in terms of a co-existence, politically, philosophically and religiously, even though this forces him to suspend a number of inevitable internal contradictions. We already touched briefly upon the social and political consequences of Molitor's sympathy for Jews and Judaism, and the following may serve as an example of exactly how far this takes him. At more than one point in the book, Molitor, a Catholic, argues passionately and at length against the (Christian) accusation that the Jews alone are guilty of the death of Christ:

> Die Verwerfung und Kreuzigung des Gott-Menschen durch seine eigenen Kinder, ist die schrecklichste That, welche seit Anbeginn vollbracht worden. Doch nicht die Juden allein haben den Heiland verworfen, die Verwerfung ist keine individuelle, sondern eine allgemeine That, woran die ganze Menschheit Theil hat und mit erniedrigt wird. [...] Theilen wir also lieber freiwillig die Schuld mit den Juden, statt dieselben wiederholt anzuklagen. Indem wir alle Schuld einzig und allein auf das jüdische Volk wälzen, so stellen wir uns als die Gerechten dar, wähnend, als hätten wir an ihrer Stelle es besser gemacht; solches aber ist ein Gräuel vor dem Herrn. (*M* I, 238–239)

The attitude which speaks from this passage seems to be very 'Christian' in its call for forgiveness and its emphatic rejection of what was the main grist to the antisemitic mill (in which sense it could also be called distinctly anti-Christian, depending on whose definition of Christianity we would go by). Yet Molitor's political-theological position towards Judaism and the Jews cannot be called liberal *stricto sensu*, because, despite his insistence on forgiveness (or, from the other perspective, because of his sole insistence on forgiveness), he still states in as many words that the Jews were wrong to have rejected the Messiah. A liberal perspective would demand a fundamental level of tolerance for the alterity of the other *in his alterity*. But, and this is the cross from which Molitor's Judaeo-Christian puppet is suspended, he effectively denies the discrete integrity of both religions, thus reducing their alterity towards each other. His calling on Christianity to take the burden of 'Jewish' guilt as its own is symptomatic of Molitor's profound interfusion of both religions, as is his insistence on the genealogical obligation of Christianity towards Judaism (an obligation echoed in the third commandment of the law which they share). Brushing against the grain of orthodoxy from both perspectives, Molitor compromises the integrity of Judaism as well as Christianity by entering them into a dialectic of sorts, making them fundamentally co-dependent. According to him, Judaism is the outward form of the inward religion that is Christianity, although the latter does not contain anything which the former did not also contain.

Judaism and Christianity: Almost a Dialectic

Throughout *Philosophie der Geschichte*, Molitor uses the image of history as a dual process of centrifugality and centripetality. In a centrifugal movement, Judaism constitutes the externalisation of the law, which is countered by the centripetal movement of Christianity as an internalisation of the same law. This twin process of alternating centrifugality and centripetality is mirrored and repeated throughout natural and human (and divine) history in several permutations. It would lead us too far to describe this complex mystical concept in any great detail, but it is important insofar as it is *not quite* a dialectic. Every time this semi-cyclical process is repeated, it essentially returns to its initial position, but not without retracing its footsteps and, in doing so, making them deeper. This process differs from a classical dialectic in that it does not sublate, but accumulate. As we have seen in the first chapter, accumulation rather than dogmatic exclusion is one of the most fundamental characteristics of the Jewish tradition, and even though it is applied here to particularly unorthodox ends, it remains the only way in which two opposites can be kept in permanent suspension, in oscillation. It is, not to put too fine a point on it, the basic structure of the *Dialektik im Stillstand*, or dialectics at a standstill, which is used here to reconcile the belief in Jesus the Messiah with the diametrically opposite belief that the Messiah is yet to come. One of the many descriptions of the relationship between Christianity and Judaism formulates the tension as follows:

> Im Christenthum giebt es gleichfalls wie im Judenthum eine allgemeine dog-matisch verbindende und eine freie mystische Lehre, die von der Kirche nicht dogmatisch befohlen, sondern der innern Forschung eines Jeden überlassen bleibt. Obwohl das Christenthum das innere aufgeschlossene Judenthum ist und daher was in demselben nur dem innern geistigen Blicke zugänglich war, in jenem dem gläubigen Gemüthe offenkundig geworden, so hat doch auch wieder das Christenthum sein höhere verborgene Seite, die nur dem aufgeschlossenen Sinne des weiter beförderten Gemüthes faßlich wird. Dies ist die höhere Mystik, auf die ohne Zweifel der Heiland zielt, wenn er zu seinen Jüngern (ehe sie den heiligen Geist erhalten hatten) spricht: 'Ich könnte euch noch Vieles sagen, aber ihr könnt es noch nicht fassen.' Joh. 16.12. (*M* I, 299)[6]

The insistence on the presence of a 'higher mysticism' which infuses Christianity is crucial. As we mentioned before, Molitor's time-scale of Jewish mysticism brings the earliest documents of the fledgling Christian church extremely close in time (and by default in space) to the *Zohar*, one of the most important texts of the Jewish mystical tradition, which he mistakenly dates back to 121 CE. This makes his claim that the New Testament shows a remarkable formal and stylistic resemblance to the *Zohar*, and thus to the tradition of Jewish mysticism, all the more acceptable, and the thought that there could be a certain correspondence between them thus does not appear particularly outlandish. But Molitor goes even further. He is not just seeking to establish a correspondence between Jewish and Christian mysticism, but a real continuity. The botanical metaphor of the bud growing into the flower takes on its full significance here, as a variation of the Jewish *theologoumenon* that everything was already contained in the one and true revelation. One needs only to 'turn it over and over, for all is in it.' As Molitor writes in the first book of *Philosophie der Geschichte:*

In dem zweiten Theile dieser Schrift werden wir es versuchen, die Existenz der mystischen Tradition im Judenthum und ihren Uebergang in das Christenthum kritisch zu beleuchten; wir bemerken daher hier vorläufig nur Folgendes. Es liegt schon in der Natur der Dinge, daß es niemals einen Sprung giebt, daß Alles, was in der Zukunft geschieht, schon in der Vergangenheit wie im Keime vorgebildet ist und sich daraus auf genetische Weise entwickelt. So lagen in den Gebräuchen des alten jüdischen Gesetzes die höchsten Geheimnisse des Christenthums alle auf symbolische Weise vorgestellt, und was das Symbol nur in seinen stummen Figuren andeutete, wurde durch den Mund der Propheten dem Verstande der Menschen wenigstens theilweise in hellerer Deutlichkeit aufgeschlossen. (*M* I, 302)

As this quotation indicates, Molitor sees the almost seamless continuity between Judaism and Christianity not only from the perspective of the latter, but also, and perhaps more surprisingly so, from the perspective of the former. Christianity undeniably uses Jewish concepts and categories in its own theology, rephrasing and reinterpreting them to create a *leicht entstellte Lehre*, a doctrine which is only slightly different from the Jewish one, and therefore, paradoxically, extremely different. *Der liebe Gott wohnt noch immer im Detail*, of course. Christians believe in the same God as Jews, but they also believe that the law this God revealed to his people has been incarnated into his son, the promised Messiah. In this respect, Molitor is correct in stating that the Christian expansion of the Jewish tradition was not 'eine Folge fremdartiger Zuthaten', as the life and meaning of Jesus are of course entirely based on interpretations of the Jewish doctrine of messianic expectation.[7] This makes it even more tempting to use the notion of the uncanny to illustrate this slight yet fundamental difference, whereby Christianity, so to speak, changed the position of one central piece of furniture in the house of Judaism, thus dramatically altering its atmosphere and making it uncomfortable to its own inhabitants. As with all analogies, this one too does not bear close scrutiny, but it expresses quite well the sense of sameness in difference which Molitor apparently seeks to convey.

From the perspective of Judaism, however, the same seamless continuity constitutes its own *Nachleben* within Christianity. If, to continue the metaphor, Christianity moved into the house of Judaism, the latter maintains a subdued but stubborn presence in a far corner, infusing the entire house with its almost unseen presence. As Molitor says on several occasions, the deepest secrets of Christianity were already contained in the oldest Jewish laws, and by extension, the oldest Jewish laws still survive in and within Christianity. In a discussion of the Christian calendar in book IV, for instance, Molitor writes:

> Bei diesem christlichen Festcyklus stellt sich ein auffallender Parallelismus mit dem des Judenthums heraus, welcher offenbar die innige Verwandtschaft zwischen Judenthum und Christenthum beweist und zeigt, daß Ersteres durch die Erscheinung des letztern nicht schlechthin aufgehoben, sondern vielmehr in dasselbe organisch aufgenommen und nur höher potenzirt wurde, wie solches auch bei den christlichen Sakramenten zu ersehen, deren Grundbasis ganz im Judenthum ruht. (*M* IV, 42)

The organic metaphor which Molitor uses to describe their relationship justifies the use of the word 'seamless' in this context, as there is no sense of '*Ostentation der Faktur*' (I, 355), or emphatic artificiality, as Benjamin calls it in *Ursprung des deutschen Trauerspiels*, in the transition between Judaism and Christianity. In fact, there is not even a transition in the real sense of the word, as Judaism is neither overcome nor overruled, but lives on at the very heart of Christianity, although, paradoxically, the latter is described as the internalisation of the former. The fact that we are so often forced to have recourse to the figure of the paradox to describe Molitor's vision of Judaism and Christianity is telling. The impression created by his vision, which is rather less systematic than our exposition, is one of a grand unified tradition, simultaneously incorporating Judaism and Christianity in one organic whole, infused by one and the same spirit which subordinates the very real differences between the two religions as mere externalities. It is easy to see how such a suspension of difference would lead to paradoxical constructions, which need not therefore become impossible constructions. It is clear that Molitor does appear to be acutely aware of the gaps and breaks between the two doctrines, especially when he is discussing the historical particularities of both Judaism and Christianity. These, however, are almost effortlessly sublated in the all-embracing concept of tradition. The title of the book, lest we forget, is *Philosophie der Geschichte oder über die Tradition*, the most concise statement of the Molitor's philosophy which quite simply equates history with tradition. In this sense, intentionally or not, his vision is in fact closer to Judaism than it is to Christianity, however eclectic and unorthodox the sum of all four volumes of the book may be even in terms of the legendarily inclusive Jewish tradition. The fact that the book presents itself as an introduction to a greater work, which has remained a promise, and that even this introduction has fundamentally remained a work in progress, may serve as further, if accidental, proof of this perspective.

Molitor goes to great and extraordinary lengths to indicate the extent of Judaism's afterlife, as we have called it, in the Christian tradition. But in doing so, he actually and possibly inadvertently puts forward the suggestion that the very substance of this Christian tradition is essentially Jewish. The casual remark, quoted above, that the gospels are formally similar to the *Zohar* is taken up again in a subsequent chapter, where he writes about the tension between the exoteric writings of the early Christian church, the first gospels composed in the late first century CE, and the esoteric oral tradition which Molitor claims underlay them.

Diese Schriften waren jedoch ursprünglich nicht für den öffentlichen, sondern zunächst für den Privatgebrauch des Einzelnen bestimmt, denn im Anfange geschah der Unterricht der Gemeinde durch die Apostel und Jünger, die noch von dem lebendig machende Geiste Gottes beseelt waren, nach der Weise des Heilandes blos durch das mündliche Wort. Man kann daher allerdings diese durch den Heiligen Geist geleisteten schriftlichen Fassungen der mündlichen Lehre gewissermaßen mit den M'gilloth S'tharim der Juden, §. 20., vergleichen, mit denen sie ihrer ganzen Bestimmung nach die größte Aehnlichkeit haben. Sie waren von und für Solche gemacht, die mit der heiligen Lehre vertraut waren, daher die vielen Lücken und Dunkelheiten, so daß nicht einmal der Tag und das Jahr der Geburt des Heilandes bemerkt ist. Späterhin fing man an, die alten M'gilloth S'tharim der Apostel nebst ihren Schreiben an die Gemeinden zu sammeln, woraus der Canon des neuen Testaments hervorgegangen, der im strengen Sinn kein geschriebenes Gesetz ist, sondern blos die schriftlich verfaßte mündliche Tradition enthält. (*M* I, 298)[8]

The formal parallel between this description of the early Christian church and the Jewish esoteric tradition as Molitor had described it earlier in the book is quite clear. In fact, if we may be allowed another parallel to gauge the import of this one, we could refer to Scholem's description of Benjamin as 'legitime[r] Fortsetzer der fruchtbarsten und echtesten Traditionen [eines Hamann und Humboldt] (*apocryphal*)' (*Briefe*, 526 and *GB* IV, 27). From the above-mentioned quotation, we can conclude that Molitor sees Jesus and his followers as 'die legitime Fortsetzer der fruchtbarsten und echtesten Traditionen eines Hillel und Schammai', essentially establishing a seamless continuity between the Jewish and Christian traditions.

This tantalising description, taken from one of Scholem's letters to Benjamin, is yet another philological curiosity we have stumbled across in the increasingly complicated Benjaminian *Quellenstudium*. In the original two-volume edition of the letters, which is the one used by Menninghaus, the passage includes a reference to Hamann and Humboldt – which is one of the arguments quoted by Menninghaus to support his hypothesis that the sources of Benjamin's language mysticism are the early German Romantics and not the Jewish tradition. In fact, *Walter Benjamins Theorie der Sprachmagie* actually opens with this very quotation, and promises to turn Scholem's subjunctive into an indicative by proving 'daß und wie weit Walter Benjamins Werk tatsächlich die genuinen sprachphilosophischen Intentionen "eines Hamann und Humboldt" sowie – vor allem – der sie vermittelnden Frühromantiker fortsetzt' (p. 7). However, in volume IV of the *Gesammelte Briefe*, the new edition of Benjamin's correspondence, published in 1998, the passage reads: […] als legitimer Fortsetzer der fruchbarsten und echtesten Traditionen' (*GB* IV, 27). The source of this edition is the original letter from Scholem which was preserved in Benjamin's *Nachlaß*, so once again, Menninghaus's argument is found wanting in evidence (and this time in a particularly painful place: the first sentence of the entire book). It still remains somewhat of a mystery where the apocryphal reference to 'Hamann und Humboldt' came from: possibly from Scholem's carbon

110

copy of the same letter, on which the first edition of the correspondence was based, and which might have been supplemented with these names, or become illegible over time. Whatever the case may be, the original obviously made no reference to the German Romantics, but merely mentions 'die fruchtbarsten und echtesten Traditionen', which, bearing in mind the inclinations of its author, would not be hard to interpret as the Jewish or even Judaeo-Christian traditions. Furthermore, the context of this letter is the 'fusion' in Benjamin's work of theology, metaphysics and materialism, resulting in an ambiguity, a 'Schwebezustand', which Scholem describes quite bluntly not as productive, but as 'Selbsttäuschung':

> wie Du selbst völlig zutreffend an Rychner, wachsen Deine eigenen und soliden Erkenntnisse aus der sagen wir kurz Metaphysik der Sprache, welche recht eigentlich das ist, womit Du, zu unverstellter Klarheit gelangt, eine hochmächtige Figur in der Geschichte kritischen Denkens sein könntest, als legitimer Fortsetzer der fruchbarsten und echtesten Traditionen. Das ostensible Bemühen dagegen, diese Resultate in einen Rahmen einzuspannen, in dem sie sich plötzlich als Resultate materialistischer Überlegungen darzustellen scheinen, gefährdet sie aufs stärkste, da es ein fremdes Form-Element hineinträgt, das zwar wohl mit Leichtigkeit von jedem intelligenten Leser loszulösen ist, das aber den von ihnen durchsetzten Produktionen den Stempel des Abenteuerlichen, Zweideutigen, ja in einigen Fällen fast Volteschlägerischen aufdrückt. (*GB* IV, 27–28)

Scholem's letter came in answer to a copy of a letter to Max Rychner, which Benjamin had sent to him, and apart from a discussion of Benjamin's preoccupation with dialectical materialism, this letter contained the following famous phrase, which Benjamin himself obviously did not consider to be in contradiction what he had written before: '[…] ich habe nie anders forschen und denken können als in einem, wenn ich so sagen darf, theologischen Sinn – nämlich in Gemäßheit der talmudischen Lehre von den neunundvierzig Sinnstufen jeder Thorastelle' (*GB*, 19–20). In the light of our investigation, it would be interesting to see which results would be yielded by a reassessment of the relationship between metaphysics and materialism in Benjamin's work – especially now it has been indicated that some of the groundwork of earlier attempts to do so was either incomplete or even mistaken.

Elsewhere Molitor notes the fact that Jesus's close circle of twelve apostles and seventy disciples is based on numbers which have a profound mystical significance in Judaism, and he believes this suggests that Jesus 'den Typus der jüdischen Hierarchie aufs Christenthum übertrug'.[9] But Molitor seeks to indicate more than a merely formal analogy between Judaism and Christianity at this stage, which can still be explained by the simple and undeniable fact that Jesus and his followers were Jews living in a predominantly Jewish land, and were thus forced to fall back on a Jewish frame of reference if they were to make themselves understood at all.[10] In his description of the relationship between Judaism and the embryonic Christian church, however, Molitor also suggests that there is a more substantial continuity, and that the essence of the Jewish doctrine is carried forward into Christianity. He goes to great lengths to refute the (antisemitic) notion that the Jewish tradition had lapsed into 'positive error' and therefore needed to be replaced with a new covenant: 'Hatten etwa damals falsche Lehren die Kirche Jisraäl verdorben, oder unsittliche Principien ihren Weg verkehrt? Nein, keiner Art von positiven Irrthümern kann die alte Kirche beschuldigt werden, weder in den Dogmen, noch in der Sittenlehre [...]' (*M* I, 231). Molitor maintains that Jesus did not attack either the Jewish tradition or the Jewish community, but rather the 'großen Übertreibungen' of the doctrine, even though these were themselves motivated by piety.[11] It is unclear whether Molitor feels forced to include some disapproving comments on Judaism so as to avoid being dismissed outright by an audience that would automatically tend to have a negative view of Jews and Judaism, or whether he himself was genuinely caught in this contradictory, catholic frame of mind which continued to cloud his judgement, as accurate as it at times may be. Whichever is the case, he takes the Pharisees as the archetypal example of these 'exaggerations' of Jewish legalism against which Jesus rebels, but then he proceeds to point out that the tractate *Sota* in the Babylonian Talmud itself distinguishes seven kinds of Pharisaism, condemning false piety and praising the love of God of the true *Perushim*. Similarly, Molitor quotes the Talmud to prove that human needs take precedence over a strict legalistic adherence to the commandment of honouring the Sabbath, thus refuting another staple antisemitic argument.[12] This leads him to the general conclusion that the 'true light' of Judaism was merely 'obscured' by the excesses of a few individuals, and that the aim of Jesus was essentially to show the way back to the 'pure doctrine' rather than to destroy Judaism and establish an entirely new religion:

> Denn wenn Christus der Herr die allgemeinen Misbräuche rügte, und die Heuchelei einzelner Pharisäer und Kirchenlehrer bestrafte, so redete er doch niemals gegen die Kirche selber. [...] Nein, die Kirche des heiligen Volkes war als solche in keinem Irrthum; denn wenn auch ihre einzelnen Theologen auf schlechten Wegen wandelten, durch unsittliches Betragen böses Beispiel gaben, oder durch Ueberfüllung des Zeremonial-Gesetzes das Volk zur todten Werkheiligkeit gewöhnten, so waren dieses [sic] blos äußere Flecken, die das reine Licht zwar verdunkelten, aber nicht auszulöschen vermochten. Denn bei allen Makeln ward die reine Lehre nie so verschroben, daß nicht ein reines Gemüth das Aechte vom Falschen hätte unterscheiden, mithin in dieser Kirche, trotz ihren Mängeln und Mißbräuchen, die Seligkeit hätte erreichen können. (*M* I, 233–234)

The strongest statement of this hypothesis comes later, however, when Molitor refers to a book by a certain Rittangel in which mention is made of 'gewissen seltenen Büchern' which he claims to have found in Poland and which convinced him that there is not a single 'Titel oder Buchstab im neuen Testament, der nicht in dem Judenthum auch zu finden sey' (*M* I, 301). In other words, the 'pure doctrine' of which Molitor speaks simply flows into Christianity, and not a word nor even a letter is added onto it. Paradoxically, again, this is a particularly Jewish notion. As we discussed in the first chapter, the task of the pious Jew was to preserve and to study the Torah, and not to change or add a single letter to it. The entire Jewish tradition from the Mishnah onwards therefore sees itself not as an addition but as an explanation of the Torah, which was deemed to contain everything already, a concept expressed by the motto 'Turn it over and over, for all is in it'. According to Molitor, this is exactly what Jesus and his followers are doing: 'Bei den Juden hat jedes einzelne Jota der Schrift dasselbe Ansehen, wie das ganze prophetische Wort, und auf diese

Heiligkeit der schriftlichen Form scheint auch Christus zu zielen, wenn er spricht, daß kein Jota vom Gesetz solle aufgehoben werden.' (*M* I, 371n). They do not add anything to the law, they merely explain it, reviving the 'pure light' that burns within it. This 'pure light', again according to Molitor, is the 'higher mystical tradition' we discussed above, which can be 'obscured' but not 'extinguished.' This higher mystical tradition is essentially the hidden allegorical meaning of the Torah, which, Molitor claims, both Jews and Christians in their different ways are trying to decipher, and it is this mystical tradition which therefore unites both Judaism and Christianity in a very fundamental way. For this tradition not only existed around the time when Jesus preached – as we saw above, Molitor brings Jewish mysticism forward in time by equating it with the oral Torah – Jesus actually referred to it and based his church on it, concluding '[d]aß Christus wirklich von der Arcan-Disciplin Gebrauch gemacht, übrigens aus mehreren Stellen der Bibel deutlich hervor[gehet]' (*M* I, 249–250). This is perhaps the most revolutionary statement of *Philosophie der Geschichte oder über die Tradition*, and one which Molitor himself proclaims with a semi-messianic air, stating that it has always been true, but that the world has never been ready for it: 'Unsere Behauptung ist also durchaus keine neue, sondern eine alt längst bekannte Idee, die man aber früher, weil ihre Zeit noch nicht gekommen war, niemals gehörig verfolgte, in den neuern Zeiten aber, wo sich der ganze Standpunkt verrückte, völlig fallen ließ.'(*M* I, 301–302).[13]

This conclusion is relevant to our argument in two rather disparate ways. Firstly because it consistently presents a picture of tradition as a homogeneous sphere, infused by a single *Lehre*. As we pointed out in the previous chapter, and will discuss again later in this chapter, this perspective on tradition is quintessentially Jewish, even if, as in the case of Molitor, it includes such an unorthodox step as the merger of Judaism and Christianity into a single tradition (the paradoxes of such radical unorthodoxy might well have been part of the reason for Scholem's lifelong fascination with Molitor).[14] Secondly, and more directly related to Benjamin, Molitor's emphasis on the Jewish character of Christianity may well explain why Benjamin did not always appear to differentiate between Judaism and Christianity whenever he addressed the matter of religion or tradition. It is not entirely implausible that this was a consequence of the impression created by Molitor's monumental attempt to fuse the two religions into one tradition. Furthermore, it would also clarify and in part support Giorgio Agamben's hypothesis that certain concepts Benjamin uses in the *Thesen über den Begriff der Geschichte* take their inspiration from the letters of Paul. In his recent book, *Le temps qui reste*, Agamben reads Paul's letter to the Romans as a specific product of a time in which Judaism and Christianity were not yet seen as emphatically distinct religions.[15] The theological background of Paul's writings could thus be described as 'Judaeo-Christianity', a notion which is of course very close to the heart of Molitor's own project. Indeed, in his discussions of the Jewish influences on Christianity, Molitor frequently mentions Paul in passing, but even in some of the more detailed accounts of these Jewish elements within the (early) Christian church, the name Paul keeps recurring. In his discussion of the methodology of the Jewish mystical tradition, Molitor writes:

> Diese hohen Geheimnisse der theoretischen und praktischen Kabbalah sind nach der Lehre der jüdischen Mystiker, alle in der Bibel, entweder mit klaren Worten hier und da ausgesprochen ausgesprochen, oder aber meistens in dunkeln Bildern, und geheimnisvollen Winken רמזים (R'masim) blos angedeutet. Der größte Theil der jüdische Mystik beruhet überhaupt auf solchen R'masim, doch nicht allein die jüdische Mystik, sondern auch manche Dogmen des Christenthums, vorzüglich diejenigen, worin gerade das Tiefste enthalten liegt.

And in a footnote to this paragraph, he adds: 'Dergleichen Erklärungen der heiligen Schrift aus bloßen R'masim findet man allenthalben in den Evangelien, besonders in den Briefen von Paulus.' (*M* I, 47–48; also *M* I, 89 and 104). Molitor again appears to suggest that the writings of the early Christian church in general, and the letters of Paul in particular, are truly informed and inspired by the Jewish mystical tradition. In fact, towards the end of the first book, Molitor says as much in as many words: 'Wir werden im Zweiten Theile aus den Schriften von Paulus im Gegentheil viele Stellen anführen, die offenbar aus der Tradition der Juden genommen sind; so wie denn auch der Heiland, in seinen Reden an das Volk, sich gleichfalls mehrerer Gleichnisse bediente, welche in der jüdischen Tradition vorkommen.' (*M* I, 446).[16] This would entail that even when he referred to specifically Christian motifs, Benjamin might have been convinced that, from a purely theological point of view, he was essentially talking about the same tradition as the tradition of Judaism. And when in the final chapter we will look closer into Benjamin's treatment and use of the concept of tradition and theology, it will become clear that it may well have been this idea of a homogeneous sphere of *Überlieferung*, tradition – for want of a better translation, which drew him to the work of Molitor and which he himself then drew from that same work. In fact, it is not just Benjamin's concept of tradition which shows great similarity to that portrayed in *Philosophie der Geschichte*, but also his writing style. Molitor's description of the so-called Rematsim, these well-hidden 'dark images and secret hints' which nevertheless contain the very essence of the mystical doctrine, is curiously similar to Benjamin's own description of the strategy he followed writing *Einbahnstraße*, as the very first paragraph says: 'Meinungen sind für das Riesenapparat des gesellschaftlichen Lebens, was Öl für Maschinen; man stellt sich nicht vor eine Turbine und übergießt sie mit Maschinenöl. Man spritzt ein wenig davon in verborgene Nieten und Fugen, die man kennen muß.' (IV, 85).

Lehre, Unterricht, Offenbarung und Beispiel

As we mentioned before, and will no doubt come to mention again, it is extremely hard to distil one main argument from *Philosophie der Geschichte*, or even to find a definition of tradition as such, let alone an unequivocal one. The four volumes of the book address a wide range of subjects and contain a wealth of information surrounding the Jewish tradition in its various guises and from various angles, so much so, even, that the connections between the four volumes are not always crystal-clear. In this respect, too, the book mimics the tradition it speaks about, giving the impression, whether this is justified or not, that it hides more than it reveals. The first volume is by far the most straightforward, presenting a more or less historical overview of the Jewish tradition in Biblical, Mishnaic, Talmudic and post-Talmudic times, not unlike the overview we presented in the first chapter, where we have sought to indicate some parallel themes and passages in the footnotes. The second volume is arguably the most kabbalist, as it is concerned mainly with theosophy and the speculative knowledge of the Godhead. This volume also introduces the theme of the third and largest volume, namely the critique of revelation. But volume three, curiously enough, also contains two very long chapters on the Jewish doctrines of bodily and spiritual impurities, or *tumoth*, and these chapters paint a meticulously detailed and highly specialised picture of the subject, which did not fail to impress even Gershom Scholem. Volume four, finally, addresses the importance of the Jewish tradition and the Kabbalah for Christianity, and finishes with an abortive discussion of Christian philosophy. But this overview is of course far from analytic. Molitor writes about a plethora of other subjects, sometimes at the most unexpected moments and with only the most tenuous of links (*Philosophie der Geschichte oder über die Tradition*, like the tradition that is its subject, is very much a book for lateral thinkers). This does not make it any easier to trace a clear line through it, as we said before, nor even to distinguish what is of primary and what is of secondary importance. Nevertheless, in this paragraph we will attempt to analyse the most important points made by Molitor with regard to the concept, the phenomenology and the methodology of tradition.

In his brief introduction, Molitor states that 'alles in der Welt auf Lehre, Unterricht, Offenbarung und Beispiel beruht' (*M* I, 5), and with this terse, authoritative statement he has essentially set the tone of the book. His analyses, although they are usually supremely know-ledgeable and highly insightful, tend to be informed by the very subject about which they are meant to be informative. As we said before, Molitor's perspective is not that of a detached historicism or scientism, but rather that of an active engagement with tradition, even if this engagement is idiosyncratic, to say the very least. The *dictum* quoted above could easily be accompanied by the statement 'Alles in diesem Buch *ist* Lehre, Unterricht, Offenbarung und Beispiel.' But it

117

is clear that the terseness and authority of Molitor's tone stems from a real belief in what he is saying. In other words, unlike Benjamin's use of similar turns of phrase, this is not merely a *Sprachfigur* or *Denkfigur*, a figure of speech or a figure of thought, there is something of the confessional in all of Molitor's statements – at times brought to the fore by his use of such phrases as 'if God wills' or the eminently Jewish 'the Holy One, blessed be He'. Nonetheless, the forceful tone of these passages shows a remarkable similarity to the tone of Benjamin's early writings, as we will discuss in the next chapters. Yet it is not just the formal similarity between Molitor and Benjamin which may raise academic eyebrows, as there are some surprising analogies with regard to the substance of their writings as well. As we will point out in this paragraph, both Molitor and Benjamin define tradition from the perspective of education or *Erziehung*. Expounding the principles of tradition, Molitor writes:

> Die menschliche Kultur, als die Erziehungsanstalt des gefallenen Menschen-geschlechts, hebt ursprünglich von einer unmittelbaren göttlichen Offenbarung selber an, und bestehet in einer fortlaufenden (obwohl durch die Einwirkung des finstern Reiches vielfach entstellten und zersplitterten) Reihe von Ueber-lieferungen, die in einer lebendig fortschreitenden organischen Entfaltung von Geschlecht zu Geschlecht übergehen, wobei die folgende Generation immer von der vorhergehenden erzogen, und die überlieferten Resultate der Ver-gangenheit die lebendigen Anfänge einer neuen Zukunft werden. (*M* I, 5)

Before discussing Molitor's theory of tradition and education in detail, we should have a closer look at the exact terms he uses, as every single one of these crucial words concerning education and tradition presents us with a problem in translation. The most obvious word is *Lehre*, which can only be translated as 'doctrine', but which has a far wider and more abstract meaning in German (or at least it is used in a far wider sense by Molitor, Benjamin and Scholem). The English word 'tradition' is the translation for both *Tradition* and *Überlieferung*, the latter of which can also be used in the sense of 'tradendum', in other words a certain element of tradition or 'something which is handed down', to use a slightly clumsier paraphrase. The major difference with regard to these words is that *überliefern* can be used as a transitive verb, designating the working of the *Überlie-*

ferung, something which is impossible to say in English. *Erziehung* is again broader than its standard translation 'education' or even 'upbringing', referring to the guided development of human beings as human beings, rather than being limited to childhood or to academic education (*erziehen* literally means 'to draw up'). *Offenbarung*, finally, is a special case. It is quite adequately translated by the word 'revelation', but it has connotations of both opening up and unveiling which the English translation lacks. Particularly in the case of Benjamin, whose theory of criticism relies heavily on the concepts of veiling and unveiling, this inevitably proves to be of some importance. For this reason, it can be unwise to rely on translated texts only in any analysis of Benjamin's work, for even if his thought does not rely quite so heavily on the particularities of the German language as the philosophy of Heidegger does, Benjamin is fond enough of plays on words and literary devices for it either to lose a considerable amount in translation or for the translation to be rather dreadful to read.

Now according to Molitor, human culture consists of a continuously progressing series of *tradenda*, 'eine Reihe von Ueberlieferungen, die in einer lebendig fortschreitenden organischen Entfaltung von Geschlecht zu Geschlecht übergehen'. This is the mode of existence of the *Lehre*, the simultaneous and reciprocal process of *lehren* and *lernen*, of teaching and learning, which cannot be located in either the teacher or the students, but must be seen as an integral and homogeneous sphere of existence – and Benjamin not only knew this, he also said that he needed Molitor's book '*anders kann ich nicht lernen*'. Again, Molitor uses the metaphor of an organic development to convey the image of a seamless continuity to describe tradition, as he did in his statement that in a traditional conception of history 'es niemals einen Sprung giebt, daß Alles, was in der Zukunft geschieht, schon in der Vergangenheit wie im Keime vorgebildet ist und sich daraus auf genetische Weise entwickelt' (*M* I, 302). This metaphor at the same time also suggests that the integrity of tradition is fundamentally maintained. From Molitor's mystical perspective, the realm of darkness may distort and fragment the continuous line of tradition, but it can never destroy the *Überlieferungen* themselves. The latter will always survive, albeit possibly in distorted or fragmented forms, so it will always be possible through contemplation and observance to restore tradition to its original form. This concept is reminiscent of the *Shevirat ha-Kelim*, or the breaking of the vessels, a doctrine from the Lurianic Kabbalah which taught that the vessels which contained the glory of the original revelation (the *Kelim*) had been broken and spread across the world to be deciphered and redeemed by the wise and the pious. This redemption obviously took the shape of a *restitutio in integrum* of the divine glory, which Luriah's followers were convinced was possible through the study and manipulation of the holy text by initiates. The importance of this image is the fact that it conceives of the *Überlieferung(en)* as something with a physical reality, a concept which, as we have discussed at length in the first chapter, infuses the entire Jewish tradition, and correspondingly finds its way into *Philosophie der Geschichte*.

One way in which Molitor conveys the concept of the physical reality of tradition is through the comparison of traditional *Erziehung* with artisanship:

> Alles Wissen war im Alterthum an das Leben geknüpft, es gab kein blos abstraktes theoretisches Wissen: das Wissen war ein Können und praktisches Ueben; die Schule eine lebendig-praktische, sittlich-scientifische Bildungs-anstalt; die nicht allein die einzelnen Verstandesfrüchte in Anspruch nahm, sondern den ganzen ungetheilten Menschen umfaßte, und mit der Wissenschaft oder Kunst zugleich den Charakter erzog. Daher standen Lehrer und Schüler in dem innig moralischen Verhältniß, wie Vater und Sohn, wie Regent und Diener, zu einander. Lange mußte sich der Schüler am Niedern üben, um den rohen, ungezügelten, natürlichen Menschen zu bändigen, und hierdurch jenen wahren, hehren Ernst, jene Gründlichkeit und reine, innere Liebe für seinen Gegenstand zu gewinnen, ohne welche nirgends ein Gedeihen möglich ist. So schritt alsdann der Lehrling nach und nach zur Stufe eines Gehülfen fort, wo er schon einen weit freiern Wirkungskreis erlangte, bis er zuletzt die Tüchtigkeit des Meisters sich erwarb, und damit die Erlaubnis erhielt, selbst wieder andere Schüler zu unterweisen. (*M* I, 7)[17]

This description emphasises the all-encompassing nature of the sphere of *Erziehung* from the perspective of the individual as well as of the activity. Education embraces all aspects of the individual, 'Wissenschaft', 'Kunst' and 'Charakter,' and it locks both teacher and pupil in a single sphere, an 'innig moralischen Verhältniß'. But it also stresses that patient contemplation of the object of study is absolutely instrumental in developing, or rather growing into knowledge, which is 'ein praktisches Ueben' rather than a 'blos abstraktes theoretisches Wissen'. What is passed on here is not knowledge for the sake of knowledge, but a 'knowing' (*Wissen* as opposed to *Wissenschaft* or *Erkenntnis*) which is most intimately linked to life itself, and which is a process that does not end until life itself ends. The pupil gradually progresses to the stage of an assistant, who, only *zuletzt*, becomes a master. But the task of this master is to teach new pupils and to enter into the same intimate moral relationship with them as his former master did with him. The people will change and pass on, but the tradition which they hand down remains fundamentally the same: the *Lehre* is a sphere of remembrance and commemoration through which all generations pass, and which itself passes through the generations.[18] Seen from the perspective of tradition, in fact, the *Lehre* is history itself. As Scholem wrote in a diary entry dated 16 October 1916: 'Im letzten wird sich die historische Skepsis nur vom Judentum aus überwinden, durch den jüdischen Begriff der Tradition. *Das Judentum ist die Historie selber.*' (*TB* I, 409; Scholem's emphasis). In book four of *Philosophie der Geschichte*, Molitor, referring back to book one and to the subject of what has now become an almost nameless tradition, reiterates the same idea practically *ipsis verbis*, but with a few interesting variations:

Wenn nun auch die kirchlich-liturgische Arcan-disciplin ihre frühere Gestalt änderte, so wurde doch die höhere spekulative Mystik fortwährend als eine Art Geheimlehre betrieben und besonders in Klöstern cultivirt, wo sie manchmal auch mit der höhern Naturkunde verbunden war. Allein nicht blos in der Kirche, sondern auch im gesammten Lebensbereiche des Mittelalters bestand, ähnlich wie im Alterthum, die Arcandisciplin. Denn da es im Mittelalter eben so wenig wie in der alten Welt ein blos abstrakt-theoretisches Wissen gab, sondern alles Wissen zugleich ein Können und praktisches Ueben war, und mit der Wissenschaft und Kunst zugleich auch der Charakter des Menschen erzogen werden sollte; so wurde der Unterricht in allen Wissenschaften, Künsten und Gewerben durchaus praktisch, und zwar meistens nach mündlicher Ueberlieferung ertheilt, wobei der Lehrer zum Schüler in einem moralischen Verhältnisse wie der Vater zum Sohn, wie der Erzieher zum Eleven stand, daher er denselben erst lange am Rohen und Niedrigen sich üben ließ und ihm nur in dem Maße von den Kunstgeheimnissen mittheilte, als er bei demselben Eifer und Fähigkeit für dieselbe fand und solcher sich zugleich durch sittliches

Verhalten derselben würdig machte. Die Genossen jeder Kunst hatten also gewisse Geheimnisse unter sich, die sie vor jedem Fremden zu verbergen suchten, und wodurch sie eine geschlossene Corporation bildeten, welche in die naturgemäße Stufenordnung von Lehrlingen, Gesellen und Meistern eingetheilt und auf diese Art organisch in sich gegliedert waren. (*M* IV, 114–115)

The *Lehre* has now not only become connected with higher physics, particularly through the activities of the monasteries, it has even become detached from the Church itself as it permeates every aspect of life in the Middle Ages. This is one modification which the concept of the *Lehre* appears to have undergone from book one to book four, becoming, as we said earlier, increasingly nameless. The presence of an unseen *Lehre* now explains the mode of experience of an entire society in a whole era, rather than merely its religious *modus vivendi*. And yet not everybody seemed to have been party to all aspects of this *Arcan-disciplin*, as there were still societies and crafts which only gradually communicated the higher secrets of this esoteric discipline to their members according to a tripartite hierarchy of apprentice, journeyman and master. But because the *Lehre* was the omnipresent defining feature of life in the Middle Ages, *dixit* Molitor, it follows quite naturally that this hierarchy should be *naturgemäß* and *organisch*. Paraphrasing Scholem, we might say: '*Die Lehre ist das Leben selber.*'

In his essay *Der Erzähler*, Benjamin made the same comparison between the dying art of storytelling and craftsmanship as Molitor did in the passages quoted above:

Die Erzählung, wie sie im Kreis des Handwerks – des bäuerlichen, des maritimen und dann des städtischen – lange gedeiht, ist selbst eine gleichsam handwerkliche Form der Mitteilung. Sie legt es nicht darauf an, das pure 'an sich' der Sache zu überliefern wie eine Information oder ein Rapport. Sie senkt die Sache in das Leben des Berichtenden ein, um sie wieder aus ihm hervorzuholen. (II, 447)

This short passage highlights the same themes as Molitor's slightly longer description. Benjamin, too, compares the act of *überliefern* with craftsmanship, this time in a dual sense, because storytelling not only takes place in the sphere of (other) manual labour, it is itself a 'handwerkliche' form of communication. This passage is written in Benjamin's characteristically apodictic style, which tends to tempt the reader into its *Bannkreis* – the word *Kreis* is eminently suitable to describe what Benjamin does and how he does it exactly because it is mercifully vague and yet powerfully eloquent – and which in this case skims over the fact that Benjamin has not given us any reason why the story should be a 'handwerkliche Form der Mitteilung'. Yet with reference to the quotations from Molitor, this statement becomes clearer. This is of course not to say that Molitor must have been the direct source for this fragment from *Der Erzähler*, but his description of the workings of tradition, in this passage and others, are most remarkably similar to what Benjamin is writing here. The similarity does not end with the analogy of storytelling and craftsmanship. Benjamin also emphasises the fact that more is communicated in the story than mere information or abstract knowledge, that it is most intimately linked to life, as was the knowledge communicated within tradition according to Molitor, in which all knowledge is 'an das Leben geknüpft.' (*M* I, 7).[19] Molitor and Benjamin also share a focus on the 'Gegenstand' of the *Erziehung* or the 'Sache' of the *Erzählung*. The pupil must be forced to contemplate his object for a long time in order to develop 'eine innere Liebe für seinen Gegenstand [...] ohne welche nirgends ein Gedeihen möglich ist', and the storyteller must allow his object to sink into his life before he can extract it again, and tell his (and its – the German is ambiguous) story. It is quite interesting in this context that Benjamin regularly used the word *Versenkung* to refer to a deep contemplation, from *Ursprung des deutschen Trauerspiels* (which was *entworfen 1916*, a year which by now ought to have a ring of familiarity) to the *Passagen-Werk*, but we will return to this subject in the next chapter.

The concept of tradition, *Tradition* or *Überlieferung*, as it comes across in *Philosophie der Geschichte*, is the same homogeneous space of the *Lehre* which we have discussed in the first chapter. Teacher and pupil, *Lehrende* and *Lernende*, pass through this sphere as they pass it on to the next generation. Yet if the *tradentes*, they who pass on, are less than permanent, the *tradenda*, or the things passed on, are given an increased sense of reality, so much so that they are referred to and treated almost as physical entities. Interestingly enough, the *tradentes* only acquire a tangible reality to the student of tradition when they become themselves *tradenda*, subjects or objects of the stories that carry tradition. In *Der Erzähler*, Benjamin referred to the subject matter of the storyteller as 'den Rohstoff der Erfahrungen' which he had to work on, *bearbeiten*, 'auf eine solide, nützliche und einmalige Art' (II, 464). The metaphor of storytelling as craftsmanship is simply taken through to its logical consequences: if the storyteller is a craftsman, he must have materials to work with. The same is true in the case of Molitor's metaphor: if the act and the sphere of tradition, *Überlieferung*, is like a craft, the materials of this craft, the *Überlieferungen*, must be at hand.

The act and art of *Überlieferung*, or tradition, is ultimately *Lehre*, or study, in the widest possible sense of the word. As Hillel said to the gentile who wanted to learn the whole of Torah while standing on one leg: 'That which is hateful to you, do not do to your neighbour. That is the whole Torah, the rest is commentary. Go and study.' (*B*. Shabbat 31a). This apodictic command, a version of *Talmud Torah*, embraces every aspect of life, and Molitor seemingly feels he cannot over-emphasise this unity of experience:

> Im Alterthum aber war der äußere und innere Mensch, mithin die äußere Legalität und innere Moralität nicht so scharf wie bei uns geschieden, daher flossen beide auch mehr in einander über, und keinem gläubigen Jisraäliten der alten Zeit fiel es ein, die doktrinelle Tradition vom Gesetz so scharf trennen zu wollen, sondern es wurde als Pflicht eines jeden Jisraäliten angesehen, sich mit der Seele des Gesetzes ebensowohl, als mit dem Leib desselben vertraut zu machen. (*M* I, 39)

The 'soul' of the law is communicated by Hillel in his first terse phrase, 'That which is hateful to you, do not do to your neighbour'; the 'body' of the law, on the other hand, is the overwhelming and ever-increasing textual corpus which gravitates around (unspoken) phrases like these. Of course, paradoxically enough, Hillel's semi-revelatory statement of the soul of the law automatically becomes part of its body by the sheer fact that it has been written, even though it is written as something which has been said.[20] It is this paradox which lies at the root of Jewish mysticism, or indeed any mysticism *pur sang*, namely the tension between infallible meaning and fallible form, between the universal and the particular, between the eternal and the historical. One solution to this paradox, requiring either an essentially unthinking leap of faith or – which is far more fascinating – an intense logical concentration and some conceptual stuntwork, is to make the particular a universal. In other words, and this phrase now becomes increasingly significant, to make language itself divine. It is now the very materiality of language which makes it divine, the one aspect which seemingly prevented it from being so. And this, as we discussed in the first chapter, is perhaps the most crucial idiosyncrasy of the already unique Jewish tradition: it invests the form with meaning to such an extent that meaning without form becomes inconceivable. This has immensely far-reaching consequences for the way language is read, studied and, quite literally, handled. One of the examples Molitor gives through which this linguistic and intellectual *tour de force* is performed is the contemplation of the holy name, through which the kabbalist is able to purify and sanctify himself and the world. This could be achieved

> [...] durch ein andächtiges Versenken der Seele in die Anschauung der heiligen Namen; denn da die Charaktere der Schriftzüge, wie die Kabbalisten sagen, die lebendigen sichtbaren Ausdrücke der göttlichen Kräfte selber sind, und das Obere sich stets dem Untern öffnet, wenn dieses sich jenem gleichförmig macht: so wird die Seele durch ein solches Versenken in die Anschauung jener geheimnißvollen Formen dermaßen in den Abdruck vergestaltet, daß sich ihm der obere Typus selber erschließt. (*M* I, 45–46)

In this quotation, the aforementioned concept of *Versenkung* appears in the context of the immersion into the sphere of language, and more particularly the divine name. As we will discuss in the next chapter, this is perhaps the most crucial aspect of Benjamin's thinking on language, tradition and intoxication, uniting these three seemingly disparate phenomena. Furthermore, it should be noted that the 'obere Typus' reveals itself to the soul after the latter has immersed itself within language and has gone up into the 'Abdruck'; or in Benjamin's words, truth is an intentionless being which cannot be attained by the predatory intellect, but only through receptive contemplation. This quotation, however, is a perfect illustration of the logical consequences of a mystical approach to language. The 'Charaktere der

Schriftzüge' are the 'lebendigen sichtbaren Ausdrücke' of the divine powers. In other words, language is not conceived of in a duality of the living and inner meaning and the outer but essentially dead or lifeless form. The very characters, rather, are alive: 'Denn die äußere Formen sind keineswegs blos etwas gleichgültig Todtes, wie der flache Unglaube gewöhnlich behauptet' (*M* I, 47).[21] The second half of the quotation is particularly mystifying. The soul, through an immersion in the contemplation of the form of language – which means individual letters or even parts of letters, becomes 'vergestaltet in den Abdruck'. The prefix *ver-* to the otherwise perfectly normal word *gestalten* can indicate a direction, a completion, an amplification or a transformation, which suggests that the soul is transported or transformed into the *Abdruck,* or consumed and completed by the *Abdruck,* i.e., the 'mark' or 'imprint', in other words, the *form* of language. It is this form of thinking to which Benjamin, too, refers when he writes about the 'Oberflachenwelt des Ornaments' or about the Chinese artist who disappears into his own painting.[22] The form is granted an objectivity which, although heading in a very similar direction, goes far beyond even the most the formalistically formulated aesthetic or poetic function of language, because it is *theological*. Benjamin's project was to import this *theologoumenon* into the sphere of the profane and still make it work, evoking *profane Erleuchtung*. As paradoxical as this may sound, even Molitor was aware that this was not impossible:

> [...] überhaupt schrieben die Alten nur weniges, dieses Wenige aber mußte den Charakter der expressiven Objektivität an sich tragen. Daher nahmen sie bei alles was sie schrieben, selbst im Profanen, auf die Form Rücksicht, die bei den Orientalen mystischer, bei den Occidentalen aber mehr ästhetischer Art war, aber überall dasselbe Princip der Objektivität zum Grunde hatte. (*M* I, 54)

This 'objectivity' should be taken very literally indeed. It means that real meaning inheres in language, rather than language merely serving as a proxy or a formal representation of an ideal and absent meaning.[23] In other words, language is not just a metaphor, and neither is the metaphor of its own objectivity or materiality just a metaphor.[24] From the perspective of the Jewish tradition, as we

126

discussed at length in the previous chapter, and as *Philosophie der Geschichte* confirms, language has a distinct and emphatic objective reality: the aim is not to go beyond or over it, or to by-pass it in some way; the aim is, as Molitor says, to go *through* it and to immerse oneself *in* it. The objectivity of language as the object of study, which is in its turn the essence of tradition, has thus established itself as the very sphere of tradition, and has assumed the same characteristics as tradition, namely a distinct spatial and material reality. In fact, it could also be said that the concept of the spatial and material reality of tradition derives from a certain way of thinking about language as its medium or mode of existence. And this, we feel, is what Benjamin attempted to do in *Über Sprache überhaupt und über die Sprache des Menschen*, and beyond, and it will be the subject of our final chapter.

Ein wahrhaft kabbalistischer Rabbi

By way of a bridge to the chapters that deal in detail with Benjamin's work, it would be appropriate to mention the essays on Franz Kafka, *Beim Bau der chinesischen Mauer* and *Franz Kafka: zur zehnten Wiederkehr seines Todestags*, from 1931 and 1934 respectively. That Benjamin was fascinated by Kafka's work is obvious from the sheer volume of notes that accompany these two essays, revealing a very intricate and multi-faceted *Auseinandersetzung*, which makes the reader think Benjamin had more essays on Kafka in him, or maybe even, as he had planned himself before fate intervened, a book.[25] In many ways, Benjamin's essays on Kafka perform an inexplicable and perhaps even unjustifiable *acte d'absence* in this book, for when we see references to Judaism, theology and Hebrew tractates strewn around Benjamin's notes, it seems odd that they do not feature more prominently here. The reason for this omission is primarily and prosaically the limitation of space, time and scope, of course. It would be extremely difficult to do the Jewish and theological aspects of Benjamin's Kafka essays justice in a single chapter, and impossible to do so without the benefit of all the other chapters. Yet even a passing reference to these essays may suffice to show not only that the theological element in Benjamin's thought was very active, but also that it was thoroughly creative. In a letter to Scholem, he recognises the possibility of a theological interpretation of Kafka, but adds:

[ich] behaupte, daß auch meine Arbeit ihre breite – freilich beschattete – theologische Seite hat. Gewandt habe ich mich gegen den unerträglichen Gestus des theologischen professional, der – wie Du nicht bestreiten wirst – die bisherige Kafka-Interpretation auf der ganze Linie beherrscht [...]' (*GB* IV, 459)

As we will see later, Benjamin's theology is idiosyncratic, paradoxical, vulnerable and always precarious, and when one becomes aware of it, it intermittently but clearly shines though that inscrutable collection of notes for his carefully written, lapidary essays.

Yet there is another link to tradition in the Kafka essays, in which Benjamin himself appears to have had a hand and which can be read as proof upon proof that it is indeed the appearance of continuity which creates the continuity of tradition. In his final essay on Kafka, there is one section entitled 'das bucklicht Männlein', which tells the story of a hunchbacked dwarf from a folk song, who, according to Benjamin, represents the form the world assumes 'im Vergessen'. As we saw above, the twin ideas of memory and remembrance are central to both the ethics and the epistemology of the Jewish tradition, as they are to the philosophy of Walter Benjamin. To forget is not only to commit a sin against the past generations who have passed on tradition and built a fence around the Torah, forgetfulness itself fundamentally stands in the way of redemption, as those who are forgotten are forever lost to history. In this sense, 'die Welt im Vergessen' is shorthand for the world in an unredeemed state, either before remembrance and redemption, or even beyond remembrance and redemption. If there were any doubt that the topic of remembrance was a specifically Jewish one to Benjamin, he himself takes that doubt away quite explicitly in his essay on Kafka, where he quotes Willy Haas's description of forgetting as the actual protagonist of Kafka's *Der Prozess*, adding: 'Daß "dieses geheimnisvolle Zentrum ... der jüdischen

Religion" entstammt, ist wohl nicht von der Hand zu weisen.' (II, 429).

The world 'im Vergessen' is out of kilter: 'Die Welt im Stande des Vergessenseins ist entstellt' (II, 1239). To Benjamin, the little hunchbacked figure is an emblem of this world and this life that we feel is not quite right: 'Dieses Männlein ist der Insasse des entstellten Lebens; es wird verschwinden, wenn der Messias kommt, von dem ein großer Rabbi gesagt hat, daß er nicht mit Gewalt die Welt verändern wolle, sondern nur um ein Geringes sie zurechtstellen werde.' (II, 432). This 'micrological messianism' continues to appear in Benjamin's work, most famously in the *Thesen über den Begriff der Geschichte*, which open with the hunchbacked dwarf in the chess machine and close with the statement, or perhaps *Lehrsatz*, that every second is the narrow gate through which the Messiah may enter. In the context of the tense kinship between Judaism and Christianity, whereby the latter is seen as a *leichte Entstellung*, rather than *Zurechtstellung*, of the former, the very concept of the Messiah becomes profoundly ambiguous, even uncanny, as the messianic world is no longer the same world which the hopeful wanted to see redeemed.[26]

It is well known that messianism as such is a concept which not only has a chequered history in the religious world of Judaism and Christianity, not in the least because Christians appropriated this eminently Jewish notion the way they did, but that the concept itself remians infused with a deep ambiguity. The appearance of false messiahs, from Jesus to Shabbatai Tsevi, has had a profound and often emphatically negative effect on Judaism and the Jews. The wait for the Messiah has been and still is long, and often filled with incomprehensible suffering and despair, as recent history has made all too painfully clear. Yet the Messiah or the messianic age cannot be brought about by mankind, as Benjamin also knew, we can only prepare ourselves, be receptive, hope and wait. After all of this, the Messiah has become not only the bringer and symbol of redemption, but also the allegory of his own absence, of the fear of what will happen if he does not come as well as of the fear of what will happen if he does. It is this cluster of anxieties that infuses Kafka's world, and which forces Benjamin into the paradox of his *Dialektik im Stillstand*, or the messianic revolution as permanent suspension.

The anonymous story of the Messiah who would put the world to right ever so slightly occurs twice in the copious notes Benjamin made in preparation for his essay on Kafka, and in both cases, it appears to be the perfect example of a 'nameless tradition' of which we spoke in the first chapter. The first note emphasises the anonymity of the story:

> Daß der Begriff der Entstellung in der Darstellung Kafkas eine doppelte Funktion hat, und welche zeigt jene jüdische Überlieferung, nach der die Welt durch die Ankunft des Messias nicht etwa durch und durch verändert sondern nur in allem 'ein klein wenig' anders werden soll als sie war. (II, 1200)

In the second note, Benjamin links the messianic theme to the *entstellte* figures in Kafka's work, Odradek, the *Katzenlamm* or Gregor Samsa in *Die Verwandlung*: 'Sie sind entstellt, wie es die Welt für jenen Rabbi war, der lehrte, das [sic] das Kommen des Messias sie nicht durch und durch verändere; "Er rückt sie nur zurecht" lehrte er.' (II, 1239). A Jewish tradition, a certain rabbi or even a great rabbi: the actual source of this story seems deliberately untraceable. That, after all, is the essence of tradition: it is always already there. But in this particular case, something slightly more prosaic may well be going on. In a letter dated 24 June 1929, an almost audibly exhausted and bitter Benjamin writes to Scholem: 'Demnächst erscheinen zwei neue Bücher von Bloch "Spuren" und "Essays", in denen ein nicht geringer Teil meiner unsterblichen Werke, z.T. etwas ramponiert, der Nachwelt überkommt.' (*GB* III, 469). There is little novelty in Benjamin's claim that Ernst Bloch constantly stole his ideas, and skimming through *Spuren* in particular, that claim does not come across as entirely implausible. Yet there is one passage in particular, from the fragment entitled 'Die Glückliche Hand', which is quite thought-provoking in the present context. Bloch writes:

> Und ein andrer Rabbi, ein wirklich kabbalistischer, sagte einmal: um das Reich des Friedens herzustellen, werden nicht alle Dinge zu zerstören sein und eine ganze neue Welt fängt an; sondern diese Tasse oder jener Strauch oder jener Stein und so alle Dinge sind nur ein wenig zu verrücken. Weil aber diese Wenige so schwer zu tun und sein Maß so schwierig zu finden ist, können das,

was die Welt angeht, nicht die Menschen, sondern dazu kommt der Messias. Dabei hat auch dieser weise Rabbi, mit seinem Satz, nicht der krauchenden Entwicklung, sondern durchaus dem Sprung des glücklichen Blicks und der glücklichen Hand das Wort geredet.[27]

This passage conveys the same concept of the 'understated apocalypse', as we have called it, and attributes it to the same mysterious rabbi, this time described as 'a great kabbalist'. Ironically, this is not a million miles away from the truth. In a letter dated 30 January 1978 to Michael Landmann on the subject of the latter's manuscript entitled 'Das Judentum bei Ernst Bloch', Scholem is quite scathing in his criticism of Bloch, stating that Landmann has not merely overseen or ignored Bloch's weaknesses, but that he has understated them. And on one subject in particular, Scholem's commentary is exceptionally enlightening:

Der Autor, der, wie sie sagen von Bloch (wie ja auch von Benjamin, Adorno und anderen) zitierten Bemerkung über den Messias – in den 'Spuren' einem 'wahrhaft kabbalistischen Rabbi' zugeschrieben –, war kein anderer als ich!! Es ist wohl der erfolgreichste apokryphe Satz, mit dem ich in die neueste Philosophie eingegangen bin. (Ich habe ihn 1916 in einem Gespräch mit Benjamin erfunden, als Gegengewicht gegen Benjamin's Vorliebe, Sätzen mit den Worten zu beginnen: Es ist eine metaphysische Wahrheit, daß...). (*SB* III, 173– 174)[28]

It is quite fascinating to find that Benjamin actually immortalised this tendency in 1916, in the essay *Über Sprache überhaupt und über die Sprache des Menschen*, where he writes: 'Es ist eine metaphysische Wahrheit, daß alle Natur zu klagen begönne, wenn Sprache ihr verliehen würde.' (II, 155). A great deal still remains to be said about the prophetically declamatory tone of Benjamin's writing in general and of this essay in particular, but we shall leave this to our final chapter.

If we recall Scholem's letter to Siegfried Lehmann, quoted above, in which he said that everyone from Moshe Rabbenu, Moses our teacher, to 'mister Lehmann himself', if he wanted to, were a part of the Jewish tradition, or rather *are* the Jewish tradition, this philological *trouvaille* throws a very small, but very meaningful light on

Benjamin's relationship with this Jewish tradition. Benjamin's nameless source quoted in the essay on Kafka turns out to be the one which is most often named as the source of his knowledge of the Jewish tradition. And by incorporating the story as an anonymous but ancient tale, Benjamin, with a characteristically midrashic overdetermination, has in fact captured the essence of being in the Jewish tradition as an intimate coexistence of past and present, where a seventeenth-century rabbi can hold discussions with the prophet Jeremiah, or where an eighteen-year-old Jewish student drinking coffee in a Berlin room can become a great kabbalist Rabbi. In those days, Benjamin and Scholem were not so much talking about the Jewish tradition as talking in the Jewish tradition. 'Nicht *durch*, sondern *in*'.

Chapter Four: Benjamin's Language Theory

By the spring of 1917, Gershom Scholem's knowledge of classical Hebrew had reached such levels that he was able to earn some money by teaching Hebrew and translating books from Yiddish and Hebrew into German. The one text he chose as his starting point to confront the rather more daunting task of translating from German into Hebrew, however, was Walter Benjamin's *Über Sprache überhaupt und über die Sprache des Menschen:*

> In den Monaten vor [Benjamins] Heirat beschäftigte ich mich einige Zeit mit dem Versuch, Teile aus der mir sehr nahegehenden Arbeit über die Sprache, in der auch Motive aus unseren Gespräche in Seeshaupt aufgenommen waren, ins Hebräische zu übersetzen. Benjamin wollte unbedingt, daß ich ihm die ersten Seiten, die ich geschrieben hatte, vorlese, um den Klang seiner Sätze in der, wie er halb scherzhaft sagte, 'Ursprache' zu hören. (*GF*, 53)

This quotation, describing what to all intents and purposes looks like a harmless intellectual *Spielerei*, can actually be read as a monad, a single, hypertropic event from which the whole of Benjamin's engagement with the Jewish tradition unfolds. It was around this time that Benjamin started studying Molitor, prompted, as we said in a previous chapter, by his intensive discussions with Scholem. It was a letter from Scholem which provoked Benjamin's extraordinary outburst of creativity in November 1916, leading him to write an eighteen-page reply which then became *Über Sprache überhaupt und über die Sprache des Menschen*, a piece in which Benjamin intends 'mich mit dem Wesen der Sprache auseinander zu setzen und zwar – soweit ich es verstehe: in immanenter Beziehung auf das Judentum und mit Beziehung auf die ersten Kapitel der Genesis' (*GB* I, 343). This essay, as we will discuss in this chapter, is itself in many ways at the heart of Benjamin's thinking about language, theology and Judaism, and it would remain so for more than twenty years. It therefore seems only fitting that it should be this text which Scholem decided to use in order to practice his budding translation skills, not least because *Über Sprache* at one point addresses the concept of translation as something which needs to be grounded 'in der tiefsten Schicht der Sprachtheorie'.[1] It seems only fitting that the text should find its way into Hebrew, the holy language; and it seems only fitting that Benjamin insisted on hearing its sounds, even though, or perhaps because, he did not understand the words.

Aber dahinter steckt viel mehr

The question of the 'jüdischer Gehalt' of Benjamin's writings, and what form it could possibly take, despite 'seiner ziemlich totalen Unwissenheit in jüdischen Dingen' (*VBJ*, 75), as Scholem himself concedes, has daunted and divided commentators for a very long time. It has prompted some of them, like Menninghaus, to give up on the matter entirely, ruling out anything but the most superficial, incidental and mostly anecdotal influence. But as Rabbi Tarfon said: 'If thou hast studied much Torah, thou shalt be given much reward.' (*M*. Avot: II, 16). This approach, unsurprisingly perhaps, also seems to lie closest to Scholem's heart, as he once explained the importance of the Jewish tradition to Benjamin's work as follows:

> Wenn wir nach dem jüdischen Element in diesem Menschen und seiner Produktion fragen, so entspricht es gerade dem vertrackten Wesen Walter Benjamins, daß, was ihm als Grund seines Wesens und zugleich oft als Ziel seines Denkens sehr bewußt war, das Jüdische, in seinem Werk fast nur in Obertönen zu vernehmen ist, freilich an sehr sichtbaren Stellen dieses Werkes, wie etwa dem Prospekt zu der von ihm geplanten Zeitschrift 'Angelus Novus' oder den geschichtsphilosophischen Thesen, seiner letzten Arbeit. Aber dahinter steckt viel mehr.[2]

'Aber dahinter steckt viel mehr'. That might have been the motto for these final chapters, because the influence of the Jewish tradition on and in Benjamin's work should be sought in the style and form of his writings as much as in their content. As we will venture to show in the following sections on *Über Sprache überhaupt und über die Sprache des Menschen, Ursprung des deutschen Trauerspiels* and *Über das Programm der kommenden Philosophie*, it is the Jewish concept of the divine, the doctrine of God and his name – *theology* in the purest sense of the word, which inspires these texts and which therefore also heavily determines the concepts of language and meaning, truth and tradition which Benjamin seeks to define in them. The importance of these texts lies in the fact that they are the only ones in which Benjamin *directly* addresses the topoi of language and philosophy. Statements about these topoi, doctrinal or otherwise, can be found punctuated throughout Benjamin's work, but *Über Sprache* and *Über das Programm* constitute his only attempts to touch upon the raw flesh of the matter, being as sparing as possible with the anaesthetic of circumspection.[3] Any subject of such an operation is bound to be extremely sensitive, and the surgeon can only approach it with a paradoxical mixture of brutality and caution.

This has distinct consequences for the style and strategy of these two essays, most notably *Über Sprache*, in which Benjamin seems to alternate between blunt 'Halakhic' statements and subtle 'Aggadic' excursions. Reading these texts thus becomes a slow and arduous task, but very necessary if we are to understand the logic, or more accurately the Λόγος, underlying much of Benjamin's work. To present such a mindful reading is what this chapter proposes to do. This does not of course amount to a comprehensive enumeration of all the instances of 'Jewishness' in Benjamin's work, which is another perfectly justifiable, if less methodical direction this book could have taken. The disadvantage of such an approach, however, is that a comprehensive catalogue of Jewish references in the work and the correspondence of Benjamin would yield a lengthy document which would not necessarily lead to a fuller understanding, because it would not reveal the underlying strategy. Scholem was quite clear about this: '*Dahinter* steckt viel mehr.' The reading we propose here, on the other hand, will provide us with a finely-tuned instrument, a precision tool with which to read some of Benjamin's most perplexing texts. In that sense, this chapter, and indeed the entire book, could be considered as the *Prolegomena zu einer künftigen Moreh Nebuchim Li-Benjamin*, the prolegomena to a future guide for the perplexed to Benjamin.

It is difficult to overestimate the importance of *Über Sprache überhaupt und über die Sprache des Menschen*, not in the least because Benjamin himself appeared to value the text beyond anything else he wrote during these early years, treating the few copies of it in circulation with almost the same reverence as one would a holy book. *Über Sprache* was, in fact, an esoteric document in every sense of the word. As far as we know, there were only four or five copies of the text in circulation at any one time, and of these copies, only three survive today (four copies, strictly speaking, but two of those are identical carbon copies of the same original).[4] Benjamin gave the text only to a small circle of close (intellectual) friends – from his correspondence it is hard to make out whether Benjamin had any friends *überhaupt* who were anything else but intellectual. First and foremost, he sent a copy to Gershom Scholem, who was in actual fact the original addressee of the text. Other copies went to Ernst Schoen, Theodor W. Adorno, and possibly to Werner Kraft and Ludwig Strauß.[5] In the case of the latter, Benjamin allowed Scholem to read *Über Sprache* to Strauß, but insisted that he should be lent a copy of Strauß's essay on ethics in return, adding: 'Ich würde was meine Arbeit angeht, Ludwig Strauß, den ich herzlich grüßen lasse, natürlich Gleiches zugestehen: vollständiges gegenseitiges Vertrauen ist hierbei Voraussetzung.'[6] It may be slightly odd that Benjamin should set conditions for the permission to read *Über Sprache* to third parties, but it is positively puzzling that he should demand 'vollständiges gegenseitiges Vertrauen' from anyone who knew of its contents. Unless, of course, we understand the significance Benjamin attached to both the content and the form of the text. Towards the end of 1917, there are four copies of the text, and in another letter to Scholem, Benjamin considers the option of having a fifth copy made:

> Von Ludwig Strauß ist noch nichts gekommen. Unter der Voraussetzung daß ich in den Besitz seiner Arbeit gelange und wenn ich dies bestätigt habe können Sie ihm ein Exemplar der Abschrift der Spracharbeit zusenden. Ein zweites kann Herr Kraft, das dritte Sie und wenn Sie keine andere Verwendung dafür haben ein viertes ich erhalten. Sonst ließe sich für mich noch ein fünftes vielleicht herstellen; aber *wer* sollte denn das vierte erhalten?[7]

Benjamin here reiterates the condition upon which Strauß is to be given a copy of the text, adding a hint of suspicion to his tone by saying that Scholem should wait until Benjamin has acknowledged the receipt of Strauß's essay. But, more importantly, he contemplates the possibility of initiating a fourth person into his *Lehre* (and it should not be just anybody: the question *wer?* is quite emphatic). This attitude is not only an early testimony to Benjamin's lifelong tendency towards secrecy and self-mystification, it is also the perfect indication of the kind of text Benjamin considered *Über Sprache* to be. In the words of Franz Joseph Molitor: 'Diese Schriften waren jedoch ursprünglich nicht für den öffentlichen, sondern zunächst für den Privatgebrauch des Einzelnen bestimmt, [...]. Sie waren von und für Solche gemacht, die mit der heiligen Lehre vertraut waren, daher die vielen Lücken und Dunkelheiten [...]' (*M* I, 298). It is clear that Benjamin considered his own text to be speaking with the authority of tradition, of the *Lehre*, or to have grown out of the same seed as the *Lehre*, and thus to be, in its own monadic *Verschränkung*, the *Lehre* itself. Perhaps he even amused himself, *halb scherzhaft* so to speak, with the idea that an untimely exposure to this text could be dangerous to the uninitiated, or that he himself was open to intellectual persecution or accusations of false messianism if the text fell into the hands of people who could not offer a 'vollständiges gegenseitiges Vertrauen'. Perhaps this was why, again in the words of Molitor,

> jeder Schüler nicht Alles [empfing], sondern nur so viel, als seine Fähigkeit zu fassen und seine Würdigkeit zu verdienen schien. [...] es [ist] auch gewissermaßen eine wahrhafte Entheiligung des inneren Geistes, das innerste Tiefste der oberflächlichen Neugierde zur öffentlichen Schau auszustellen; – weßwegen denn das sinnvollere Alterthum über alles einen Schleyer des Geheimnisses zog, und den Zugang dazu nur denen verstattete, die der Weihe würdig befunden worden [sic]. (*M* I, 8)

Benjamin started referring to *Über Sprache* as an esoteric document towards the end of 1917, less than five months after he acquired *Philosophie der Geschichte*. It is tempting to think, considering the temporal as well as the semantic proximity of the passages quoted above, that reading Molitor might have influenced Benjamin's understanding of himself as a thinker at this point. A letter from Benjamin to Scholem dated 12 June 1938 confirms that the former did indeed consider his own work to have both an esoteric and an exoteric side, as he writes about a long letter on Kafka: 'Natürlich kannst du ihn [Adorno] mitteilen [...]. Allenfalls könntest Du ihm erklären, daß Du den Brief für Dein Archiv meiner esoterischen Schriften von mir erwirkt hättest.' (*GB* VI, 116).[8] This rings particularly true when we take into account that Molitor's observations on the *Lehre* and on esoteric knowledge as such are made entirely in the context of education, knowledge and language, topics which were high on the agenda in Benjamin's correspondence and conversation in 1917 and 1918, as we already mentioned in a previous chapter. At the time, he appeared to have found a twin focal point for his thought in the concept of the *Lehre* and in the work of Kant, both through Hermann Cohen and in the original. At several points in his correspondence, he states the necessity to synthesise the two as well as his own intention to do so, an attempt which resulted in *Über das Programm der kommenden Philosophie* (1918), a text we will discuss later on in this chapter. But we must not rush ahead of ourselves. Exactly how crucial *Über Sprache* remained to this project in Benjamin's own estimation is voiced in a letter to Ernst Schoen, dated 28 February 1918:

> Vor allem: für mich hängen die Fragen nach dem Wesen von Erkenntnis, Recht, Kunst zusammen mit der Frage nach dem Ursprung aller menschlichen Geistesäußerung aus dem Wesen der Sprache. Dieser Zusammenhang ist es eben der zwischen den beiden vorzüglichen Gegenständen meines Denkens besteht. In Hinsicht der ersten Gedankenreihe ist auch schon mehreres aufgeschrieben was aber noch nicht communicabel ist. Kennen sie eigentlich schon meine Arbeit vom Jahre 1916 'Über Sprache überhaupt und über die Sprache des Menschen'[?] Falls nicht könnte sie Ihnen, vorläufig leider nur leihweise zugestellt werden. Sie bildet den Ausgangspunkt aller weiterer Arbeit an den erstgenannten Problemen für mich. (*GB* I, 437) [9]

Benjamin here characterises *Über Sprache* as the 'Ausgangspunkt aller weiterer Arbeit' on the question of the 'sprachliche Grundlagen des kategorischen Imperativs', which is the first problem he refers to (*GB* I, 436, yet again Kant and language). Seventeen years later, in two letters to Gershom Scholem, he still mentions the early essay as the point of departure for his thoughts on language, this time referring to the composition of *Lehre vom Ähnlichen*, a piece which he says would become 'ausführbar allein [...] wenn ich vorher einen Vergleich dieser Notizen mit jenen frühen "Über Sprache überhaupt und über die Sprache des Menschen" vornehmen könnte' (*GB* IV, 214). He reiterates this condition quite emphatically a week later, on 31 May 1933, saying: 'Nur muß ich unbedingt die erste [Spracharbeit] vorher einsehen.' (*GB* IV, 223). This remarkable longevity of what at first may seem to be a youthful burst of creativity – he wrote *Über Sprache* in the week running up to 11 November 1916 – is a good indication of the extraordinary importance Benjamin attached to the essay. And when he writes to Scholem about the infamous *Erkenntnis-kritische Vorrede*, the prologue to his first published book *Ursprung des deutschen Trauerspiels* (1925), we are given an idea as to the status of *Über Sprache* in Benjamin's own intellectual development:

> Diese Einleitung ist eine maßlose Chuzpe – nämlich nicht mehr und nicht weniger als Prolegomena zur Erkenntnistheorie, so eine Art zweites, ich weiß nicht ob besseres, Stadium der frühen Spracharbeit, die Du kennst, als Ideen-lehre frisiert. Übrigens werde ich mir die Spracharbeit dafür noch einmal durch-lesen. (*GB* III, 14)

Benjamin not only describes the new version of the language essay using the Yiddish word *Chuzpe*, or chutzpah, he also confesses to be uncertain as to whether he has done the original version justice, and whether or not the new version is an improvement on the first concise and authoritative statement. The second page of the *Erkennt-niskritische Vorrede*, which presents itself as a self-consciously anti-quated *Traktat*, already gives us a clue as to why Benjamin might have thought his attempt at rewriting *Über Sprache* failed to a certain extent: 'Traktate mögen lehrhaft zwar in ihrem Ton sein; ihrer inner-sten Haltung nach bleibt die Bündigkeit einer Unterweisung ihnen versagt, welche wie die Lehre aus eigener Autorität sich zu behaupten vermöchte.' (I, 208). We can conclude from this that Benjamin did in fact consider *Über Sprache* to have the *Bündigkeit einer Unter-weisung* which qualified it as being part of the *Lehre*, or indeed as being the *Lehre* of the essence of language. However much Benjamin thought of the *Erkenntniskritische Vorrede* as a 'maßlose Chuzpe', it is, in a way, far less ambitious than its predecessor. It is *lehrhaft*, but it lacks the terseness of the *Lehre*. Just as Benjamin had qualified the stories of Franz Kafka as Aggadah without Halakhah, his own *Erkenntniskritische Vorrede* can be read as the Aggadah to the esoteric and hidden Halakhah that is *Über Sprache*.

When Benjamin wanted to hear the sound of his own sentences in the 'holy language', Scholem tells us he asked this only 'halb scherzhaft', which suggests that there was more to this request than a mere harmless diversion. And when Molitor writes the following words in book one of *Philosophie der Geschichte*, Benjamin might well have recognised in them not only his own request, but even the *Lehrsatz* that is *Über Sprache* itself:

> Die biblischen Namen haben alle einen mystischen Sinn, der sich freilich nur aufschließen läßt durch die Zurückführung des Wortes auf seine Wurzel. Bei der bisher gewöhnten unkorrecten Behandlung dieser Namen in den Uebersetzungen ging natürlich ihre Bedeutung verloren, und sie sind uns jetzt alle lauter Worte ohne Sinn. Aus dieser Ursache haben wir den Versuch gewagt, die ebräischen Namen nach ihrer wahren eigenthümlichen Weise auszudrücken. Mag auch solches der Ungewohntheit wegen anfangs hart und auffallend klingen, so glauben wir doch, daß sich nach und nach unser europäisches Ohr an die Töne jener heiligen Sprache gewöhnen, und in denselben jenen tief verborgenen Sinn allmählich erfassen wird. (*M* I, 127n)

To Benjamin, the self-confessedly assimilated Jew, the confrontation of his holy language and his European ear must have been an almost schizophrenic experience, but one that summarises what *Über Sprache* is trying to do, with all its ambiguities and paradoxical constructions.[10] What Benjamin wanted to hear, says Scholem, was the '*Klang* seiner Sätze [...] in der Ursprache' (my emphasis). It did not seem to matter that, not knowing Hebrew, Benjamin would not understand the words: Scholem's reading evidently communicated something to him which was not so much expressed *through* the language, but *in* the language. The very sounds of 'jener heiligen Sprache' would have communicated a 'tief verborgenen Sinn' which goes beyond lexicon and grammar, much as Molitor claims the biblical names in their original and slightly alienating tones would do. And this is in fact precisely what Benjamin announces in the characteristically declamatory tone of *Über Sprache*: 'Der Name hat im Bereich der Sprache einzig diesen Sinn und diese unvergleichlich hohe Bedeutung: daß er das innerste Wesen der Sprache selbst ist. Der Name ist dasjenige, *durch* das sich nichts mehr, und *in* dem die Sprache selbst und absolut sich mitteilt.' (II, 144).

These intentionally mystifying sentences attempt to define an idea around which the whole of *Über Sprache* is constantly circling without actually touching it. This circumambulatory strategy has everything to do with the the fact that *Über Sprache* approaches language from a theological perspective, and this comes with its own epistemology which is used, but not thematised, in the 1916 essay. However, this is the case in the *Erkenntniskritische Vorrede*, which, as mentioned before, is extremely closely related to *Über Sprache* and which explicitly addresses the theological epistemology which Benjamin presupposes in the earlier essay.[11] Before we proceed with our analysis of the language essay, it would be useful to explore this epistemology in greater depth, as it has important consequence for Benjamin's entire methodology. In the *Erkenntniskritische Vorrede*, knowledge and truth are defined as ontologically very different entities, and, to a certain extent, even incompatible. Knowledge, Benjamin says, is a 'having': 'Ihr Gegenstand selbst bestimmt sich dadurch, daß er im Bewußtsein – und sei es transzendental – innegehabt werden muß. Ihm bleibt der Besitzcharakter.' (I, 209). Knowledge can be had, it can be appropriated, imparted and questioned, and as such it can be classified, divided and arranged. Knowledge, according to Benjamin, is always the knowledge of something, and this objective aspect, this 'dinghafte', is also a property of knowledge itself: knowledge is an object which may be manipulated in every sense of the word. Truth, on the other hand, is defined as a 'being', it does not have any of the objectivity of knowledge and thus cannot be displayed, held or conveyed in the same way. Truth is autonomous in the sense that it has no need of us to represent it, indeed, Benjamin describes it as a being which, unlike anything else, is 'ein Sich-Darstellendes' (I, 209).[12] Truth, in other words, takes the form of a revelation, in particular a revelation which reveals itself, and as such it cannot be of human making, nor can its revelation even be wanted by human beings, it can only be received. Benjamin writes in one of the seminal passages of the *Erkenntniskritische Vorrede*:

> Wahrheit tritt nie in eine Relation und insbesondere in keine intentionale. Der Gegenstand der Erkenntnis als ein in der Begriffsintention bestimmter ist nicht die Wahrheit. Die Wahrheit ist ein aus Ideen gebildetes intentionsloses Sein. Das ihr gemäße Verhalten ist demnach nicht ein Meinen im Erkennen, sondern ein in sie Eingehen und Verschwinden. Die Wahrheit ist der Tod der Intention. (I, 216)

As 'ein Sich-Darstellendes', truth is not even there for us, it merely is. The only way the truth can ever be revealed to us is if we are prepared to receive it and totally surrender ourselves to it. As if the definition of truth as pure being was not enough to single out this construct as a theological one, Benjamin goes one step further and specifies it as 'das aller Phänomenalität entrückte Sein', and this being is 'das des Namens' (I, 216).[13] If the being beyond all phenomenality almost automatically characterised the construction out as a theological one, the addition that this being is that of the Name specifies it as a Jewish theology. Here, the proximity of Benjamin's line of thinking to the philosophy of Maimonides – and through him, and to a lesser degree, of Aristotle – is quite astounding.

First of all, as we mentioned in our first chapter, *Ursprung des deutschen Trauerspiels* casts itself very deliberately (and *unzeitgemäß*, one might say) in the antiquated form of the medieval, scholastic tractate. Benjamin claims that neither the philosophical system-building of the nineteenth century nor the positivist philosophies of his day and age are able to approach the truth, and he attributes their failing to the fact that these philosophies seek to lead the reader to know the truth, rather than to show it in themselves. And in order to show the truth, philosophy again needs to become an exercise in thinking by closely following its very own traditional, esoteric form of the tractate. Typically, Benjamin again suggests that the correct way of reaching one's objective is to keep one's eyes on the road, not on one's destination. He calls the scholastic tractate the indispensable 'Propädeutik' which leads to the truth because it does not overtly and directly aim to do so, but rather reaches it through contemplation of its own method: 'Darstellung ist Inbegriff ihrer Methode. Methode ist Umweg. Darstellung als Umweg – das ist denn der methodische Charakter des Traktats. Verzicht auf den unabgesetzten Lauf der Intention ist sein erstes Kennzeichen' (I, 208).[14] If we compare this to the *Directions for the Study of this Work* which Maimonides gives in his *Guide for the Perplexed*, the similarity of the writing strategy is striking:

> If you desire to grasp all that is contained in this book so that nothing shall escape your notice, consider the chapters in connected order. In studying each chapter, do not content yourself with comprehending its principal subject, but attend to every term mentioned therein, although it may seem to have no connection with the principal subject. For what I have written in this work was not the suggestion of the moment; it is the result of deep study and great application. [...] Do not read superficially, lest you do me an injury, and derive no benefit for yourself. You must study thoroughly and read continually; [...][15]

Neither the *Guide for the Perplexed* nor *Ursprung des deutschen Trauerspiels* head directly for the point they are hoping to make, but instead approach it carefully, methodically and reverently, and the similarity of their approach can be attributed largely to similarities in the way their respective authors conceive of their subject. Even though Maimonides at first sight appears to be more explicit about the theological nature of his discourse than the famously more circumspect Benjamin, it soon becomes clear that an almost identical collection of *caveats* are applied by both. Maimonides's conception of God is that of an Aristotelian unmoved mover, a prime cause and end who is independent of man and world and whose essence cannot be truly known by man. For instance, Maimonides says that we can only speak negatively of God's attributes, as any positive statement about God's essence, quality or relation would deny his unity, his autonomy or his uniqueness. The only attributes which can be predicated of God without compromising his divine essence are those of action, which is to say that man can only know God through his actions. However, and this is where Maimonides supreme scholastic subtlety comes into play, the only way in which we know of God's actions is through the Torah, which Maimonides declares, quoting a Talmudic saying, speaks the language of men. In other words, even though we are able to speak about God, his unity, his goodness and the like, what we say about God does not apply to him in the same way that it would apply to us: 'the term existence, when applied to God and to other beings, is perfectly homonymous. In like manner, the terms Wisdom, Power, Will and Life are applied to God and to other beings by way of perfect homonymity, admitting of no comparison whatever.'[16]

Maimonides established such an enormous conceptual and epistemological distance between God and man that everything we can say about his actions is metaphorical and every word we use to describe him is a homonym, bearing no real relationship to God's actual essence, which remains unknowable. However, Maimonides allows these two fundamentally dissimilar spheres of the human and the divine one point at which they seem to touch, and that is in the act of studying and thinking. Whereas God's intellect is one, its subject, object and action one and the same, human intellect is at first only a potentiality which needs the intellect of God to become a reality, and this is the point where the two spheres intersect, if only momentarily. Obviously, this cursory gloss does not quite do justice to the complexity of Maimonides's philosophy, but it is enough to illustrate the scholastic kind of theological thinking which permeates Benjamin's *Über Sprache* and its later permutation *Erkenntniskritische Vorrede*, as well as two texts which can be situated somewhere in between those, namely the *Theologisch-politisches Fragment*, written around 1921, and the only published, but fairly sanitised version of Benjamin's language theory, the 1923 essay *Die Aufgabe des Übersetzers*.

In all four of these texts, which are among the most important of Benjamin's very small collection of theoretical writings, we find the same recurring pattern of the two spheres or planes of the divine and the profane which do not touch, save in one very tangential or even asymptotic point. In *Ursprung des deutschen Trauerspiels*, the two spheres are truth and knowledge, which correspond to the spheres of ideas and phenomena respectively. Ontologically fundamentally different, they can nevertheless enter into a constellation in which the otherwise unknowable ideas become apparent, and in which the otherwise disparate and mute phenomena become meaningful and, in Benjamin's words, redeemed: 'Die Ideen [...] bleiben dunkel, wo die Phänomene sich zu ihnen nicht bekennen und um sie scharen. Die

144

Einsammlung der Phänomene [vollendet] ein Doppeltes: die Rettung der Phänomene und die Darstellung der Ideen.' (I, 215). As extreme ends of a philosophical or epistemological spectrum, these two spheres do not touch, not does one enter into the other, but as a constellation of extremes, the whole becomes apparent, meaningful and redeemed. We find the same pattern again in the *Theologisch-politisches Fragment*, but this time from the perspective of a *Heilsgeschichte* in which the opposing poles are the order of the profane and the order of the messianic. Similar to Benjamin's concept of truth in the *Erkenntniskritische Vorrede*, the messianic cannot be wanted, it can only reveal itself:

> Erst der Messias selber vollendet alles historische Geschehen, und zwar in dem Sinne, daß er essen Beziehung auf das Messianische selbst erst erlöst, vollendet, schafft. Darum kann nichts Historisches von sich aus auf Messianisches beziehen wollen. (II, 203)[17]

Just as the epistemology of the *Trauerspiel*-book revolved around the concept of the 'death of intention', the advent of the Kingdom of Heaven is made dependent on eliminating the desire for its coming. Nevertheless, the order of the profane can come closer to the order of the messianic by concentrating on the (profane) idea of human happiness: 'Das Profane also ist zwar keine Kategorie des Reichs, aber eine Kategorie, und zwar der zutreffendsten eine, seines leisesten Nahens' (II, 204). However, this approach, exactly like the constellation of ideas and phenomena, is manifestly not a contact or a convergence, instead it is asymptotic, like two lines moving ever closer towards one another into infinity without ever touching.

In *Aufgabe des Übersetzers*, Benjamin actually uses the image of a tangential line touching a circle at only one single point, before moving off into infinity, to describe the relationship between a translation and the original. In this text, the opposition between translation and original is used to illustrate the two poles of human language and pure language or 'reine Sprache'. The latter is clearly a theological construct, modelled on the Jewish concept of the *Leshon ha-Qodesh* or the Holy Language, which knows no distinction between meaning and form, and which, according to one of the most fundamental doctrines of the Jewish tradition, is also the language God used to create the world. 'In dieser reinen Sprache', Benjamin writes, 'die nichts mehr meint und nichts ausdrückt, sondern als ausdrucksloses und schöpferisches Wort das in allen Sprachen Gemeinte ist, trifft endlich alle Mitteilung, aller Sinn und alle Intention auf eine Schicht, in der sie zu erlöschen bestimmt sind' (IV, 19). All human languages share an 'überhistorische Verwandtschaft', as Benjamin calls it (IV, 13). They all derive from the pure language – before Babel, there was only one language – and it is also the vanishing point towards which all human languages are (still) orientated, although they can only reach that point 'a[m] messianische[n] Ende ihrer Geschichte' (IV, 14). To Benjamin, translation has a messianic quality in that it reveals the kinship of all languages in the idea of the pure language. A good translation is therefore not one that manages to convey the meaning of the original, but one that allows the idea of the pure language to shine through, and because of, the translatability of the text: 'Die wahre Übersetzung ist durchscheinend, sie verdeckt nicht das Original, steht ihm nicht im Licht, sondern läßt die reine Sprache, wie verstärkt durch ihr eigenes Medium, nur um so voller aufs Original fallen.' (IV, 18). Again it is in a constellation of opposites that the theological mystery reveals itself.[18]

In *Über Sprache*, finally, the opposition is between what Benjamin terms the 'geistige Wesen' of an entity, or its spiritual – we might say metaphysical – essence, and its 'sprachliche Wesen' or its linguistic essence. According to Benjamin, man, God and world all have both a metaphysical and a linguistic essence, which are situated at either end of a spectrum, much like truth and knowledge, idea and phenomenon or the messianic and the profane. And again like in the other patterns we described, there is a point in which both spiritual and linguistic essence come together in a constellation, which in this case is the Name. As we will discuss in the next paragraph, Benjamin not only follows the doctrine of Genesis in that he defines man as the namer of God's creation, he also says that in this act of naming both creation and himself, spiritual essence converges with linguistic essence. However, this convergence is of course not absolute, at least not for either man or world. Referring explicitly to scholastic philosophy, Benjamin reveals the only place where the perfect convergence may be found:

> Für die Metaphysik der Sprache ergibt die Gleichsetzung des geistigen mit dem sprachlichen Wesen, welches nur graduelle Unterschiede kennt, eine Abstufung allen geistigen Seins in Gradstufen. Diese Abstufung […] führt daher auf die Abstufung aller geistigen wie sprachlichen Wesen nach Existenzgraden oder nach Seinsgraden, wie sie bezüglich der geistigen schon die Scholastik gewohnt war. Die Gleichsetzung des geistigen mit dem sprachlichen Wesen ist aber in sprachtheoretischer Hinsicht von so großer metaphysischer Tragweite, weil sie auf denjenigen Begriff hinführt, der sich immer wieder wie von selbst im Zentrum der Sprachphilosophie erhoben hat und ihre innigste Verbindung mit der Religionsphilosophie ausgemacht hat. Das ist der Begriff der Offenbarung. (II, 146)

Revelation and the Name

Benjamin's preoccupation with what we could call metaphysical entities, such as truth, pure language, and the messianic, not only informs the contents, but also the form and style of his texts in a very particular way, a way which can be called theological in the strictest sense of the word, as they attempt to define or circumnavigate the ineffable. With its exploration of spiritual and linguistic essence, as well as the classical philosophical triad of man, world and God, *Über Sprache* is no exception. The text constitutes Benjamin's first thorough exploration of a profoundly complex way of thinking which would continue to shape his work, through several phenomenological mutations, until his death. After all, the dwarf in the chess machine, however abject and ugly, is still the allegory of theology. This is the reason why a close reading of *Über Sprache*, upon which we are about to embark, can provide us with the keys, or perhaps in his own words the *Vorschule* to Benjamin's *Lehre*. One can seek and succeed to grasp knowledge, but not a metaphysical truth, and it is clearly the latter which *Über Sprache*, with all the paradoxicality of a self-proclaimed prophecy, believes to reveal. This may be what Benjamin meant when he suggested that the text of *Über Sprache* should be treated with the utmost care, as it is a theologically dangerous text, slowly but very steadily making its way into the conceptual twilight zone between orthodoxy and heresy.[19] And this also explains the semi-revelatory tone of *Über Sprache* itself. If the text is to be concerned with truth rather than knowledge, revelation rather than discovery must be its model. As Benjamin again states in the *Erkenntniskritische Vorrede*: '[...] Wahrheit [ist] nicht Enthüllung, die das Geheimnis vernichtet, sondern Offenbarung, die ihm gerecht wird.' (I, 211). We find a very similar concept in *Philosophie der Geschichte*, where Molitor writes about the nature of the mystical truths contained in the Bible:

> Diese hohen Geheimnisse der theoretischen und praktischen Kabbalah sind nach der Lehre der jüdischen Mystiker, alle in der Bibel, entweder mit klaren Worten hier und da ausgesprochen, oder aber meistens in dunkeln Bildern, und geheimnisvollen Winken רמזים (R'masim) blos angedeutet. [...] Denn das Tiefste und Heiligste, das seiner Natur nach dem äußern Sinne verborgen, ist in der heil. Schrift stets mit dem Schleyer des Geheimnisses bedeckt. [...] weil das Tiefste und Allerheiligste äußerlich nicht begriffen, sondern mit gläubigem Gemüthe aufgefaßt, und nur im Innersten erkannt werden kann. (*M* I, 47–48)

The idea that truth is a 'dark image' which cannot be grasped by the predatory intellect – a postlapsarian phenomenon – but must be contemplated so that it might reveal itself, is very much akin to Benjamin's statements on truth in the *Erkenntniskritische Vorrede*, where he compares the 'transzendente Wucht [...] der Wahrheit' with the contemplation of a mosaic: 'Die Relation der mikrologischen Verarbeitung zum Maß des bildnerischen und des intellektuellen Ganzen spricht es aus, wie der Wahrheitsgehalt nur bei genauester Versenkung in die Einzelheiten eines Sachgehalts sich fassen läßt.' (I, 208). The 'truth content' of a work of art will only allow itself to be grasped – and the metaphor clearly has an erotic undertone – if it is approached with a meticulous and loving attention to detail that can only be called religious. If, to continue the metaphor, the work of art takes note of any dishonourable intentions in the mind of the critic, it will turn away, and the critical intention will be destroyed. Truth is a vision, an image granted to someone who approaches it *mit gläubigem*

148

Gemüthe. The fragile and precarious nature of this truth as an image is conveyed by the same image of a veil concealing the deepest and holiest truth that was used by Molitor, although Benjamin chooses Schiller's poem *Das verschleierte Bild zu Sais* as its point of reference. This poem relates the story of a young man who travels to Egypt, consumed by an insatiable desire to know its secret wisdom. In the temple of Isis, he is shown an gigantic statue covered by a veil, which the priest tells him conceals the truth. The priest also tells him that no mortal soul is allowed to lift this veil, but driven by 'des Wissens brennende Begier', the young man returns to the temple during the night to do just that. The next morning, he is found pale and lifeless at the foot of the statue:

> Eben das kann ja die Fabel von einem verschleierten Bilde, zu Sais, besagen, mit dessen Enthüllung zusammenbricht, wer die Wahrheit zu erfragen gedachte. Nicht eine rätselhafte Gräßlichkeit ist's, die das bewirkt, sondern die Natur der Wahrheit, vor welcher auch das reinste Feuer des Suchens wie unter Wassern verlischt. (I, 216)[20]

As a basic prerequisite to be able to address its subject, *Über Sprache* does indeed use certain models or moulds into which to cast itself, and this is a strategy which Benjamin would continue to use throughout his work. Just as the *Erkenntniskritische Vorrede* presented itself nine years later as a *Traktat*, *Über Sprache*, both implicitly and explicitly, mimics the form of the *Lehrsatz* or doctrinal statement, of the *theologoumenon* or theological proposition (or the 'metaphysical truth' of which Benjamin was so fond), and even of the midrash. The latter seems the more tentative suggestion of the three, but *Über Sprache* can nevertheless be read as a midrash, since Benjamin finds a 'tiefer verborgenen Sinn' in a passage from Genesis – and this is exactly how Molitor defined midrash. With reference to the special status of the human name in the first chapters of Genesis, and by extension in the theory of language as such, illustrated by the fact that man names all creatures without being named himself, Benjamin writes: 'Vielleicht ist es kühn, aber kaum unmöglich, den Vers 2,20 in seinem zweiten Teile in diesem Zusammenhang zu nennen: daß der Mensch alle Wesen benannte, "*aber* für den Menschen ward keine

Gehilfin gefunden, die um ihn wäre'" (II, 149). This, as we discussed extensively in the first chapter, is an eminently midrashic strategy: lifting a verse out of its original context and inserting it, seemingly seamlessly, into a new one, where it takes on a further and deeper meaning, without losing its 'original' contextual meaning. Benjamin appears to have been well aware of both the audaciousness and the validity of his interpretation, as is witnessed by his preamble 'vielleicht ist es kühn, aber kaum unmöglich'.

There are other instances where Benjamin picks the text of Genesis apart to reveal hidden meanings – the 'rhythm' of the act of creation, for example: 'Es werde – Er machte (schuf) – Er nannte', or the passage where Benjamin discusses the material out of which man was made (II, 147–148) – but the first case is particularly interesting because Benjamin self-consciously recognises the interpretation as a daring one, as an instance of lateral thinking, so to speak, which conforms perfectly to the dynamic of midrashic interpretation, or 'wie das vor sich geht'; the very dynamic which Scholem had sought to explain to Benjamin the year before (*GF*, 24). In one paragraph of *Über Sprache* Benjamin makes it very clear that he consciously and intentionally used theological texts as a model or a conceptual pattern, in this case the Bible:

> Wenn im folgenden das Wesen der Sprache auf Grund der ersten Genesiskapitel betrachtet wird, so soll damit weder Bibelinterpretation als Zweck verfolgt noch auch die Bibel an dieser Stelle objektiv als offenbarte Wahrheit dem Nachdenken zugrunde gelegt werden, sondern das, was aus dem Bibeltext in Ansehung der Natur der Sprache selbst sich ergibt, soll aufgefunden werden; und die Bibel ist *zunächst* in dieser Absicht nur darum unersetzlich, weil diese Ausführungen im Prinzipiellen ihr darin folgen, daß in ihnen die Sprache als eine letzte, nur in ihrer Entfaltung zu betrachtende, unerklärliche und mystische Wirklichkeit vorausgesetzt wird. Die Bibel, indem sie sich selbst als Offenbarung betrachtet, muß notwendig die sprachlichen Grundtatsachen entwickeln. (II, 147)[21]

The reason why Benjamin uses the Bible, and specifically the first chapters of Genesis, which relate the creation stories, is because it presents itself as revelation, and must therefore necessarily explore the nature and fundamental characteristics of language. Revelation, as we have seen, is the medium in which truth exists, and the locus of truth is language, or more precisely, the name: 'Das höchste Geistesgebiet der Religion ist (im Begriff der Offenbarung) zugleich das einzige, welches das Unaussprechliche nicht kennt. Denn es wird ausgesprochen im Namen und spricht sich aus als Offenbarung.' (II, 147). This identification of revelation and the name as the highest sphere of religion echoes a familiar topos from the Jewish tradition, namely that God created the world by speaking or revealing his own name, and that this revelation is at the same time Torah, in other words, that the whole of the Torah *is* the name of God.[22] It would follow from Benjamin's formulation that, if the Bible conceives of itself as revelation, it must be a name, for this is how revelation expresses itself; and if the Bible, as Benjamin says it does, must necessarily explore the *Grundtatsachen*, the fundamental facts of language, it follows that name, revelation and language are one. This does indeed seem to be the idea around which *Über Sprache* is circling, and which is suggested or expressed in many different ways throughout the essay, perhaps most concisely in the following *theologoumenon*: 'Im Wort wurde geschaffen, und Gottes sprachliches Wesen ist das Wort.' (II, 149). The 'sprachliches Wesen' is juxtaposed at the beginning of the essay with the 'geistiges Wesen', which is expressed as 'sprachliches Wesen' *in* rather than *through* language. The two are not identical, but the 'geistiges Wesen' as such is unknowable and incommunicable: 'Was an einem geistigen Wesen mitteilbar ist, das ist sein sprachliches Wesen.' (II, 142).[23]

Benjamin himself appears to a certain extent to be struggling with the paradox, as he reiterates the idea twice in very similar terms, but each time with different emphases: 'Das geistige Wesen ist mit dem sprachlichen identisch, nur *sofern* es mitteil*bar* ist.' (II, 142). And: 'Es wird das geistige Wesen also von vornherein als mitteilbar gesetzt, oder vielmehr gerade *in* die Mitteilbarkeit gesetzt, und die Thesis: das sprachliche Wesen der Dinge ist mit ihrem geistigen, sofern letzteres mitteilbar ist, identisch, wird in ihrem "sofern" zu einer Tautologie.' (II, 145). The relationship Benjamin postulates between 'sprachliches' and 'geistiges Wesen' is quite similar to the Kantian distinction between *phenomenon* and *noumenon*. 'Geistiges Wesen' and *noumenon*, or 'das Ding an Sich', are knowable only insofar as they are communicable in language, thus becoming 'sprach-liches Wesen' rather than 'geistiges Wesen', or insofar as they can appear as a *phenomenon*. The very act of inquiring into their essence either turns them into a complete unknowable or, *insofar* as something can be said about them, into their complement. Benjamin, however, appears to be entirely equivocal about the epistemological limitations that this construct entails, much in the same way that Maimonides simply accepted the unknowability of God as an inevitable conse-quence of his being. This attitude is summarised beautifully in the choice of modal in Wittgenstein's so-called *Schweigegebot* that con-cludes the *Tractatus Logico-philosophicus*: 'Wovon man nicht sprechen kann, darüber muß man schweigen.'[24] The fact that Wittgen-stein chose the verb *müssen* rather than *sollen* perfectly expresses both the inevitability and the moral neutrality of the statement, and hence the term *Gebot* seems a complete misnomer. If we paraphrase the argument in Benjamin's terms, even if we wanted to communicate the 'geistiges Wesen' as such, it would simply not be possible, and thus we are forced to express it insofar as it can become 'sprachliches Wesen'.[25]

What follows from this is that the only knowable and com-municable essence of God, his 'sprachliches Wesen' in other words, is the word, or language itself.[26] And again we are back to the focal point – or rather vanishing point – of the essay: language. As Benjamin states at the very beginning of *Über Sprache*: 'Ein Dasein, welches ganz ohne Beziehung zur Sprache wäre, ist eine Idee; aber diese Idee läßt sich auch im Bezirk der Ideen, deren Umkreis diejenige Gottes bezeichnet, nicht fruchtbar machen.' (II, 141).[27] This distinctly odd formulation, in which the grammar seems to mimic the content of the sentence, is a circumnavigation of an unspecified centre, and this circumnavigation or penumbra, we are told, is the idea of God.[28] This idea and its form are characteristic of *Über Sprache*. Everything is related in some way to language, but language, in a sense, remains the great unknown (and some of the ambiguities or even obscurities in Benjamin's language are indeed extremely hard to unravel). The clearest statement of the fundamental principles of language comes later in the essay, when Benjamin writes about the 'tiefe deutliche Beziehung des Schöpfungsaktes auf die Sprache':

Mit der schaffenden Allmacht der Sprache setzt er ein, und am Schluß einver-
leibt sich gleichsam die Sprache das Geschaffene, sie benennt es. Sie ist also
das Schaffende, und das Vollendende, sie ist Wort und Name. In Gott ist der
Name schöpferisch, weil er Wort ist, und Gottes Wort ist erkennend, weil es
Name ist. 'Und er sah, daß es gut war', das ist: er hatte es erkannt durch den
Namen. Das absolute Verhältnis des Namens zur Erkenntnis besteht allein in
Gott, nur dort ist der Name, weil er im innersten mit dem schaffenden Wort
identisch ist, das reine Medium der Erkenntnis. Das heißt: Gott machte die
Dinge in ihren Namen erkennbar. Der Mensch aber benennt sie maßen der
Erkenntnis. (II, 148)[29]

Language opens the act of creation, or rather *is* the act of
creation, and completes creation by naming it (through mankind).
Language is both *schöpferisch* and *erkennend*, it is divine, human and
objective. It is divine in that language originates with God, and insofar
as the 'sprachliche Wesen' of God actually *is* the word. Language is
human because, after having served as the medium of mankind's
creation, it is bestowed upon mankind to name the whole of creation:
'[...] im Menschen entließ Gott die Sprache, die *ihm* als Medium der
Schöpfung gedient hatte, frei aus sich' (II, 149). And language is
objective, finally, because the objects communicate their 'sprachliche
Wesen' in their own mute, objective language to mankind so it might
be translated into human language. We can find a similar idea in
chapter seven of the first book of *Philosophie der Geschichte*, where
Molitor also appears to characterise language as a divine medium,
mediating between God, man and world: 'Die Ursprache und Urschrift
ist weder eine menschliche Erfindung noch eine Nachahmung der
äußern Natur, sondern eine Nachahmung Gottes, eine Nachbildung
des göttlichen Redens und Schreibens.' (*M* I, 341). The *Ursprache* of
which Molitor speaks may be taken to correspond to Benjamin's
concept of the *reine Sprache*, which he defined in *Über Sprache* and
in *Die Aufgabe des Übersetzers*, as both the prelapsarian and messianic state of language. Molitor not only speaks of a pure language
which gradually declines as a result of the Fall, or the decline of which
constitutes the Fall, but also emphasises unity, spontaneity and immediacy as characteristics of the 'reinen Bildersprache', all of which are
lost and replaced by the mediation of the 'artificial' process of human
thought:

Denn wenn die alte Zeit Alles in der Total-Einheit erkannte, das Aeußere und Innere damals völlig eins war, so war dem Menschen die ganze Natur und göttliche Offenbarung gleichsam eine für sich verständliche, aber eben darum völlig bewußtlose Symbolik. Als aber der Mensch aus der Einheit getreten, das unmittelbare Verständnis jener reinen Bildersprache verloren, und durch die Reflexion die Uebereinstimmung zwischen dem Aeußern und Innern künstlich auffinden mußte, so ward ihm erst jetzt das Aeußere als ein Symbol des Innern zum bewußten Objekte, und damit erwachte das Streben und Bemühen, überall mit Absicht hinter dem äußern, sinnlichen Bilde die höhere geistige Idee aufzusuchen, und alles Sichtbare auf unsichtbare, intellektuelle Verhältnisse zu beziehen. (*M* I, 188–189)

Mankind leaves the 'holy' state of language at the moment of the Fall, when the *'menschliches Wort'* is born and language becomes both a means to an end as well as a means to judge: 'Indem der Mensch aus der reinen Sprache des Namens heraustritt, macht er die Sprache zum Mittel [...]' (II, 153; Benjamin's emphasis). It is important to draw this analogy, as Benjamin proceeds to define the (human) name, which corresponds to the prelapsarian *reine Sprache* or Molitor's *Ursprache*, as '[d]as tiefste Abbild diese göttlichen Wortes und der Punkt, an dem die Menschensprache den innigsten Anteil an der göttlichen Unendlichkeit des bloßen Wortes erlangt [...]. Der Eigenname ist die Gemeinschaft des Menschen mit dem *schöpferischen* Wort Gottes' (II, 149–150; Benjamin's emphasis).[30] Molitor states this community of human language with the creative word of God in a for him uncharacteristically apodictic definition: 'Wie das menschliche Denken ein Gleichnis zu der ewigen urbild-lichen Idee in Gott, so ist das Sprechen gewissermaßen das Bild des unendlichen Schaffens, oder das Hervorbringen der ewigen urbild-lichen Idee als ein Daseyn außer Gott.' (*M* I, 338). It is quite interesting to note here that Molitor also appears to locate the realm of ideas within God, or, in other words, that God is the *Umkreis* of the realm of ideas. Any manifestation of the ideas outside of this divine penumbra seems either to be a quasi-platonic imitation or a more mystical-kabbalist invocation of the idea insofar as it can exist 'außer Gott'.

Regardless of whether we can speak here of a direct or an in-direct influence of these Jewish theological topoi on *Über Sprache*, it does appear to be the case that both Benjamin and Molitor, however disparate they may be in time and place, see eye to eye as far as their conception of the 'sprachlichen Grundtatsachen' are concerned.[31] But the similarities in their *Lehre* do not end there. When we take a closer look at *Über Sprache* and Molitor's chapter entitled *Ueber den Ursprung der Sprache und Schrift bei den Ebräern*, we find that they agree on three other important points, namely the arbitrariness of the sign, the aforementioned status of human knowledge versus divine knowledge, and the abstract concept of the *Ursprache* and its necessary characteristics. Starting with the latter, it may be surprising to find that Molitor, too, did not take tradition literally. Just as Benjamin used the Bible as an illustration of the fundamental principles of language, Molitor at this point dismisses any reference to empirical knowledge and states that, in these matters, we need *in principle* to turn to the idea: 'Die erste Erfindung der Schrift verliert sich in das Dunkel der Geschichte, wohin, weil es an allen Erfahrungs-Daten fehlt, die gewöhnliche Kritik mit ihrer Beurtheilung nicht hinreichet, und also die Idee nur allein zu entscheiden vermag.' (*M* I, 335–336). Thus Molitor reads tradition as a conceptual construct from the Bible, which presents itself as revelation and must therefore propound certain *Grundtatsachen* with regard to language:

> Ja die jüdische Tradition steigt noch höher hinauf, und behauptet, das Ebräische sey die erste Ursprache gewesen, die Adam im Paradiese gesprochen. Obgleich nun solches nicht nach dem buchstäblichen Sinne genommen werden darf, indem die Ursprache, welche der Mensch in seiner Geistigkeit vor dem Falle geredet, von ganz anderer Art als alle jetzt bestehende Sprachen gewesen, so muß doch, wenn die Bibel das Buch der göttlichen Offenbarung seyn soll, die ebräische Sprache ein zwar geschwächter verkörperter, aber doch treuer Abdruck jener ersten, reinen Ursprache seyn. Denn gleichwie der Mensch auch noch in seinem gefallenen Zustand den Abglanz seiner ehemaligen geistigen Hoheit an sich trägt, so muß auch seine Sprache wenigstens die Spuren jenes magischen Schöpfungsgeistes der frühern Ursprache noch behalten haben; die in seinen Nachkommen sich immer mehr degenerirte, je tiefer das Menschengeschlecht nach und nach sank. (*M* I, 329–330)

First and foremost, Molitor consciously leaves the sphere of literal interpretation to state that what he is about to say must necessarily follow from the Bible insofar as it conceives of itself as divine revelation, or in the words of Benjamin, 'indem sie sich selbst als Offenbarung betrachtet'. Secondly, he paints a picture, similar to Benjamin's, of a prelapsarian human language which was characterised by a greater degree of divinity than its postlapsarian counterpart, and which gradually degenerated into a language in which words and concepts proliferated, but in which the intensity and immediacy of meaning steadily declined:

> So vermehrte sich mit jedem Jahrhundert die Masse der Verstandes-Begriffe, und der Kreis des Wissens nahm immer mehr an Reichthum und Mannichfaltigkeit zu, verlor aber in demselben Maaße an Tiefe und Intensität. Was der Mensch ehemals auf einem Blick sah und ihm aus der unmittelbaren Anschauung verständlich war, mußte jetzt seinem Verstande in viele Begriffe zergliedert dargestellt werden. (*M* I, 189)[32]

If we compare this to Benjamin's description of postlapsarian language, the similarity in their respective doctrines becomes very striking indeed:

> Das Wort soll *etwas* mitteilen (außer sich selbst). Das ist wirklich der Sündenfall des Sprachgeistes. Das Wort als äußerlich mitteilendes, gleichsam eine Parodie des ausdrücklich mittelbaren Wortes auf das ausdrücklich unmittelbare, das schaffende Gotteswort, und der Verfall des seligen Sprachgeistes, des adamitischen, der zwischen ihnen steht. (II, 153)

The crucial concept shared by these two descriptions is *Unmittelbarkeit*, immediacy, which sheds light on what are in essence the necessary *Grundtatsachen* of a language theory which models itself on a theological pattern. Benjamin will use the concept of *Unmittelbarkeit* to develop the contrasting notions of language as a *Mittel*, a means to an end, and language as a *Medium*, as we will discuss below.

In the longer passage from *Philosophie der Geschichte* quoted above, Molitor mentions the 'magischen Schöpfungsgeistes der frühern Ursprache', the former, prelapsarian magic of language which still adheres in scattered traces to the postlapsarian human language.

He reiterates this idea later, in the aforementioned seventh chapter, where he writes:

> So wie das Wort der Ursprache ein reiner Abdruck des Gedankens ist, und das Wort ursprünglich selber eine magische Kraft hat, so war auch die Urschrift des Menschen, wie jegliches Werk und jegliche That, der figurirte Ausdruck des magischen Wortes, und darum selber magisch in ihren Wirkungen. (*M* I, 341)[33]

The 'magic' Molitor writes about is intimately linked to the creative power of the Word of God, which we mentioned above. God speaks, and what he has spoken comes into being. True to the Jewish doctrine of *creatio ex nihilo*, this means that nothing exists before language, that language is the *immediate* cause of creation and that everything must thus necessarily exist *in* language, and, as we said before, that language therefore *is* creation in both act and substance. This also sheds light on Benjamin's insistence that language is never a mere *Mittel* but always a *Medium*: language is not only the means by which God creates the world, it is also the medium in which the world exists. Towards the end of the essay, Benjamin expresses this linguistic omnipresence in the following terms: 'Die Sprache eines Wesens ist das Medium, in dem sich sein geistiges Wesen mitteilt. Der ununterbrochene Strom dieser Mitteilung fließt durch die ganze Natur vom niedersten Existierenden bis zum Menschen und vom Menschen zum Gott.' (II, 157). In other words, because it is the divine language which creates the world from nothing, the creation itself is a form of language. It is this idea which lies at the basis of the notion of the 'book of the world', according to which the whole of creation, as does the whole of the Torah with which it was created, contains a divine message.[34] Benjamin's statement that the objects communicate themselves to mankind, so that the latter is able to name them as was decreed by God, is fundamentally akin to this notion (II, 143).[35] So much so, in fact, that we find Molitor's description of 'die Spuren jenes magischen Schöpfungsgeistes', which are meant still to adhere to human language, echoed extremely closely in *Über Sprache* as the 'Residuum des schaffenden Gotteswortes', which permeates the whole of nature as a mute, nameless language.[36] One interesting detail here is the slight shift in emphasis between these two phrases. Whereas

Molitor talks about the 'Schöpfungs*geist*', Benjamin prefers the term 'Gottes*wort*', and it is perhaps this detail which reveals Molitor as a Christian author and which sees Benjamin taking a more characteristically 'Jewish' approach. As became apparent from Benjamin's epistemological and methodological emphasis on the 'sprachliches Wesen' over the 'geistiges Wesen' in *Über Sprache*, the central category in his thought, theological or otherwise, must ultimately be language, *Sprache*, not *Geist*. Scholem, too, recognised this emphasis as a fundamentally Jewish trait of Benjamin's philosophy, referring to 'die tiefe Bindung des echten theologischen Denkens der Juden an die Sprache [...], wie sie immer wieder bei ihm zum Vorschein kommt' (*GF*, 219).

Benjamin's description of language differs from Molitor's in one respect only, yet it is an aspect which is absolutely crucial in understanding not only Benjamin's language theory, but in fact his entire work. Whereas Molitor approaches the subject from the perspective of humanity and its language, Benjamin appears to pay attention to both world and man, but not always in equal measure. As a direct consequence of his conception of tradition and the immanence of his critique, Benjamin's focus is more on the object and its language. This is an emphasis which Benjamin would maintain throughout his work, from *Über Sprache* and *Ursprung des deutschen Trauerspiels* to *Berliner Kindheit um Neunzehnhundert* and his pieces on the figure of the collector, as well as the unfinished *Passagen-Werk* and the so-called *Haschisch-Protokolle*. Nowhere is Benjamin's focus on the object more clear than in this remarkable collection of texts, where his emphasis with the objective perspective leads him to the 'verwunderte Notiz': 'Wie die Dinge den Blicken standhalten.' (VI, 587 and IV, 416). This perspective is the profane complement of the theological concept of the 'book of the world', as mentioned by Molitor in *Philosophie der Geschichte*, and Benjamin was clearly aware of this. In the notes for the *Passagen-Werk*, a project which presented itself as an attempt to redeem the 'Abfall der Geschichte', the immense and ever increasing collection of outmoded and discarded commodities, Benjamin writes: 'Die Rede vom Buch der Natur weist darauf hin, daß man das Wirkliche wie einen Text lesen kann. So soll es hier mit der Wirklichkeit des neunzehnten Jahrhunderts gehalten werden. Wir schlagen das Buch des Geschehenen auf.' (V, 580). It is in this project that the profane and the theological come together into the paradoxical fusion that is 'profane Erleuchtung', or as Scholem once phrased it so succinctly: 'Seine Einsichten sind die eines ins Profane verschlagenen Theologen.'[37]

Sprachmagie

The language theory, if indeed theory it is, of both Benjamin and Molitor circles around the idea of a language which in which meaning and form somehow coincide. As we discussed in the previous paragraph, both Benjamin and Molitor are aware that such a language is a theological construct first and foremost, and both authors accordingly use the notion of an original, holy language or a hypothetical pure language as the keystone of their respective theories. Benjamin and Molitor are also quite conscious of the paradoxical nature of such a construct, and both refer to the unity and immediacy of this language as its 'magic'. This magic, according to Molitor, derives firstly from the creative power of the word, from the fact that the language of God becomes the world, or in more christological terms, the word becomes flesh. In such a paradigm, as we shall discuss later, there is neither room for a mediation between sign and meaning nor for the arbitrary nature of their relationship. There can, in fact, not even be a 'sign' as such: there must be a fundamental identity between language and world. This is true whether we use the Saussurean, Peircean or Derridean definition of the sign as something which stands for something else in its absence: if a sign becomes illegible in the absence of its referent, the presence or existence of the latter would become a *conditio sine qua non* for the sign to be able to fulfill its function. If, for instance, a word would be meaningless if it was not uttered in the proximity of its referent, it would become entirely obsolete as a signifier.[38]

The best example of the theological reinterpretation of the sign, if we may be allowed another christological excursion, is the fact that Jesus was taken up into heaven with his earthly body. The word had become flesh, they were identical, hence there could no longer be a disjunction between God and man in Christ after the Incarnation. It is testament to the complexity and enormity of this paradox that Christianity's first five hundred years were consumed by often intense christological debates, and that most of the earlier and later heresies circled around the definition of the person of Christ. The most common group of heresies sought to separate the earthly, bodily Jesus from the heavenly, 'ethereal' Jesus in some way, with the most radical even going so far as to deny the humanity of Jesus, as was the case in Eutychian and Julianist Monophysitism. These heresies, inspired to a greater or a lesser degree by gnosticism, a manichean dualism or quite simply a neo-platonic dislike of the body, proved to be very resilient and continued to resurface throughout the centuries, with Albigensianism perhaps its most (in)famous manifestation.[39] The reason why these heresies were considered heretical was the fact that, in order both to deny the notion that the body of Christ ascended into heaven and to avoid a logical inconsistency, they tended in some form to deny the Catholic doctrine of the incarnation.

Interestingly enough, Benjamin himself refers to this very same paradox of the Λόγος in his explanation of the difference between 'sprachliches' and 'geistiges Wesen', locating it at the very root of linguistic theory. Thus the most fundamental problem of language theory becomes, again, a fundamentally theological one:

> Die Unterscheidung zwischen dem geistigen Wesen und dem sprachlichen, in dem es mitteilt, ist die ursprünglichste in einer sprachtheoretischen Untersuchung, und es scheint dieser Unterschied so unzweifelhaft zu sein, daß vielmehr die oft behauptete Identität zwischen dem geistigen und dem sprachlichen Wesen eine tiefe und unbegreifliche Paradoxie bildet, deren Ausdruck man in den Doppelsinn des Wortes Λόγος gefunden hat. Dennoch hat diese Paradoxie als Lösung ihre Stelle im Zentrum der Sprachtheorie, bleibt aber Paradoxie und da unlösbar, wo sie am Anfang steht. (II, 141–142)

Just as the unthinkable concept of the *reine Sprache* functioned as the guarantor of the translatability of all languages, the seemingly impossible union of the materiality of the sign and the 'immateriality' of meaning, of 'sprachliches' and 'geistliches Wesen', must stand at the centre of a language theory that cannot give up on meaning. What is even more fascinating is the fact that Benjamin insists that this paradox remains unsolvable 'wo sie am Anfang steht', as there is one particular instance where this is indeed the case: the paradox of the Λόγος as proclaimed in the opening verses of the gospel according to John, is, in both senses of the word, the most *ursprüngliche* mystery of Christianity: ''Εν ἀρχῇ ἦν ὁ λόγος, καὶ ὁ λόγος ἦν πρὸς τὸν θεόν, καὶ θεὸς ἦν ὁ λόγος. οὗτος ἦν ἐν ἀρχῇ πρὸς τὸν θεόν. πάντα δι' αὐτοῦ ἐγένετο, καὶ χωρὶς αὐτοῦ ἐγένετο οὐδε ἕν ὃ γέγονεν' (Joh 1, 1–3).[40] The first two words, 'Εν ἀρχῇ, already suggest that the evangelist actually intended his words to stand at the origin, or rather that they were meant to echo and thus replace an older origin, namely the book that had started with the words בראשית, *Bereshith*. The concise passage can again be read as a statement of the linguistic essence or existence of God (and the Son), as we discussed it in our first chapter in relation to the vocalisation of the tetragrammaton. The concept of the Λόγος , the Word incarnate, expresses the fundamental unity and identity of the Father and the Son, so profound that the Λόγος,, the Word or the Son, rhetorically if not necessarily theologically pre-exists the Father, a paradox which is suspended, but of course manifestly not solved, in the second verse which states that God *is* the Word. Locating this paradox at the very origin of the faith is a way of circumnavigating the otherwise insoluble problem of the relationship between signifier and signified, and by extension the problem of the relationship between *geistiges* and *sprachliches Wesen*. In fact, using these terms Benjamin comes closer to the original mystery of Christianity than to the Saussurean mystery of the signifier/signified relationship, as the Son, or Λόγος, can be said to be the *sprachliches Wesen* of God, i.e., his *geistiges Wesen* insofar as it expresses itself, insofar as it becomes flesh.

Benjamin recognises the necessity of putting the paradox of form and meaning at the centre of his language theory, if either are to be salvaged, but he also recognises the even more pressing necessity of keeping the paradox unsolved and suspended: '[...] diese Ansicht als

Hypothesis verstanden, ist der große Abgrund, dem alle Sprachtheorie zu verfallen droht, und über, gerade über ihm sich schwebend zu erhalten ist ihre Aufgabe' (II, 141). When Benjamin discusses what he calls the 'bürgerliche[n] Ansicht der Sprache' (II, 150), according to which the relationship between the sign and the thing to which it is assigned rests solely on convention, he reverts to the same figure of the paradox, refusing to countenance the replacement of the 'bourgeois' view by a mystical theory of language. He opts instead for a third alternative constructed out of the suspension of the only two choices which seem available. Benjamin rejects the Saussurean *arbitraire du signe*: 'Die Sprache gibt niemals *bloße* Zeichen' (II, 150). Yet he does not support the view of straightforward language mysticism, according to which the word expresses the essence of the thing. The emphasis in the lapidary statement quoted above is on '*bloße*', not on 'Zeichen'. In other words, he does not deny that language is made up of signs, but he maintains that the relationship of these signs with their referents is less uncomplicated than *mere* representation. What Benjamin does here is to suspend us again over the abyss of a third, unknowable alternative, gaping between the two extremes of the bourgeois theory and the mystical view, between science and religion, between man and God. This third unknowable, in many ways typical of Benjamin, comes from the perspective of the object, and rests on the literally inconceivable notion that objects communicate their essence, bestowed on them by God, to mankind in their own mute language:

> [...] die Sache an sich [hat] kein Wort [...], geschaffen ist sie aus Gottes Wort und erkannt in ihrem Namen nach dem Menschenwort. Diese Erkenntnis der Sache ist aber nicht spontane Schöpfung, sie geschieht nicht aus der Sprache absolut uneingeschränkt und unendlich wie diese; sondern es beruht der Name, den der Mensch der Sache gibt, darauf, wie sie ihm mitteilt. Im Namen ist das Wort Gottes nicht schaffend geblieben, es ist an einem Teil empfangend, wenn auch sprachempfangend, geworden. Auf die Sprache der Dinge selbst, aus denen wiederum lautlos und in der stummen Magie der Natur das Wort Gottes hervorstrahlt, ist diese Empfängnis gerichtet. (II, 150)

Mankind's assignation of signs cannot be an arbitrary activity because man does not *have* language *stricto sensu*. Mankind exists *in*

162

language, language is its medium, in the same way as truth exists *in* language but can never be communicated *through* it. Language is bestowed upon humankind by God, and the 'sprachliches Wesen' which this language will express can only be expressed after the objects which human language names have communicated their 'geistiges Wesen' to mankind. Thus mankind finds itself suspended over the epistemological abyss between an unknowable God and an unknowable objective essence, without which, nevertheless, meaning as such is necessarily inconceivable and inexpressible. God ensures that language is able to *mean* and the object ensures that language is able to mean *something*. If it would be possible to detach language from its guarantors, God and world, language would not signify and would signify nothing, an idea which, as Benjamin himself said, cannot be made fruitful. Or *wovon man nicht sprechen kann, darüber muß man schweigen.*

A similar notion is expressed by Molitor when he describes the prelapsarian stage of human existence as a 'Seyn und Leben [...] in einer realen aber harmonischen Natur, für die es weder Nothwendigkeit noch Willkühr gab, sondern alles eine reine reflexionslose That war' (*M* I, 135). If we apply this pattern to the question of language and meaning, we are led to the same conclusion reached by Benjamin of an excluded, unnamed third alternative. Language is neither a question of *Nothwendigkeit*, i.e., given by God to mankind without the latter having any hand in the matter, nor is it a question of *Willkühr*, of mankind simply assigning names to objects on its own account. If we reject both God, *Nothwendigkeit*, and man, *Willkühr*, as the source of language, it must necessarily originate from a third source, namely the object itself. In this respect, it is interesting that Molitor should have described the behaviour of mankind as 'eine reine reflexionslose That', emphasising receptivity rather than intention. In fact, a subsequent discussion by Molitor of the concept of arbitrariness is particularly enlightening in this matter, as he writes:

Die Urschrift bestand daher eben so wenig aus willkührlichen Zeichen, als die Ursprache aus willkührlichen Tönen; so wie es denn an sich gar keine willkührlichen Töne und Zeichen giebt, sondern alle Töne, Formen und Gestalten der Ausdruck gewisser Ideen und Qualitäten sind, und also Leben und Wirksamkeit in sich haben. Doch beruhet ihre Wirkung stets auf der Intention des Wirkenden, und auf dem Rapport und Empfänglichkeit dessen, auf den die Wirking gerichtet ist. (*M* I, 341)

This passage, quite deceptively, may sound as if Molitor is simply restating the received opinion of traditional language mysticism, saying that there is no such thing as an arbitrary sign (which is in itself a deceptive formulation, as *l'arbitraire du signe* does not refer to the sign, but to the relationship between signifier and signified). But on closer inspection, we find that Molitor is in fact talking about nature as a signifier. On the previous page, he had defined the whole of nature, visible and invisible, as a sign: 'Alle Formen in der äußern Natur sind lauter göttliche Schriftzüge, die ganze sichtbare Natur ist die eingegrabene Schrift Gottes oder das äußere schriftlich offenbarte Wort, das mündliche hingegen ist blos innerlich im Geiste vernehmbar' (*M* I, 340). This entails that the 'Intention des Wirkenden' of the previous passage actually refers to nature, in other words to the object, and the 'Rapport und Empfänglichkeit' commensurate to this intention thus refers to mankind. This inevitably leads us to the conclusion that, in Molitor's view, too, the object communicates itself to mankind, which then proceeds to name it.[41]

One important difference between Molitor's version and Benjamin's is that the former suggests that it is in fact God who is communicating himself to mankind through nature, whereas Benjamin's essay appears to leave the role of God open in this respect, choosing instead to concentrate on the medium, *Sprache überhaupt*. Yet this does not necessarily mean that Molitor and Benjamin are incompatible on this point, on the contrary, the latter's shift of emphasis is merely dictated by his own distinction between *geistiges Wesen* and *sprachliches Wesen*. When Benjamin apparently refuses to talk about God as such, this is merely because, according to his own definition, God's essence, his *geistiges Wesen*, can only be known insofar as it expresses itself in language and thus becomes his *sprachliches Wesen*, his linguistic essence. This retreat of God into language or into the essence of language is a characteristically Jewish turn of thought. As we saw in chapter one, catachretically, the Talmud needs only the letter *heth* to conclude that God lives in the heights of the wor[l]d. It is partly this very doctrine of the linguistic essence of God and its consequences which, according to Benjamin, explained why the name of God was conspicuously absent from Kafka's work – and indeed his own: 'Es wurde darauf hingewiesen, daß im ganzen Werke Kafkas der Name "Gott" nicht vorkommt. […] Wer nicht versteht, was Kafka den Gebrauch dieses Namens verbietet, versteht von ihm keine Zeile' (II, 1219).

Yet Benjamin is far from silent on this subject, although he too, prompted by the prohibition generated by his own thought as much as by the Jewish tradition, religiously avoids addressing the name of God, reverting instead to speculations about the Word of God or about his 'sprachliches Wesen'. In *Über Sprache* he expounds a doctrine, which we quoted above, which is in fact extremely similar to the one found in *Philosophie der Geschichte*:

> Im Namen ist das Wort Gottes nicht schaffend geblieben, es ist an einem Teil empfangend, wenn auch sprachempfangend, geworden. Auf die Sprache der Dinge selbst, aus denen wiederum lautlos und in der stummen Magie der Natur das Wort Gottes hervorstrahlt, ist diese Empfängnis gerichtet' (II, 150)

In this passage, Benjamin says that the word of God shines forth in the 'mute magic of nature', and it is this 'word of God' which he himself defined on the previous page of *Über Sprache* as 'Gottes sprachliches Wesen' (II, 149). This means, in other words, that in Benjamin's view, too, nature is the expression of God's essence insofar as it can be known to mankind, just as Molitor states in *Philosophie der Geschichte*. Still there remains an important distinction between Benjamin and Molitor, which, as we mentioned before, is the former's emphasis on language as the focal point of his essay: *Wort* and not *Geist*. God, to continue the pictorial metaphor, is the vanishing point of *Über Sprache*, knowable only in his effects, which are necessarily *sprachlich*. Even in his description of the word of God as it shines forth in nature, Benjamin stresses the fact that we have to go through, or rather *into* language. The very word of God becomes *sprachempfangend*: after creation, language passes into the hands of mankind in the form of the names which mankind gives to creation, and these names, as we said before, are translations from the mute language of objects into human language. In Molitor's version, it is mankind which becomes receptive to the language of nature. In Benjamin's account, it is the word of God which becomes receptive, *through* mankind fulfilling its task to name creation. This slight shift in emphasis deeply embeds God into language, much more so than is the case in *Philosophie der Geschichte*. Language becomes the medium of existence as such, not just of man and world, but now also of God. And this is the magic of (divine) language which pervades language as such: the world is created in language and continues to exist in language. Human language, as a naming language, still has traces of this magic because it was bestowed on humankind by God, and because the very task of naming and thereby completing creation is a God-given task. Language, in other words, is magical because of its immediacy and ubiquity, because it *is* and because it is everything and everywhere. Or in the words of Benjamin himself:

> [...] jede Sprache teilt sich *in* sich selbst mit, sie ist im reinsten Sinne das "Medium" der Mitteilung. Das Mediale, das ist die *Unmittel*barkeit aller geistigen Mitteilung, ist das Grundproblem der Sprachtheorie, und wenn man diese Unmittelbarkeit magisch nennen will, so ist das Urproblem der Sprache ihre Magie. Zugleich deutet das Wort von der Magie der Sprache auf ein anderes: auf ihre Unendlichkeit. Sie ist durch die Unmittelbarkeit bedingt. Denn gerade, weil *durch* die Sprache sich nichts mitteilt, kann, was *in* der Sprache sich mitteilt, nicht von außen beschränkt oder gemessen werden, und darum wohnt jeder Sprache ihre inkommensurable einziggeartete Unendlichkeit inne. Ihr sprachliches Wesen, nicht ihre verbalen Inhalte bezeichnen ihre Grenze. (II, 142–143)

This concept of 'Medium' is, in the most theological sense of the word, the 'mystery' of Benjamin's language essay. 'Die Sprache eines Wesens ist das Medium, in dem sich sein geistiges Wesen mitteilt' (II, 157). It is this concept, as the attribute of language, which the essay circumnavigates – as we phrased it before. The reason for this strategy of circumnavigation, *Umkreisung*, is that the concept of 'Medium' is essentially a theological one, and, in a way, also a divine one. It designates not only the sphere of existence of language, but also the sphere of existence of God. God, like truth and like language, cannot be grasped, named, pinpointed, located or acquired. To say that God has attributes – as we said of language a few sentences ago – is impossible. Thus it also becomes impossible to posit any attributes of language as such, because the original Language, *Sprache überhaupt* or the *reine Sprache*, which all forms of language take as their ideal, is also divine. This is why we have to continue to circumnavigate, delay and deny, rather than state. One of the most fundamental tenets of Maimonides's theology is that it is both prohibited and impossible to state anything else about God apart from his existence, which is not an attribute but a state, *ein Sein*. And, to paraphrase Benjamin himself, Maimonides's theology in this respect is *nicht unjüdisch*, unsurprisingly. Through a combination of radical monotheism, the strict prohibition of graven images, and a subsequent reliance on language in general as well as the language of the Torah, Judaism comes to a definition of God which appears fundamentally to cross the borders of the expressible and the thinkable. This leads the Jewish tradition into the most intricate and simple paradox of human thought – so much so that naming this paradox requires a paradox, so it becomes a tautology – which is the *Inbegriff*, the quintessence, of theological thought as such. God becomes everything and nothing, both and neither at the same time.

Chapter Five: Medium

Das Denken der Lehre

In November 1917, a year after writing *Über Sprache* and six months after acquiring his own copy of *Philosophie der Geschichte*, Benjamin started writing *Über das Programm der kommenden Philosophie*, a text which is in many ways the metaphysical and epistemological counterpart to the earlier language essay. *Über das Programm* represents Benjamin's first and only thorough *Auseinandersetzung* with Kant, and, characteristically, it is rather more impressionistic than scholarly. Benjamin appears to have been full of admiration for the style of Kant's writings, expressing his conviction that Kant's prose represents 'einen limes der hohen Kunstprosa' (*GB* I, 390).[1] But, more importantly, Benjamin consistently defines Kant's philosophy in terms of the elusive concept of the *Lehre*. To Benjamin, Kant's table of categories, which he says claims to stand on its own as an accurate and complete reflection of knowledge and experience, should itself rather be seen as a part of an even larger *Lehre von den Ordnungen*, an all-encompassing sphere which can both accommodate and order the whole of human *Geistesleben*, for want of a better term (II, 166). That this form of the *Lehre* closely mirrors the Jewish concept of tradition is obvious, with its effortless combination of the legal, the philosophical, the theological but also the all-too-human, the comical and even the whimsical. And this is perhaps the most striking point made by the essay – which names Benjamin as 'legitimer Fortsetzer der fruchtbarsten und echtesten Traditionen [eines Molitors]', to paraphrase Scholem – namely that even such at first sight radically heterogeneous manifestations as the philosophy of Kant and the collages of the Surrealists should be seen in the light of the *Lehre*. 'Benjamin', Scholem writes,

sind Mystiker und Satiriker, Humanisten und Lyriker, Gelehrte und Mono-
manen gleicherweise der philosophische Versenkung wert. Unversehens geht
dabei die Betrachtung vom Profanen ins Theologische über, spürt er doch die
genauen Konturen des Theologischen noch da, wo es vollends ins gänzlich
Weltliche aufgelöst erscheint.[2]

Much as Molitor, perhaps for strategic purposes, refused to
recognise Judaism and Christianity as discreet and distinct entities, as
we discussed extensively in previous chapters, Benjamin refuses to
acknowledge the idea of the division of labour which had been
creeping into the fields of the humanities and sciences since the
Enlightenment, and which he attributes to a Neo-kantian misreading
of the intention of Kant's system.[3] To him, there remained one overarching principle, one ἀρχή, which united even the most disparate
manifestations of thought, and that was the medium in which thought
as such, by definition, had to exist: *die Lehre*. In a letter dated 22
October 1917, less than a month before the composition of *Über das
Programm der kommenden Philosophie*, Benjamin's correspondence
again seems to bear witness to intense mental activity, as it had the
year before. Admitting that he does not yet have any proof for his
intuitions, he nevertheless states, with the same doctrinal authority
that spoke from *Über Sprache*:

> In der Tat sehe ich nur die Aufgabe wie ich sie eben umschrieben habe klar vor
> mir daß das *Wesentliche* des Kantischen Denkens zu erhalten sei. Worin dieses
> Wesentliche besteht und wie man sein System neu gründen muß um es hervor-
> treten zu lassen weiß ich bis heute nicht. Aber es ist meine Überzeugung: wer
> nicht in Kant *das Denken der Lehre selbst* ringen fühlt und wer daher nicht mit
> äußerster Ehrfurcht ihn mit seinem Buchstaben als ein tradendum, zu Über-
> lieferndes erfaßt (wie weit man ihn auch später umbilden müsse) weiß von
> Philosophie garnichts. (*GB* I, 389; Benjamin's emphasis)

The two most crucial elements in the project that became *Über
das Programm* are, firstly, the intimate connection between philosophy and the *Lehre* which Benjamin attempts to establish, and
which will – embryonically at least – take the form of *philosophia
ancilla doctrinae*, and secondly Benjamin's firm belief that philosophy must be able to accommodate all manner of experience without
renouncing its claim to speak with the certainty of 'systematische

170

Einheit oder', in other words, 'die Wahrheit'.[4] This claim to speak in truth, as we discussed before and will continue to explore later, automatically brings philosophy into a theological frame of mind, and the argument of *Über das Programm* is no exception. Indeed, towards the end of the essay, Benjamin says that the mandate of any future philosophy should be to create a concept of knowledge which corresponds to the concept of an experience 'von der die Erkenntnis Lehre ist' (II, 168). This centrifugal and centripetal movement from knowledge to experience and back describes the constant and unending interchange between two poles that we could designate as the metaphysical and the physical, the divine and the profane, which keeps the process of tradition or *Lehre* dynamic. Benjamin clearly realised that this new and dynamic concept of philosophy would either have to be theology or would indeed transcend theology in that it also included history and philosophy: 'Eine solche Philosophie wäre entweder in ihrem allgemeinen Teile selbst als Theologie zu bezeichnen oder wäre dieser sofern sie etwa historisch philosophische Elemente einschließt übergeordnet.' (II, 168). Yet in stating this, Benjamin must also have been aware that the ideal model for such a future philosophy already existed. *Das Denken der Lehre*, the 'thinking of the doctrine', becomes the metaphor for a form of thought which is not only disembodied from both subject and object, but also encompasses all manifestations of consciousness, a form of thinking which is extremely close to the *Gedankenbewegung* of the Jewish tradition.

In May 1918, when Scholem visited Benjamin in Bern, much of their conversation was still centred on *Über das Programm*, and particularly the concept of experience which Benjamin elaborates in this text. At that point Benjamin formulated the following, according to Scholem, 'extreme' definition: 'Eine Philosophie, die nicht die Möglichkeit der Weissagung aus dem *Kaffeesatz* einbezieht und explizieren kann, kann keine wahre sein.' (*GF*, 77). This 'extreme' formulation is also extremely straightforward in the context of Benjamin's epistemology, which we discussed in the previous chapter. Truth, unlike knowledge, cannot be appropriated or possessed, it simply is. Any philosophy which claims to speak in truth must therefore *be* in truth, it must partake of the sphere which is truth. This seemingly mystical conception of philosophy becomes far more lucid

171

when we connect the concepts of truth and experience. This connection is nowhere more obvious than in the essay *Erfahrung und Armut*, written in 1933, which opens with the following parable:

> In unseren Lesebüchern stand die Fabel vom alten Mann, der auf dem Sterbebette den Söhnen weismacht, in seinem Weinberg sei ein Schatz verborgen. Sie sollten nur nachgraben. Sie gruben, aber kein Spur von Schatz. Als jedoch der Herbst kommt, trägt der Weinberg wie kein anderer im ganzen Land. Da merken sie, der Vater gab ihnen eine Erfahrung mit: Nicht im Golde steckt der Segen, sondern im Fleiß. (II, 213–214)

As was the case with *Über Sprache*, this opening paragraph mimics the form of the tradition which it discusses. It refers to an untraceable source, but, crucially, it mentions a source, thereby labelling this parable as 'überliefertes Wissen', which in turn becomes 'überlieferbar', according to Benjamin's own definition of traditional knowledge. As we have seen in the first chapter, this sense of continuity is of supreme importance in the Jewish tradition, as it preserves the integrity of revelation, on a physical as well as on a spiritual level, regardless of whether this is strictly philologically justified. Benjamin himself was well aware of this wilful suspension of disbelief inherent in the traditional world-view, yet rather than seeing it as incidental and possibly deplorable, he acknowledged that maintaining the appearance of a continuity was in fact at the very heart of tradition. As he wrote in one of the notes for the *Passagen-Werk*: 'Mag sein, daß die Kontinuität der Tradition Schein ist. Aber dann stiftet eben die Beständigkeit dieses Scheins der Beständigkeit die Kontinuität in ihr.' (V, 609). By the same token, the people of which the parable speaks remain unnamed, although they are entirely plausible. In other words, they *could* be real, even though the unspoken convention of the parable is that its protagonists are subservient to the story and therefore remain emblematic, or perhaps rather symptomatic. This parable is also a perfect illustration of the methodological detour which is so typical of Benjamin's self-confessed writing strategy, which performs a double function here in a kind of a *mise-en-abyme*. Benjamin's essay on the concept of experience opens with a little story in which the protagonists are indirectly taught the value of hard work through experience, which in turn shows Benjamin's reader the kind of experience which he considers to be under threat. So rather than start with a thesis and a clear definition of his terms of reference, Benjamin opens his essay with a little snippet of *aggadah*, which he then uses to illuminate his *halakha* or his *Lehre*.

But most importantly, and of course very closely related to this methodological detour, this parable demonstrates what Benjamin said sixteen years earlier about the nature of truth and experience. Truth, let us say it once more, cannot be had, it can only *be*. This is illustrated perfectly by the parable, which circumnarrates the point it wants to make, the experience it wants to bring across, the truth it seeks to reveal, without actually stating it. There is no point even in this very short parable where the truth or the experience can be situated: its image grows in its telling. Benjamin uses the same organic metaphor to describe how Kafka's stories unfold: 'Kafkas Parabeln entfalten sich aber [...] wie die Knospe zur Blüte wird' (II, 420).[5] What Kafka's stories 'unfold', Benjamin says, is 'die wolkige Stelle in ihrem Innern'. They intimate a mystery hidden deep within, with the added complication in Kafka's case, as we suggested before, that we no longer possess the *Lehre* which his parables are supposed to illustrate: 'Besitzen wir die Lehre aber [...]? Sie ist nicht da; wir können höchstens sagen, daß dies und jenes auf sie anspielt' (II, 420). This is particularly true in the case of Benjamin's parable, as the lesson 'nicht im Golde steckt der Segen, sondern im Fleiß' is manifestly not the point, which is rather to illustrate the concept of traditional knowledge and experience. And even the illustration of the concept of experience can be said to be subordinate to the subliminal, perhaps even esoteric aim of the passage, which seems to be to hint at the form of truth as such, a treasure of a different, less palpable kind, which reveals and manifests itself in the passage. In *Ursprung des deutschen Trauerspiels*, Benjamin called truth, with that wonderfully clear yet entirely untranslatable expression, 'ein Sich-Darstellendes', something which represents, manifests or establishes itself.[6] This is why the quotation from Benjamin's Kafka essay is particularly apt in the context of the parable, as we cannot 'possess' the *Lehre* or the truth by its very nature. If, Benjamin seems to suggest, truth does not want to be revealed, it will not be revealed, just as in Schiller's poem the truth can only be seen when Isis chooses to lift its veil. The way to touch upon the *Lehre* must therefore be through references, illustrations or hints, in the words of Molitor: 'dunkeln Bildern, und geheimnisvollen Winken' (*M* I, 47–48).

This concept of truth may also in part explain the importance of the Jewish or, to a lesser extent, Judaeo-Christian tradition to Benjamin's theory of knowledge and experience. As we indicated above, the Jewish tradition is often at pains to retrace its links to revelation, thereby establishing a tangible continuity and effectively preserving the *Wahrheitsgehalt* of revelation within itself like a liquid in a vessel. This means that all knowledge which can be recognised as 'überliefert' will speak with the authority of revelation, but it also means that retracing the gradual expansion of tradition since its inception, study, becomes a religious duty. Or as Benjamin wrote in the notes to the *Passagen-Werk*: 'Methode ist Umweg', the detour through the strict propaedeutic that is tradition. The delaying strategies of the *Passagen-Werk* have often been interpreted as an influence of modernist and surrealist techniques such as montage and collage, but it can quite justifiably be seen as a direct consequence of working with traditional and theological concepts, which, as we already saw and will discuss further below, either simply preclude the direct statement or make it impossible without its mirror opposite – because all is contained within tradition.

In a letter to Scholem dated 6 September 1917, approximately two months before the composition of *Über das Programm*, Benjamin draws the strands of truth, experience and education together in the eminently Jewish concept of the *Lehre*. Again, truth cannot be located in any particular communication or example given by the teacher to the pupil, rather it exists in the activity of the *Lehre*, in the ambiguity of the German word *lehren*: 'Wenn man also sagt der Lehrer gibt das "Beispiel" zum Lernen so verdeckt man durch den Begriff Beispiel das Eigentümliche, Autonome im Begriff solchen Lernens: nämlich das Lehren.' (*GB* I, 382)[7] Any translation of the words *lernen* and *lehren*, *study* and *teach*, must necessarily be deceptive, as neither of these terms refers to a one-sided activity. In the German-Jewish consciousness, *lernen* designates the engagement with the text within tradition, or rather the engagement with the text that is tradition.

Benjamin himself used the word to describe his reading of Molitor and Baader, whose works he wanted to have in front of him simultaneously, writing to Scholem: 'anders kann ich nicht lernen' (*GB* I, 357). As we discussed in the first chapter, the Jewish concept of study, *lernen*, does not refer to a silent and solitary reading of a text, but to a communal activity in which the teacher, the *Lehrer*, is engaged as much as his pupils. It does not refer to the passing on of quantifiable information, which is readily available to the teacher, to ignorant pupils. The verb *lernen* in this (Jewish) context does have an object, but this (grammatical) object cannot be objectified, partly because it cannot be named. In *Geschichte einer Freundschaft*, Scholem defines the 'object' of the *Lehre* not as 'den wahren Stand und Weg des Menschen in der Welt', but as 'den transkausalen Zusammenhang der Dinge und ihr Verfaßtsein in Gott'.[8] The *Lehre*, in other words, does not communicate information, it reveals ideas. *Lernen* and *lehren*, the same 'Ringen des Denken der Lehre' which Benjamin detected in the writings of Kant, refer to an activity which will reveal truth, a truth which is not sought but granted. The metaphor which is often used in this context is that of a journey on which both teacher and pupil embark, and which would not necessarily lead them to where they thought they were going.[9] Nevertheless, if teacher and pupils were ready for it, once they had cultivated, in the words of Molitor, 'jenen wahren, hehren Ernst, jene Gründlichkeit und reine, innere Liebe für seinen Gegenstand' (*M* I, 7), their *Umwege* through the text would lead them to a revelation, in the same way as the three sons learned of the blessings of toil on their quest for easy money.

In the same letter to Scholem, Benjamin gives an uncharacteristically precise and very eloquent definition of the terms *Lehre*, education and tradition, and how these relate to one another. The words and images he uses are quite poignant in our present context, hence it seems well worth quoting the passage in full:

Ich bin überzeugt: die Tradition ist das Medium in dem sich *kontinuierlich* der Lernende in den Lehrenden verwandelt und das im ganzen Umfang der Erziehung. In der Tradition sind alle Erziehende und zu Erziehende und alles ist Erziehung. Symbolisiert und zusammengefaßt werden diese Verhältnisse in der Entwicklung der Lehre. Wer nicht gelernt hat kann nicht erziehen denn er sieht nicht an welcher Stelle er einsam ist, wo er also auf seine Weise die Tradition umfaßt und lehrend mitteilbar macht. Wer sein Wissen als überliefertes begriffen hat in dem allein wird es überlieferbar, er wird in unerhörter Weise frei. Hier denke ich mir den metaphysischen Ursprung des talmudischen Witzes. Die Lehre ist wie ein wogendes Meer, für die Welle aber (wenn wir sie als Bild des Menschen nehmen) kommt alles darauf an sich seiner Bewegung so hinzugeben, daß sie bis zum Kamm wächst und herüberstürzt mit Schäumen. Diese ungeheure Freiheit des Übersturzes ist die Erziehung, im eigentlichen: Der Unterricht, das Sichtbar- und *frei* werden der Tradition: ihr Überstürzen aus lebendiger Fülle. Es ist so schwer über Erziehung zu reden weil deren Ordnung mit der Religiösen Ordnung der Tradition ganz zusammenfällt. Erziehen ist nur (im Geiste) die Lehre bereichern; nur wer gelernt hat kann das: darum ist es unmöglich für die Kommenden anders als Lernend zu leben. Die Nachkommen sind aus dem Geist Gottes (Menschen), sie steigen aus der Bewegung des Geistes wie Wellen auf. Unterricht ist der eine einzige Punkt der freien Vereinigung der ältern mit der jüngern Generation, wie Wellen die im Ineinandergehen den Schaumkamm werfen.

Jeder Irrtum in der Erziehung geht darauf zurück daß man in irgend einem letzten Sinne unsere nachkommen von *uns* abhängig denkt. Sie sind von uns nicht anders abhängig als von Gott und der Sprache in die wir uns daher um irgend einer Gemeinsamkeit mit unsern Kindern willen versenken müssen. (*GB* I, 382–383; Benjamin's emphasis)[10]

Erinnerung ist ein Bad

This letter is one of the first times after writing *Über Sprache* that Benjamin again uses the term *Medium*, this time referring to tradition or the unfolding of the *Lehre*. He defined the concept of *Medium* before in the context of language as the medium of its own communication: language, so to speak, as a 'Sich-Darstellendes', which already elevates it to a privileged position.[11] He went on to qualify this existence of language as a medium, *das Mediale*, as both *unmittelbar* and *unendlich*, or immediate and infinite. Tradition, he now says, is the medium of *Erziehung*, education, and it would therefore follow that the sphere of education is also *unmittelbar* and *unendlich*. Since tradition is a medium, in other words, it is not restricted by the constraints of a passing, linear time. Everything that is part of tradition remains as new, as alive and as accessible to us as on the day it was first written or said. This doctrine actually has its precedent or counterpart in the Jewish tradition itself. Six months after receiving this letter, Scholem records the following note in his diary, in which he interprets a passage from B. *Pesahim* in the context of the medial nature of the *Lehre*: 'In der Thora gibt es kein Vorher und Nachher, בתורה אין מוקדם ומאוחר d.h. der Talmud kennt die *mediale* Natur der Lehre' (*TB* II, 151).[12]

The way Benjamin describes the individual's relationship with tradition supports this notion. Firstly, as we said before, because the *Lehre* is the sphere in which truth exists, there can be no intentionality in the quest for the true knowledge of tradition, neither on the part of the subject nor from the perspective of the object. As we mentioned before, the student of tradition must approach his object with a humble and open mind, empty and ready to accept the revealed truth of tradition. He must not, as many Jewish stories of *hybris* in the face of the divine make clear, confront tradition with an aggressive, predatory intention, eager for knowledge that may be of some benefit to him. For the true treasure of tradition will retreat from him, and more often than not, he will be punished, for it lies in the nature of truth, 'vor welcher auch das reinste Feuer des Suchens wie unter Wassern verlischt' (I, 216).[13] In other words, truth in the *Lehre* becomes immediately available, *unmittelbar*, insofar as it is not seen as a means to an end, *un-mittel-bar*.

But the immediacy, *Unmittelbarkeit*, also refers to the fact that truth within tradition assumes the form of revelation, which, by definition, cannot be mediated. The light of revelation must shine *through* the prophet, as it does in the case of Moses, so the word of God may reach the faithful in an unadulterated form, or, better still, the prophet must *be* the word of God, as in the case of Jesus, the Λóγος incarnated. The term *Erleuchtung*, illumination, which Benjamin uses with reference to both religious and profane experiences, illustrates the fact that he conceives of this experience as immediate and unmediated. This is why, in the *Passagen-Werk*, Benjamin feels himself drawn to the receptive immediacy of the dream, which is one of the profane counterparts of the theological concept of *Erleuchtung*. As he writes in a note on the figure of the collector:

Im Grunde lebt der Sammler, so darf man sagen, ein Stück Traumleben. Denn auch im Traum ist der Rhythmus des Wahrnehmens und Erlebens derart verändert, daß alles – auch das scheinbar Neutralste – uns zustößt, uns betrifft. Um die Passagen aus dem Grunde zu verstehen, versenken wir uns in die tiefste Traumschicht, reden von ihnen so als wären sie uns zugestoßen. (V, 272)[14]

However, this immediacy can take a rather less mystical form than its name may suggest. The parable of the old man and his three sons is a good example of this, as its 'lesson' is revealed to the three sons in a flash of insight, a very ironic *Aha-Erlebnis* so to speak, as they come across a truth when they were actually looking for something entirely different. Significantly, however, they were in the ritual 'Kreis des Handwerks', performing manual labour which, according to Benjamin, is the sphere of distracted learning, allowing experiences to sink into their consciousness and take root. As Benjamin's metaphor of the sea and the waves makes clear, the individual must abandon himself to the movement of the infinite sea of tradition – this movement is the *Gedankenbewegung* which we have called study – and only then does tradition become wholly visible and wholly free. This is the second characteristic of tradition as a medium: its infinity. Strictly speaking, it is impossible for a finite being to encompass an infinite entity, yet that is exactly what happens in Benjamin's description of tradition. This, with a characteristically Benjaminian and also characteristically Jewish turn of thought, is essentially a paradox, a juxtaposition of opposites which is not resolved in a dialectical *Aufhebung*, but is instead kept in suspension. This suspension can be construed as the conceptual or philosophical equivalent of a leap of faith. In *Über das Programm*, a text whose self-confessed aim is to elaborate and extend the Kantian concept of experience so that it will be able to accommodate and explain religious experience,[15] Benjamin attempts to systematise the juxtaposition and suspension of opposites in the concept of non-synthesis, which is to be added to the Kantian paradigm: 'Jedoch wird außer dem Begriff der Synthesis auch der einer gewissen Nicht-Synthesis zweier Begriffe in einem andern systematisch höchst wichtig werden, da außer der Synthesis noch eine andere Relation zwischen Thesis und Antithesis möglich ist.' (II, 166).

The true import of the paradoxical confrontation of a finite human experience with an infinite tradition lies in Benjamin's statement that he who has understood his knowledge as *überliefert* becomes 'in unerhörter Weise frei'. This must seem like quite a counterintuitive qualification, for how can anybody who is carrying the whole weight of the Jewish tradition, with every single one of its legal complexities, be 'free as never before'? The opposite rather seems to be true, the individual appears to be bound hand and foot by an unsurveyable quantity of legal and religious requirements. This anxiety is expressed in those famous words of Micha Joseph Berdyczewski which we quoted in the first chapter: 'Our eyes are not our own, our dreams and our thoughts are not our own, our will is not the one implanted in us; everything we were taught long ago, everything has been handed down to us.' Yet the freedom of which Benjamin speaks is intimately linked to the infinity of tradition becoming *sichtbar*, visible. There is a way in which the finite individual can encompass an infinite tradition, namely by becoming part of it. By entering into the sphere of the *Lehre*, the individual 'umfaßt die Tradition auf seine Weise' and makes it 'lehrend mitteilbar'. It is the initial humility in the face of the Law or the *Lehre* which makes a liberated light-heartedness possible. As Benjamin said in the letter quoted above: 'Hier denke ich mich den metaphysischen Ursprung des talmudischen Witzes' (*GB* I, 382).[16]

The talmudic joke indeed has its origin in the unmediated confrontation of the sacred and the profane, of a finite humanity and an infinite divinity, which can make the former seem momentarily divine and the latter seem almost human, exemplified by an ironically smiling God in the tractate *Baba Meziah* when the rabbis use his own law against him: 'He laughed and said "my children have overcome me!"' (59b). This paradoxical, potentially subversive combination of the sacred and the profane that is the irreverent talmudic joke is the precursor of Benjamin's abovementioned concept of *profane Erleuchtung*, which is an inversion of its talmudic counterpart. Whereas the talmudic joke uses a profane concept to achieve sacred ends, *profane Erleuchtung* uses theological concepts to achieve profane ends. This is voiced very clearly in the *Haschisch-Protokolle*, in which Benjamin describes his experiences under the influence of hashish in terms of a changed attitude towards time and space, and more particularly towards eternity, which is no longer perceived to be quite as daunting: 'Nun kommen die Zeit- und Raumansprüche zur Geltung, die der Haschischesser macht. Die sind ja bekanntlich absolut königlich. Versailles ist dem, der Haschisch gegessen hat, nicht zu groß, und die Ewigkeit dauert ihm nicht zu lange.' (IV, 410).[17] The initial, perhaps instinctive humility of 'der winzige, gebrechliche Menschenkörper' (II, 439) in the face of an unforgiving eternity has turned into a knowing lightheartedness which 'auf seine Weise die Tradition umfaßt und lehrend mitteilbar macht'. The fact that Benjamin did indeed see these profane effects of intoxication from an explicitly theological perspective becomes abundantly clear in the 1929 essay *Der Sürrealismus*, in which he writes:

> Die wahre, schöpferische Überwindung religiöser Erleuchtung aber liegt nun wahrhaftig nicht bei den Rauschgiften. Sie liegt in einer *profanen Erleuchtung*, einer materialistischen, anthropologischen Inspiration, zu der Haschisch, Opium und was immer sonst die Vorschule abgeben können. (Aber eine gefährliche. Und die der Religionen ist strenger.) (II, 297)

It is obvious that Benjamin saw a great structural affinity between religious education, study or *Erziehung*, and the nature of experience under the influence of intoxicating substances. A careful analysis of these structural affinities in fact reveals something which Benjamin had hitherto confined to 'dunkeln Bildern und geheimnisvollen Winken', namely how he conceives both of the sphere of tradition and the state of intoxication. The long passage from the letter which we quoted above contains another pointer in this direction. Benjamin says that in order for the older generation to educate itself as it is educating its children, it must immerse itself in God and language, in other words revelation and tradition: '[zu] Gott und der Sprache in die wir uns daher um irgend einer Gemeinsamkeit mit unsern Kindern willen versenken müssen'. The crucial term here is *Versenkung*, which is usually translated as contemplation or absorption and which represents the causative-egressive aspect of the German word *sinken*, to sink. Thus it continues an almost fluid metaphor of immersion or submersion, a very synaesthetic form of perception which brings together both subject and object in a single, all-encompassing sphere. Nor is this metaphor limited to only one 'stage' in Benjamin's intellectual development, whether this should be the so-called 'theological' *Frühschriften* or the allegedly marxist–materialist *Spätwerk*. On the contrary, if we survey the whole of Benjamin's work, we find that this metaphor keeps recurring in different guises and permutations, yet it always remains manifestly and probably intentionally recognisable. If Benjamin does indeed have his own esoteric doctrine, this concept of the fluid medium of language, experience, truth and tradition may in fact be it.

In *Ursprung des deutschen Trauerspiels*, for example, the seminal description of truth as 'ein aus Ideen gebildetes intentionsloses Sein' is followed by this admonition: 'Das ihr gemäße Verhalten ist demnach nicht ein Meinen im Erkennen, sondern ein in sie Eingehen und Verschwinden.' (I, 216). This 'Eingehen und Verschwinden' is a more abstract version of the immersion metaphor, but it is nevertheless eminently recognisable as such. In this epistemology, the subject does not remain a discreet entity, but voluntarily immerses himself within truth, and appears even to become part of its sphere. A more literal and more liquid example can be found in the letter to Scholem quoted above, where Benjamin refers to the 'wogendes Meer' of tradition to which man, represented as an individual wave, is to abandon himself:

> [...] für die Welle aber (wenn wir sie als Bild des Menschen nehmen) kommt alles darauf an sich seiner Bewegung so hinzugeben, daß sie bis zum Kamm wächst und herüberstürzt mit Schäumen. Diese ungeheure Freiheit des Übersturzes ist die Erziehung, im eigentlichen: Der Unterricht, das Sichtbar- und *frei* werden der Tradition: ihr Überstürzen aus lebendiger Fülle. (*GB* I, 382)

Again, we see the same recurring characteristics of this privileged form of experience or knowledge: tradition is an awe-inspiring, viscous whole, and the disappearance of the subject within it serves as the consommation of his initiation into its mystical doctrine, if we may be allowed the use of this rather ambiguous term. This passage is particularly thought-provoking, because here Benjamin links the 'aqueous' form of experience very explicitly to the Jewish tradition. It constitutes one of his first revelations of the doctrine of *profane Erleuchtung*, which is yet to become entirely profane, at least on the surface level. Throughout his work, Benjamin shows a very keen awareness of the *Unzeitgemäßheit* of explicitly theological language to the modern mind, which is partly why the concept of *Erleuchtung* undergoes a strategic profanisation. However, it would be wrong to assume that the concept of *profane Erleuchtung* is only secular for strategic reasons, or that its innermost essence somehow remains exclusively theological. As with so many of Benjamin's ideas, the concept of *profane Erleuchtung* derives its power from the intentionally unresolved juxtaposition of opposites, the suspended paradox, lending the concept a certain dynamism which is paradoxically absent from a traditional dialectic. The development of *Profane Erleuchtung* takes place predominantly in the *Haschisch-Protokolle* and in the long gestation process that resulted in the vast compendium of quotes we now know as the *Passagen-Werk*. In his writings on intoxication, the metaphors of water, sea and waves are quite prominent. As Egon Wissing, one of the doctors attending to Benjamin during his experiments, wrote in his notes: 'Das Wasser beherrscht die Bildwelt weiter, die Vorstellung des Meeres, die bei den Wellen zu Grunde lag, tritt aber nunhmehr gegen die von Strömen zurück' (VI, 594). In the same *Versuchsprotokoll*, he recorded one apodictic statement which reveals the full extent of the connection which existed in Benjamin's mind between religious and intoxicated experience, a statement which again unites the Jewish concept of tradition, as a labour of remembrance, with a very physical concept of immersion as the essence of the experience of intoxication: 'Erinnerung ist ein Bad' (VI, 596).[18] This short *Lehrsatz*, written about ten years after *Über Sprache* and *Über das Programm*, shows a remarkable continuity in Benjamin's thought and at the same time summarises the basic intention of the project which would occupy most of his time until his death in 1940, the *Passagen-Werk*.

The unpublished *Protokolle zu Drogenversuchen*, which can be found in volume six of the *Gesammelte Schriften*, have always been read, if at all, as a quaint anomaly, a mystifying dead end in Benjamin's *oeuvre*, unconnected to any of his main works and altogether unworthy of scholarly attention.[19] As was the case with

182

Molitor, this unwillingness yet again bears witness to an inexcusable academic myopia, not only because certain fragments from the *Protokolle* found their way into the notes for the *Passagen-Werk*,[20] but also because Benjamin himself explicitly states that these *Protokolle* are very closely related to his philosophical writings, as he says in a letter to Scholem dated 30 January 1928:

> [...] ich [bin] nun schon zweimal in die Bezirke des Haschisch eingegangen [...]. Die Aufzeichnungen, die ich teils selbständig, teils im Anschluß an die Versuchsprotokolle darüber gemacht habe, dürften einen sehr lesenswerten Anhang zu meinen philosophischen Notizen geben, mit denen sie, und z.T. sogar die Erfahrungen im Rausch, die engsten Beziehungen haben. Diese Nachricht aber möchte ich im Schoß der Familie Scholem beschlossen wissen. (*GB* III, 324)

More than ten years after *Über Sprache*, Benjamin again places an esoteric text at, or at least very near, the centre of his thoughts, admonishing Scholem not to tell anyone of the existence of the *Protokolle*. In the same letter, he mentions another text which never saw the light of day, 'den äußerst prekären Versuch "Pariser Passagen. Eine dialektische Feerie"', which he is hoping to finish within the next few weeks, and about which Benjamin is reluctant to reveal anything as yet: 'Verraten kann ich dich im übrigen von dieser Sache nocht nichts, habe noch nicht einmal genaue Vorstellungen vom Umfang' (*GB* III, 322–323).[21] This time, however, Benjamin's secretiveness has surpassed itself: more than four years later, the *Haschisch-Protokolle* are still subject to a *Schweigegebot*. In a letter to Scholem of 26 July 1932, in which he writes about his four 'major unfinished works', Benjamin again mentions his experiments with intoxication, again names them as one of the focal points of his thought, and again swears Scholem to silence: 'Es sind die "Pariser Passagen", die "Gesammelten Essays zur Literatur", die "Briefe" und ein höchst bedeutsames Buch über das Haschisch. Von diesem letztern Thema weiß niemand und es soll vorläufig unter uns bleiben.' (*GB* IV, 113).[22]

In the context of Benjamin's preoccupation with the epistemological notion of tradition as an almost physical form of immersion, it is hardly surprising that he felt himself drawn to the concept of intoxication. In the drug-induced *Rausch*, he found the empirical counterpart, so to speak, to his intuitive philosophical speculations. Here, he could experiment with the notion of *Versunkenheit* first hand, and especially the first few *Haschischversuche* frequently talk about different forms of immersion, physical and otherwise, as well as of the consequences of finding oneself 'tiefer drinnen'.[23] One of his more remarkable impressions, which would become a crucial part of Benjamin's perspective on the Parisian arcades, finding itself reiterated in different guises throughout the notes, is the aversion the subject begins to cultivate for the very thought of the 'outside': 'Vielleicht ist es keine Selbsttäuschung zu sagen, daß man in diesem Zustand eine Abneigung gegen den freien sozusagen uranischen Luftraum bekommt, der den Gedanken des "Draußen" beinah zur Qual werden läßt.' (VI, 561).[24] Furthermore, like the viscous sphere of tradition before it, this *Versunkenheit* into the sphere of intoxication is given a privileged epistemological status, as unexpected connections and correspondences reveal themselves within this sphere. These correspondences, however, are sometimes ghostly and macabre, and the sphere of intoxication as well as the atmosphere of the arcades with which it becomes associated, is something of a *tremendum fascinans* to Benjamin, exuding an almost literally haunting influence over the last years of his work. The passage quoted above continues:

> Es ist nicht mehr, wie voriges Mal das freundliche gesellige Verweilen im Raum aus Freude an der Situation wie sie ist sondern ein dichtes sich eingewebt sich eingesponnen haben, ein Spinnennetz in dem das Weltgeschehen verstreut wie ausgesogene Insektenleiber herumhängt. Von dieser Höhle will man sich nicht trennen. Hier bilden sich auch Rudimente eines unfreundlichen Verhaltens gegen die Anwesenden, Angst, daß sie einen zerstören, herauszerren könnten. (VI, 561)[25]

Die Höhlentiefe ihrer Passagen…

In November 1938, when the *Passagen-Werk* had been occupying Benjamin's mind for more than ten years without its end being even remotely in sight, Adorno expressed his concern that it might never see the light of day and wrote, quoting the words of his wife: 'Gretel hat einmal im Scherz gesagt, daß sie die Höhlentiefe ihrer Passagen bewohnten, und darum vorm Abschluß der Arbeit zurückschreckten, weil sie fürchteten, den Bau dann verlassen zu müssen.'[26] A few months earlier, Gretel Adorno herself had written to Benjamin: 'Ich habe nur die Befürchtung, daß es Dir in den Passagen so gut gefällt, daß Du Dich von diesem Prachtbau gar nicht mehr trennen willst, […].'.[27] What is particularly interesting about these letters is the fact that Gretel Adorno – and possibly her husband – actually knew of Benjamin's experiments with hashish, and that they therefore might have been referring implicitly, but directly, to his *Haschisch-Protokolle*. It is certainly thought-provoking that a combination of both Gretel's and Theodor's sentences all but yields a carbon copy of Benjamin's original sentence: 'Von diese[r] Höhle[ntiefe] willst du dich [gar] nicht mehr trennen.'[28] But there is more to suggest that the mystifying *Protokolle zu Drogenversuchen* and the no less mysterious *Passagen-Werk* share a common logic, and that this logic in its turn has the same basic characteristics that Benjamin attributed to the concept of tradition. In the early notes for the *Passagen-Werk*, made at the same time as the early *Protokolle*, the immersion metaphor we mentioned before recurs several times. In one of these notes, it is extremely explicit and quite revealing, as Benjamin writes: 'Motiv der Traumzeit: Atmosphäre der Aquarien. Wasser Widerstand verlangsamend?'[29] and another note reads: 'Erdatmosphäre als unterseeisch' (V, 1031).[30] Benjamin saw the antiquated Parisian arcades as the allegory of the nineteenth century: in the ruins of the arcades, all the dreams, expectations and aspirations of the collective unconscious still lingered, and the historian had to immerse himself, as well as his object, into this dream atmosphere to bring out the truth about both the recent past and the present: 'Um die Passagen aus dem Grunde zu verstehen, versenken wir sie in die tiefste Traumschicht […]' (V, 1009).[31]

Benjamin's 'Motiv der Traumzeit' is an ambiguous one. On the positive side, it refers to the abovementioned utopian expectations of every era, on the negative side, the motif of the dream refers to the numbness of the collective in capitalism, a state of anaesthesia brought about and symbolised by the magical spectacle of the commodity, the *Phantasmagorie der Ware*. In this particular collective dream, the capitalist system manages to present itself as a natural phenomenon rather than an artificial construction, lulling the people into an inert and unquestioning sense of acceptance, *ennui* or *Langeweile*.[32] One of Benjamin's intentions with the *Passagen-Werk* is to attempt to wake the collective from its dream, exposing it to the reality of its condition. Exactly how this awakening was meant to be brought about remains a mystery, and it is quite possible that Benjamin himself, at the time of his death, did not yet have a clear idea of how to bring together the very disparate elements needed for such a conceptual *tour de force*.[33] What is clear, however, is that Benjamin was obviously convinced that the *Traumdeutung* of the *Passagen-Werk* would tap into the power of remembrance that lay concealed within tradition, turning it into a profane force that could be used for utopian ends:

> Das Erwachen als ein stufenweiser Prozeß, der im Leben des Einzelnen wie der Generation sich durchsetzt. Schlaf deren Primärstadium. Die Jugenderfahrung einer Generation hat viel gemein mit der Traumerfahrung. Ihre geschichtliche Gestalt ist Traumgestalt. Jede Epoche hat diese Träumen zugewandte Seite, die Kinderseite. Für das vorige Jahrhundert sind es die Passagen. Während aber die Erziehung voriger Generationen in der Tradition, der religiösen Unterweisung, ihnen diese Träume gedeutet hat, läuft heutige Erziehung einfach auf die 'Zerstreuung' der Kinder hinaus. Was hier im folgenden gegeben wird, ist ein Versuch zur Technik des Erwachens. Die dialektische, die kopernikanische Wendung des Eingedenkens (Bloch). (V, 1006)

This 'kopernikanische Wendung des Eingedenkens', a profanisation of the Jewish concept of remembrance, is the form of profane illumination proposed in the *Passagen-Werk*: the moment of awakening as the shock of recognition fused with alienation. It is partly this sudden flash of insight, provoked by a careful, strategic circumnarration of the object – the nineteenth century as epitomised in the Parisian arcades – which is the particularly theological component of this strategy. True to its theological form, the truth about this recent past

186

cannot be stated, it must be revealed. As Benjamin so famously wrote in *Konvolut N*: 'Ich habe nichts zu sagen. Nur zu zeigen' (V, 574). This perspective on the nature of historical truth is a direct descendant of Benjamin's *Lehre* about the nature of philosophical truth, or truth as such, which we discussed above. Not only is this epistemological perspective, as we have shown, a fundamentally theological one, it also continues to play a crucial and central role in Benjamin's thought up to the very end. In one of the notes for *Über den Begriff der Geschichte*, probably composed no earlier than 1939, he writes:

> Das wahre Bild der Vergangenheit *huscht* vorbei. Nur als Bild, das auf Nimmerwiedersehn im Moment seiner Erkennbarkeit eben aufblitzt, ist die Vergangenheit festzuhalten. Seiner Flüchtigkeit dankt es, wenn es authentisch ist. In ihr besteht seine einzige Chance. Eben weil diese Wahrheit vergänglich ist und ein Hauch sie darinrafft, hängt viel an ihr. (I, 1247)[34]

It is quite rare for Benjamin to write about the nature of truth in such explicit terms, which is possibly why the last three sentences did not make it into the 'final' version of *Über den Begriff der Geschichte*. As we have shown, he tends to reveal his hidden doctrine, sometimes even to his closest friends, only once every ten years. In 1916–1918, he had done so in *Über Sprache* and *Über das Programm*, in 1925, the doctrine was restated in *Ursprung des deutschen Trauerspiels*, and in 1939, it finds its way, quite emphatically, into *Über den Begriff der Geschichte*. What we have in between these dates and texts are usually the by now quite familiar 'dunkle Bilder und geheimnisvolle Winken', which can be found throughout the massive collection of notes for the *Passagen-Werk*, like so many 'schlechte Stichen' which weave together its quotations (VI, 596). But there is one more *locus classicus* of Benjamin's epistemological *Lehre*, and one that has remained undiscovered for quite a long time. In the second *Haschisch-Impression*, from which we have already quoted several passages, Benjamin writes:

> Was aber unser eigenes Abgleiten, Abspringen vom Gesprächsgegenstand angeht, so sieht das Gefühl, das der physischen Kontaktunterbrechung entspricht, etwa so aus: wovon wir gerade zu sprechen vorhaben, das lockt uns unendlich; was uns intentional vorschwebt, danach breiten wir liebend die Arme aus. Kaum haben wir es berührt, so enttäuscht es uns gänzlich: der Gegenstand

unserer Aufmerksamkeit welkt unter der Berührung der Sprache plötzlich hin. (VI, 564)

This emphasises yet again Benjamin's by now well-documented aversion towards the direct statement, and his conviction that it is both philosophically and methodologically unfruitful. It also highlights the connection which continued to exist in Benjamin's thought between the concepts of revelation, tradition and intoxication, and their shared claim to speak, or rather to *be*, in truth. The pattern behind Benjamin's description of the object of his fascination which whithers away the very instant he starts to describe it, or literally the very instant language touches it, is reminiscent of his earlier descriptions of truth as a revelation. Yet this time, it is not the inquisitive individual who collapses and dies in the face of revelation, as in Schiller's poem, it is the object of revelation itself which escapes us the moment we seek to own it. Although the pattern is indeed reversed, the logic or the *Lehre* behind it remains fundamentally the same: knowledge is a having, but truth is a being.

Shunning the direct dogmatic statement in the same way, the *Passagen-Werk* intends to illuminate through the most eminently Jewish methods of tradition, the methods which in fact constitute the construction and the corpus of tradition: quotation and commentary. *Konvolut N*, subtitled *Erkenntnistheoretisches, Theorie des Fortschritts*, leaves little doubt about the role of this traditional, theological method for the *Passagen-Werk*. Its form was to be a commentary on the nineteenth century, a transposition of the Talmudic methodology to reality: 'Sich immer wieder klarmachen, wie der Kommentar zu einer Wirklichkeit (denn es handelt sich um den Kommentar, Ausdeutung in den Einzelheiten) eine ganz andere Methode verlangt als der zu einem Text. In einem Fall ist Theologie, im andern Philologie die Grundwissenschaft' (V, 574). What this commentary on reality was meant to reveal exactly, as we said before, is not entirely clear, but at the end of this final chapter, we can propose a tentative hypothesis. A central, recurring theme in the *Protokolle zu Drogenversuchen* is the so-called *Kolportagephänomen*, a concept about which even the first word remains to be said.[35] At first sight, it is anything but obvious what cheap, popular or even trashy fiction, sold

188

door to door, might have in common with the Jewish tradition and profane illumination. Yet in the second *Protokoll*, Benjamin describes the phenomenon as follows:

Auf das Kolportagephänomen des Raumes zurückzukommen: es wird simultan die Möglichkeit aller potentiell in diesem Raume etwa geschehnen Dinge wahrgenommen. Der Raum blinzelt einen an: Nun, was mag hier mir wohl zugetragen haben? Zusammenhang dieses Phänomens mit der Kolportage. Kolportage und Unterschrift. So vorzustellen: man denke sich einen kitschigen Öldruck an der Wand und im unteren Teile des Rahmens einen länglichen Streifen herausgeschnitten. Durch die untere Leiste liefe ein Band und nun erschienen in dem Spalt Unterschriften die einander ablösten: 'Ermordung Egmonts', 'Kaiserkrönung Karls des Großen' etc. [...] Zusammenhang der Kolportage-Intention mit den tiefsten theologischen. Sie spiegeln sich getrübt wieder, versetzen in den Raum der Kontemplation, was nur im Raume des tätigen Lebens gilt. Nämlich: daß die Welt immer wieder dieselbe sei (daß alles Geschehen im gleichen Raume sich hätte abspielen können). Das ist im Theoretischen trotz allem eine müde, welke Wahrheit (trotz aller scharfen Sicht, die darin steckt) aufs höchste aber bestätigt sie sich im Dasein des Frommen, dem wie hier der Raum der Phantasie zu allem *Gewesenen*, so alle Dinge zum *Besten* dienen. So tief ist Theologisches hier in den Bereich der Kolportage gesunken. (VI, 565–566)[36]

The crux of this passage is the word *simultan*. All the events which potentially might have taken place in this space – the word *Raum* means more than just room – are perceived simultaneously. This form of simultaneity, which we discussed extensively in the first chapter, is one of the most fundamental characteristics of the Jewish tradition, with its insistent, almost stubborn tendency to keep a record of minority decisions, to accumulate interpretations and to immerse itself in the text, revealing correspondences between its seemingly most disparate aspects. As David Stern summarised it:

a fundamental tendency of midrash [is] the urge to unite the diverse parts of Scripture into a single and seamless whole reflecting the unity of God's will. This tendency derives directly from the rabbinic ideology of the canonical Torah – Pentateuch, Prophets and Writings – as the inspired word of God, a timeless unity in which *each and every verse is simultaneous with every other, temporally and semantically*; as a result, every verse, no matter how remote, can be seen as a possible source for illuminating the meaning of any other verse.[37]

Benjamin's fusion of this high theological motif with the extreme banality of *Kolportage* – 'So tief ist Theologisches hier in den Bereich der Kolportage gesunken' – is the quintessence, *der Inbegriff*, of profane illumination. The *Kolportagephänomen* defies the limitations of both time and space, transporting the canonical highpoints of history into the present-day banality of a bourgeois sitting room, familiarising the former and defamiliarising the latter. It is probably the escapist or even utopian function of the *Trivialliteratur* peddled from door to door in which Benjamin saw the greatest potential, as it contains a transformation of the desire for a better world, whether this should be in the past or in the future, to which the *Passagen-Werk* sought to appeal. Much like the Jewish tradition, this phenomenon does not so much refuse to acknowledge the linearity of history, as refuse to accept the unidirectionality of this linearity. In the space of the Talmud, as we have seen, prophets as well as ordinary rabbis can move back and forth in history, intervening in discussions, supporting a ruling, serving as an intermediary between the divine and the human, or even providing some light relief. Most importantly, however, when a past occurrence is inserted in such a way in a present-day discussion, it honours and redeems the decision of the majority as well as the opinion of the individual. A prime example of this is the passage from *Baba Meziah*, which we quoted in the first chapter and mentioned again in this chapter to illustrate the concept of the Talmudic joke. Disputing whether a particular oven should be considered clean or unclean, Rabbi Eliezer finds himself in a minority position against all the other sages. In his exasperation, he calls for a number of miracles to occur to prove him right:

> Again he urged: 'If the *halachah* agrees with me, let the walls of the school-house prove it', whereupon the walls inclined to fall. But R. Joshua rebuked them, saying: 'When scholars are engaged in a *halachic* dispute, what have ye to interfere?' Hence they did not fall, in honour of R. Joshua, nor did they resume the upright, in honour of R. Eliezer; and they are still standing thus inclined. (B. *Baba Meziah*, 59b)

The seemingly precarious state of suspension of the walls, which, according to the Talmud, has nevertheless lasted until this day, may serve as an allegory of the particular form of the suspension of judgement in the Jewish tradition, where the observance of the *Halakhah* is accompanied by the remembrance of the fruits of *Talmud Torah* (and of course the remembrance of past injustice, as in the *Pesach Haggadah*). It is this twin perspective, which acknowledges that history may be a *fait accompli* to a certain extent, but refuses to accept that it cannot be counterbalanced in the act of remembrance, which lies at the very basis of Benjamin's elusive *Kolportagephänomen*, and indeed the project of the *Passagen-Werk*. Benjamin referred to this phenomenon as the *Unabgeschlossenheit der Geschichte*, the refusal to approach history with the maxim 'look, but don't touch!'[38] The concept of remembrance *does* touch historical events, lifting them out of the continuity of history and holding them up as a mirror to the present and future. This is the theological element which Benjamin imported into his philosophy of history, convinced that history could not be understood properly in any other sense. It is also one of the main points on which some members of the *Institut für Sozialforschung*, with which Benjamin was always loosely affiliated, begged to differ.

In a letter dated 16 March 1937, Max Horkheimer wrote an elaborate commentary on Benjamin's major essay on the collector, *Eduard Fuchs: Sammler und Historiker*, in which Benjamin had written about the task of historical materialism, characterising its outlook with the phrase: 'Das Werk der Vergangenheit ist ihm nicht abgeschlossen.' (II, 477). Horkheimer confessed that he could not see how such a concept was viable: 'Das vergangene Unrecht ist geschehen und abgeschlossen. Die Erschlagenen sind wirklich erschlagen. Letzten Endes ist Ihre Aussage theologisch. Nimmt man die Unabgeschlossenheit ganz ernst, so muß man an das jüngste Gericht glauben.' (*GB* V, 495). Benjamin responded to this letter twice. He sent one answer to Horkheimer himself, in which he explains in conspicuously secularised terms what the ramifications of the *Unabgeschlossenheit der Geschichte* might be. Benjamin's response is again quite characteristically, if covertly, Jewish. Admitting that there is a certain finality to defeat, he maintains that it is after all not the dead who should remember, but that it is the responsibility of the survivors to honour their obligation towards the past by remembering that they have a place in history only because others have not. The vanquished, Benjamin maintains, may have lost the war, but they did not and should not lose their history:

> Sehr bedeutsam ist für mich Ihr Exkurs über das abgeschlossene oder aber offene Werk der Vergangenheit. Ich glaube ihn durchaus zu verstehen, und irre ich mich nicht, so kommuniziert Ihr Gedanke mit einer Überlegung, die mich öfter beschäftigt hat. Mir ist immer die Frage wichtig gewesen, wie die merkwürdige Sprachfigur zu verstehen sei: einen Krieg, einen Prozeß *verlieren*. Der Krieg, der Prozeß sind ja doch nicht der Einsatz sondern der Akt der Entscheidung über denselben. Ich habe mir das zuletzt so zurechtgelegt: wer den Krieg, den Prozeß verliert, für den ist das in dieser Auseinandersetzung umfaßte Geschehen wirklich abgeschlossen und somit *seiner Praxis* verloren; für den Partner, der gewonnen hat, ist das nicht der Fall. Der Sieg trägt seine Früchte ganz anders als die Niederlage die Folgen einheimst. (*GB* V, 486–487)

A second response, however, Benjamin reserved for his most esoteric collection of notes, the theoretical foundation of the *Passagen-Werk* now known as *Konvolut N: Erkenntnis-kritisches, Theorie des Fortschritts*. In this particular section of the *Passagen* manuscript, Benjamin is often uncharacteristically direct and explicit about the philosophy and the methodology underlying his work, as he was in *Über Sprache*. For this reason alone we may safely asume that, no matter what the finished article would have looked like, the notes in *Konvolut N* would not have retained their exceptional immediacy. In one of these notes, which also answers Horkheimer's question, Benjamin does not seek to conceal the fact that his work is theologically inspired. On the contrary, this is one of those extremely rare moments when Benjamin makes the extent of this theological inspiration very, and very bluntly explicit. But, perhaps even more crucially, Benjamin counters Horkheimer's reservations, not with a (superficially) secularised version of his *Geschichtsphilosophie*, but with a reflection on the strategic concealment of theology, the necessity of which he considers to be as compelling as the necessity of theology as such in order to understand history:

192

Das Korrektiv dieser [Horkheimer's] Gedankengänge liegt in der Überlegung, daß die Geschichte nicht allein eine Wissenschaft sondern nicht minder eine Form des Eingedenkens ist. Was die Wissenschaft 'festgestellt' hat, kann das Eingedenken modifizieren. Das Eingedenken kann das Unabgeschlossene (das Glück) zu einem Abgeschlossenen und das Abgeschlossene (das Leid) zu einem Unabgeschlossenen machen. Das ist Theologie; aber im Eingedenken machen wir eine Erfahrung, die uns verbietet, die Geschichte grundsätzlich atheologisch zu begreifen, so wenig wir sie in unmittelbar theologischen Begriffen zu schreiben versuchen dürfen. (V, 589)

This strategic consideration came to dominate Benjamin's thought during his last few years, as work on the *Passagen-Werk* slowed down to a crawl, his handwriting became increasingly miniaturised and his health gradually deteriorated. The crucial question no longer seemed to be *what* the message of the *Pariser Passagen* could be, but *how* his projected magnum opus was to proceed. As Benjamin eventually ran out of time, with the work not even approaching completion, he turned his attention towards another project, the manuscript of which he valued more than his own life.[39] This was the text now known as *Über den Begriff der Geschichte*, which incorporated some material from the *Passagen-Werk*, as well as several ideas from his essays on Kafka, Baudelaire and Eduard Fuchs. The text contains eighteen theses and two addenda, apodictic and parabolic statements circling around the concepts of history and historiography. They were no doubt intended both as an extremely condensed summary of the *Passagen-Werk*, which he already considered to be lost, and as a key to the aborted project, if ever it should be found again (which it was after the war, thanks to the efforts of Georges Bataille, then librarian of the *Bibliothèque Nationale* in Paris). The opening paragraph of *Über den Begriff der Geschichte* is, in its turn, the key to the elusive *Thesen* as well as the allegorical *Verschränkung* of Benjamin's method. This thesis, here in the first version, is Benjamin's final answer to the objection put forward by Horkheimer three years earlier:

Es lief bekanntlich eine zeitlang die Legende von einem Automaten um, der so wunderbar konstruiert sei, daß er auf jeden Zug eines Schachspielers von selbst mit dem richtigen Gegenzuge erwidere. Eine Puppe in türkischem Gewand, eine Wasserpfeife im Munde saß vor dem Brett, das auf einem Tisch ruhte. Ein

System von Spiegeln erweckte die Illusion, man könne durch diesen Tisch hindurchsehen. In Wahrheit saß ein buckliger Zwerg darinne[n], der ein Meister im Schachspiel war und die Hand der Puppe an Schnüren lenkte, wenn er den Gegenzug einmal gefunden hatte. Jeder der mit der Puppe sich messen wollte, konnte den leeren Sitz einnehmen, der ihr gegenüber errichtet war. Ich könnte mir ein pendant zu dieser Apparatur in der Philosophie umso leichter vorstellen, als der Streit um den wahren Begriff der Geschichte wohl in Gestalt einer Partie zwischen zwei Partnern sich denken läßt. Gewinnen soll, wenn es nach mir geht die Türkenpuppe, die bei den Philosophen Materialismus heißt. Sie kann es ohne weiteres mit jedem Gegner aufnehmen, wenn die Dienste der Theologie ihr gesichert sind, die heute ohnehin klein und häßlich ist und sich nirgends sehen lassen darf. (I, 1216)[40]

This opening image of Benjamin's last writings can be read as the opening to his entire work. It is his own condensed, miniaturised, monadological guide for the perplexed to his own work, a paradoxically direct oblique statement of the impossibility of the direct statement. It was as close as Benjamin came to the revelation of his *Lehre*, reluctantly and persistently suggestive to the last, as indicated by his further condensation of the first thesis. Ever the meticulous and keen stylist, Benjamin made a number of cosmetic improvements to the text as it was to appear in its last version, but he also left out the explicit reference to the 'Streit um den wahren Begriff der Geschichte' as well as every single use of the first person singular. Instead, the final version simply states that one could imagine the puppet having a 'Gegenstück in der Philosophie', which is followed by the very terse *Lehrsatz*: 'Gewinnen soll immer die Puppe, die man "historischen Materialismus" nennt.' (I, 693). One last time, in this dark image and with these secret hints, Benjamin brings together all the suggestions and allusions that we find throughout his work on truth, knowledge, history and tradition, and the rest is silence.

194

Urgrund und Inbegriff

As much as it may appear that he is trying to dissemble it himself, there is an overarching logic in Benjamin's intuitions regarding the concepts of tradition, knowledge and truth, or at least a certain continuity which cannot be overlooked, and which suggests that he is indeed trying to construct the 'reines systematisches Erfahrungs-kontinuum' (II, 164), which he feels to be the greatest potential or the greatest promise of the Kantian system. Throughout this chapter, and indeed throughout this entire book, we have been looking at how Benjamin's hidden assumptions, theories and hypotheses affect not only the content, but also the form of his thought, and we have come to the conclusion that their influence runs deep and that their – albeit distant – horizon exhibits Jewish family traits. Yet, like Benjamin, we have been skirting around the issue in a manner which is entirely appropriate. If we consider the characteristics which all these concepts share, the overarching logic, the Ἀρχή or the Λόγος, reveals itself as a parallel to the most strictly theological concept of all, and at the same time the most unnameable, which has sometimes been called God. The reason why our reluctance to address this subject directly is appropriate is not just because to do so would be a theological impos-sibility or philosophical hybris. That in itself never stopped anyone. The main reason is that for Benjamin too, in spite of all the implicit hints and references, God never played an explicit part. In the words of Albert Salomon, to Benjamin 'the throne of God was empty' (*SB* II, 261). This, however, does not mean that the idea or the concept of the divine is not of central importance to Benjamin, but it is only and emphatically as an absent centre that we find God in the middle of his work.

It is quite conspicuous that Benjamin never really defines the theological or metaphysical concepts he is working with in the trad-itional sense of the word *definition*. As Benjamin's answer to Hork-heimer's objection suggests, the *Feststellung* of a scientific mode of thinking is not entirely appropriate here. This is because the name of God and the true revelation which derives from it, even if they are merely used as a conceptual framework regardless of their confessional religious meaning, cannot be caught within the limits of a definition. To do so would be to demote them to the status of a 'mere' concept themselves, which is not necessarily the wrong thing to do, but which would make the power that the concepts of God, revelation and tradition undoubtedly have or have had impossible to harness. Yet this is exactly what Benjamin was after. In 1918, the very year *Über das Programm der kommenden Philosophie* was written, Scholem wrote a note in his diary much to the same effect: 'Die Lehre (תורה) kann nicht definiert, sie kann nur gelehrt werden. Die Lehre anders als in ihr selber definieren (was ja als Limes der Definition eben selbst keine mehr ist), heißt den entscheidendsten Irrtum im Bereich des Judentums begehen.' (*TB* II, 343).

For this very reason, Benjamin finds himself in the paradoxical position of seeking to draw on the idea of the divine and to channel the utopian hopes that it holds, but being unable to name it, lest it should dissolve and disappear. He often describes, or rather circumscribes, the concepts of tradition or *Lehre*, God, truth and language, but he never delimits them; more crucially still, he never sets them off against one another. Paraphrasing Benjamin's own remark on the absence of the name of God from Kafka's work, we might say: 'Wer nicht versteht, was […] den Gebrauch dieses Namens verbietet, versteht [da]von keine Zeile.' The reason for this, as we mentioned in the previous chapter, is that he sees these concepts in theological terms. As he states quite explicitly in *Ursprung des deutschen Trauerspiels*, Benjamin is convinced that it is impossible even to think the concept of truth without a 'wenn auch latenten Hinweis auf die Gegenstände der Theologie'.[41] This 'although latent reference' to theology will have its implications for the structure of Benjamin's thought, literally informing its most basic and fundamental tenets, yet remaining mysteriously concealed in its most profound depths. He described this double bind, which both demands the presence of theology and requires its concealment, in another famous passage from the *Passagen-Werk*: 'Mein Denken verhält sich zur Theologie wie das Löschblatt zur Tinte. Es ist ganz von ihr vollgesogen. Ginge es aber nach dem Löschblatt, so würde nichts was geschrieben ist, übrig bleiben.' (V, 588).

In *Über das Programm der kommenden Philosophie*, Benjamin says that it should be the task of a future philosophy to create a concept of perception or knowledge – *Erkenntnis* – which will make it possible to think the concept of God: 'Damit soll durchaus nicht gesagt sein daß die Erkenntnis Gott, wohl aber durchaus daß sie die Erfahrung und Lehre von ihm allererst ermöglicht.' (II, 164). This, as we said not long ago, is why God has not taken centre stage in this study. Benjamin was not primarily interested in God himself, but in the experience or the *Lehre* of God, and theology *stricto sensu* is exactly that: the doctrine of God.[42] But this logos, this *Lehre*, does not ask the question *whether* God exists – that is the domain of religion – but, if he were to, *how* God would exist, what his existence would be like, and how we could know or experience God. Defined as such, theology in general, and Benjamin's theology in particular, is the phenomenology and epistemology of the divine, however one would wish to define this divinity.[43] In *Über Sprache*, Benjamin used the Bible in order to explore the essence of language, not because he took the book as gospel truth, but because it presented itself as revelation, and thus saw language as 'eine letzte, nur in ihrer Entfaltung zu betrachtende, unerklärliche und mystische Wirklichkeit' (II, 147). Conceiving of itself as revelation, Benjamin says, the Bible simply has to come up with a fundamental theory of language.[44] Similarly, *Über das Programm* is not interested in the question of the existence of God, but in the possibility of thinking the concept of God, and how the possibility of this concept would affect thought as such. To Walter Benjamin, as we have seen, God is indeed a conceptual possibility. In fact, he uses the concept of the divine as a decisive factor in his language theory, and he uses the concept of God – but therefore not God himself – as the keystone to his thought on truth and tradition.

Benjamin never provides us with a direct definition of God, because, as we indicated before, this would be a theological impossibility in the *Sprache des Menschen*. In this sense, to paraphrase Scholem again, his disposition is not un-Jewish. The only thing which can be predicated of God within the Jewish tradition is existence, which, even in grammatical terms, would not even be a predicate. *God is* is the naked, tautological statement of God's being, his identity with himself, his unity. This identity and unity is stressed in the Shema:

'Hear, O Israel: The Lord is our God, the Lord is One' (*Dt*: 6, 4). In the Hebrew original, 'יהוה אלהינו יהוה אחד', quite literally 'God Lord God One', the absence of the copula in the so-called construct state – the juxtaposition of two nouns to designate identity – puts an even greater emphasis on the tautological nature of the statement. As we mentioned before, these ideas were developed philosophically by Maimonides, who reacted strongly against any attempt to anthropomorphise God, as this would detract from his divinity. We find a similar warning in the second volume of *Philosophie der Geschichte*, which sounds as if it might well have been influenced by this particular strand of Maimonidean thinking:

> Bei dieser Betrachtung der Gottheit als Schöpfer und Erhalter des creatürlichen Daseyns, wornach dieselbe als das ewige Princip und der lebendige Urtypus des endlich Geschaffenen erscheint, dürfen wir jedoch nicht stehen bleiben; sondern müssen, um uns zu der Idee der unendlichen alle creatürliche Fassung übersteigenden Erhabenheit Gottes anbetend zu erheben, und unser eignes Seyn in seiner ganzer Negativität zu erkennen, von allem Geschaffenem abstrahiren, und so weit es unserer endlichen beschränkten Vernunft möglich ist, die Gottheit außer allen Relationen, in ihrem reinen, ewigen, absoluten An- und Fürsichseyn uns denken. (*M* II, 56)

The clearest expression of the divine tautology is the name, the sign which can refer to one thing only, and thus ceases to be a sign. In the case of God, this tautology – the logos referring to the same entity – is expressed *à coup redoublé* in the ineffable tetragrammaton YHWH. The vocalisation of this name of God is unknown, and in readings it is substituted by *Adonai*, meaning 'the Lord'. But more importantly, the tetragrammaton is explained in Exodus 3:14 with the phrase אהיה אשר אהיה, *I am who is* or *I am that I am*.[45] The exceptional nature of this phrase lies in the fact that it is the smallest possible self-contained logical system, missing out one step of the Cartesian *cogito* and the Kantian *Ich denke* (namely the disjunction between subject and action). *I am that I am*, the statement of existential identity, is the juxtaposition of extremes that constitutes the two-step dialectic which Benjamin termed *Dialektik im Stillstand*. There is no object in *I am that I am*, and consequently the role of the subject itself changes. The subject does not find itself opposed to an object which it is trying to master or reduce to a relationship in which the object, passively, lies before the subject. Nor does the subject become aware of itself as a thinking subject, thus creating a rift within itself which, to a certain extent, compromises the integrity of the subject (but nevertheless remains paradoxically necessary for the subject to come into being in the first place). This question is structurally identical to the necessary disjunction between the sign and the signifier, without which there can be no sign. It is this very same disjunction which is overcome, or anticipated – depending on one's point of view, in the concept of the Λογός, the word made flesh. Even more so, *I am that I am*, or YHWH, is not only a name which can refer to only one entity, it is also the one name which refers only to the fact its own existence. The subject of *I am that I am* is like the self-contained, non-predatory subject of the experience of existence within tradition, as Benjamin described it before, with the one difference that *I am that I am* is the alpha and omega of tradition itself. And in *Über das Programm*, it is this specifically theological concept of identity which Benjamin tries to name as the ground of the new *Sphäre der Erkenntnis* which he himself had defined as the *Lehre*:

> Die Fixierung des bei Kant unbekannten Begriffes der Identität hat voraussichtlich in der transzendentalen Logik eine große Rolle zu spielen, insofern er in der Kategorientafel nicht steht, dennoch vermutlich den obersten Begriff der transzendentallogischen ausmacht und vielleicht wahrhaft geeignet ist die Sphäre der Erkenntnis jenseits der Subjekt-Objekt-Terminologie autonom zu begründen. (II, 167)

This is where we come to the core of the essay. Benjamin has named the possible ground for the new 'Sphäre der Erkenntnis', which a coming philosophy must be able to think, as the concept of identity. From a Jewish perspective, it would be possible to conclude that this 'oberste Begriff', this highest concept of transcendental logic would therefore coincide with the idea of God, as he is the very concept of identity, pure being without being something. This however, would be a religious statement, for a theological conclusion could never hope to be so direct, so blunt in fact, as to point straight towards the divinity. *Über das Programm der kommenden Philosophie* is no different. The idea of God is suggested obliquely, but never indicated. On the same page as the passage quoted above, Benjamin writes: 'Die Konvergenz der Ideen auf den obersten Begriff der Erkenntnis ist nachzuweisen.' (II, 167). This tells us that the 'oberste Begriff' is to be found at the centre of the realm of ideas, that it is, in other words, both the ground of the new sphere of knowledge as well as the destination of its ideas. In a letter to Scholem dated 31 January 1918 – an esoteric document, in the most original sense of the word – Benjamin states quite explicitly what he understands both this 'oberste Begriff' and the 'höchste Sphäre' to be:

> [...] metaphysisch ist diejenige Erkenntnis die a priori die Wissenschaft als eine Sphäre in dem absoluten göttlichen Ordnungszusammenhang, dessen höchste Sphäre die Lehre und dessen Inbegriff und Urgrund Gott ist zu erkennen trachtet, und die auch die 'Autonomie' der Wissenschaft als sinnvoll und möglich nur in diesem Zusammenhang betrachtet. (*GB* I, 422)

God is both 'Inbegriff' and 'Urgrund' of the sphere of knowledge, a sphere which is defined in terms of an 'absoluten göttlichen Ordnungszusammenhang'. All these terms are in need of some clarification, as a simple translation cannot hope to do them justice. The 'Ordnungszusammenhang', firstly, could be translated, rather clumsily, as 'interrelated' or 'structured order', although it may be better to use the more general term 'order', as this has the benefit of a certain vagueness which is also present in the original. At face value, it is not entirely clear what this 'absolute divine order', which is meant to encompass the sphere of knowledge, might be, but it would become more obvious if we recall Scholem's definition of the Jewish tradition as the study of 'den transkausalen Zusammenhang der Dinge und ihr Verfaßtsein in Gott' (*GF*, 73).

The study of the Jewish tradition is not the study of a thing or an object, but of a sphere, an order, a set of relationships, in other words *eines Zusammenhangs*; and the student of the Jewish tradition is a part of that coherence, he is immersed in it to such an extent that he ceases to be merely or exclusively an autonomous subject. Benjamin says that the 'autonomy' of science or knowledge – the term *Wissenschaft* is extremely ambiguous – can only be thought in the context of the sphere of tradition or the *Lehre*. This is because the sphere of tradition is autonomous in the deepest sense of the word: it provides its own law, it *is* the law from the first to the last letter. All is the word, all is Torah. And, finally returning to what we have called the simplest, most intricate paradox of human thought, the law is God because the word is God. God is the *Urgrund*, the first cause or the ground of this law, but he is also its *Inbegriff*, its epitome or its inclusion. The word *Inbegriff*, which Benjamin uses several times to designate the status of God within the *Lehre*, is oddly ambiguous. It would normally be translated, admittedly slightly metaphorically, as the epitome or the quintessence, but it literally means the *Gesamtheit*, the all, or the sum of all concepts, *Begriffe*, encompassed by a single one. This almost mystical description may become clearer when we recall the enigmatic circumscription of God in *Über Sprache*, via the 'Bezirk der Ideen, deren Umkreis diejenige Gottes bezeichnet' (II, 141). This means that the ideas both converge on the 'oberste Begriff' and are circled, circumscribed by it. This is what it means for God to be both the *Urgrund* and the *Inbegriff*. God is both the *Inbegriff* of and the *Begriff in* the heart of tradition, the alpha and omega.[46] With this foundation, the whole of tradition becomes divine. As we discussed in the first chapter, God, Torah and tradition thus become interchangeable and in a sense indistinguishable. The appropriate way to approach God thus also becomes the appropriate way to approach tradition, and *vice versa*. As Benjamin writes in *Über das Programm der kommenden Philosophie*:

> Die Philosophie beruht darauf daß in der Struktur der Erkenntnis die der Erfahrung liegt und aus ihr zu entfalten ist. Diese Erfahrung umfaßt denn auch die Religion, nämlich als die wahre, wobei weder Gott noch Mensch Objekt oder Subjekt der Erfahrung ist, wohl aber diese Erfahrung auf der reinen Erkenntnis beruht als deren Inbegriff allein die Philosophie Gott denken kann und muß. Es ist die Aufgabe der kommenden Erkenntnistheorie für die Erkenntnis die Sphäre totaler Neutralität in Bezug auf die Begriffe Objekt und Subjekt zu finden; mit andern Worten die autonome ureigne Sphäre der Erkenntnis auszumitteln in der dieser Begriff auf keine Weise mehr die Beziehung zwischen zwei metaphysischen Entitäten bezeichnet. (II, 163)[47]

Crucially, the theological shift in Benjamin's philosophy away from the subject manifestly does not translate into the appearance of God on the centre stage of his thought. On the contrary, having established the divine as the keystone in the edifice of tradition, Benjamin proceeds to lose interest in God in the same way that Scholem confessed the existence or non-existence of the centre of all things was utterly equivocal to him. What is of far greater interest to Benjamin is what happens to tradition once its vanishing points have been defined as the divine, and so the same movement that took him away from the subject on the one side and towards the divine on the other side now takes him back to the middle, to the *Lehre*, to the all-encompassing *Medium*.

In June 1918, a few months after Benjamin wrote *Über das Programm der kommenden Philosophie*, Scholem planned to write '95 Thesen über Judentum und Zionismus', in imitation of Luther's ninety-five Wittenberg theses, as a present for Benjamin's twenty-fifth birthday. These theses, which read as if they were a condensation of Benjamin's and Scholem's discussions and correspondence over the years, were indeed written, dated 15 July 1918 with the admonition 'mit 15jähriger Diskussionsfrist', but never given to Benjamin. Nevertheless, they will no doubt provide a very fertile ground to continue the study of Benjamin's work in the light of the Jewish tradition, although we have now come to the point where this study must take the form of a *potentialis* rather than a *realis*. Yet this should not be the cause of undue anxiety, for as we know, every book is but a commentary waiting to become the subject of another commentary, and as such neither it nor its author need worry where would be the most felicitous place to conclude. Tradition, like the sea Benjamin compared it to, does not conclude, it merely pauses temporarily so as to allow the waves to reach their crest before they crash down and rejoin the water. There is something oddly comforting in the awareness that even though we cannot comprehend infinity, we are at least part of it, and in our own unique way, *auf unerhörte Weise*, free. The most poignant summary of this notion of tradition, and indeed the perfect summary of our own argument, is provided by Gershom Scholem in one of his ninety-five theses. In a mere twelve words, less than a drop in the vast ocean of tradition, it nevertheless epitomises the very idea of tradition which Benjamin, Molitor and he himself found so endlessly fascinating and fruitful. Encompassing infinity in its delicate yet emphatic contraction, it says, with the merciful brevity of the doctrinal *Lehrsatz*: 'In der Lehre gibt es weder Objekt noch Subjekt. Sie ist Medium.' (*TB* II, 302).[48]

Epilogue

Il ne me reste pas assez de temps pour écrire
toutes ces lettres que j'eusse voulu écrire.

Ὦ Κρίτων τῷ Ἀσκληπιῷ ὀφείλομεν
ἀλεκτρυόνα· ἀλλὰ ἀπόδοτε καὶ μὴ
ἀμελήσητε.

As we have come to the end of our exploration, very little remains to be said that could and should still be said within the small space traditionally allocated to a conclusion. Hence these final pages contain not so much a conclusion as an epilogue and an apology. It is an epilogue *sensu proprio*, as all the conclusions drawn from our research were already put before the reader in the preceding pages, and it is an apology for very much the same reason.

Five chapters and two hundred pages ago, we set out to investigate to which extent Walter Benjamin's thought and writing could be said to have been influenced, to a greater or lesser degree, by his own Judaism or by the philosophical, theological, epistemological and methodological complex which we have called the Jewish tradition. Aside from Benjamin's own work and biography, the one tangible crutch we have used in this investigation was Franz Joseph Molitor's book *Philosophie der Geschichte oder über die Tradition*, a book Gershom Scholem characterised as 'das von einem christlichen Theosophen und Anhänger Franz von Baaders stammende, bemerkenswerteste deutsche Werk über die Kabbala'.[1] In the course of these five chapters, we have aimed to present as detailed an analysis as the usual constraints would permit of the Jewish tradition and Jewish thought itself, of Molitor's discussion of this Jewish tradition and its mystical as well as its more 'mundane' sides, and of Walter Benjamin's and Gershom Scholem's *Auseinandersetzung* not just with this 'bemerkenswerteste deutsche Werk über die Kabbala', but through it also with their own experience of Judaism as a religion and the Jewish tradition as a system and a reservoir of thought which they were able to explore, dip into and use.

Throughout the book, by way of so many interim conclusions, we have drawn attention to a number of concepts and ideas from a considerable number of texts, passages and fragments from the work of Benjamin, Scholem and Molitor which we felt pointed towards certain affinities, correspondences or similarities. These, in turn, we hoped could shed light on what remains an obscure episode in the German *Ideengeschichte* and could provide fresh insights into the thought of Walter Benjamin and his intellectual friendship with Gershom Scholem. In this context we have re-read some of the key texts of Benjamin's oeuvre, such as *Über Sprache überhaupt und über die Sprache des Menschen, Ursprung des deutschen Trauerspiels* and the *Passagen-Werk*, and we have sought to present interpretations which both were as coherent and exhaustive as is philologically feasible and took into account themes, topics and considerations which had hitherto not received an inordinate amount of scholarly attention. Thus we discussed Benjamin's concept of the *Lehre* as a multi-dimensional intellectual sphere, the idea of language as a physical reality, the concept of *profane Erleuchtung* and the notion of *Medium* as a methodological refinement of the *Lehre*, and the pervasive yet elusive water metaphor, which Benjamin uses so often to dramatic effect. All of these concepts and themes, we argued, were influenced to some degree by his own study, understanding and interpretation of Jewish-theological motifs. At least in part true to Benjamin's own stated aim 'nichts zu sagen, nur zu zeigen', we have shown that in order to become as rich and meaningful as they are, these concepts also require patient study and careful contextualisation. In this sense, this epilogue can only be just that: an afterword ruminating on the realisation that if there was any insight at all, it will have already flashed before our eyes, leaving this text to be little more than the 'langnachrollende Donner'.

These afterthoughts *en lieu* of a conclusion, as we said before, also constitute something of an apology, both pre-emptive and post facta. Inevitably, there is a limit to what one sensibly can and arguably ought to discuss in a single book. For every subject raised and for

206

every text read, there are many others to which we could not do justice within the confines of our chosen framework. Although we have sought to give a comprehensive account of the possible Jewish influence on Benjamin's epistemology and methodology, we have thus been unable to discuss the ethical dimension of his philosophy of history in any detail, although this too could be said to have more than just a casual tinge of Judaism.[2] Similarly, although we have examined what we considered to be the most salient parts of Benjamin's and Scholem's biography in terms of their discovery and exploration of Judaism, there remain questions which we have not been able to address directly. Their involvement in various youth movements and discussion groups, from the *Jugendbewegung* to *Jung Juda*, for instance, is not only something which brought them together, but also something which undoubtedly played a crucial role in shaping their intellectual outlook and horizons. After all, it was through Gustav Wyneken's *Schulgemeinde* that Benjamin claimed fundamentally to have discovered his Judaism: 'Von Wickersdorf aus, nicht spekulativ, nicht schlechthin gefühlsmäßig, sondern aus äußerer und innerer Erfahrung habe ich mein Judentum gefunden.' (*GB* I, 71).

Benjamin's attempts at learning Hebrew and his often stated intention to emigrate to Palestine are two issues which would equally merit further attention, as they are in many ways perfect examples of his often ambiguous relationship to Judaism which we have examined throughout this book. Hans Puttnies' and Gary Smith's marvellous self-styled 'scrapbook' *Benjaminiana* features a wonderful reproduction of Benjamin's Hebrew writing exercises from 1924, meticulous vocalisations included, and as late as 1929, Scholem assures us, 'lief Benjamin wirklich, wie mir von mehreren Seiten bestätigt wurde, immer mit einer hebräischen Grammatik herum'(*GF*, 193).[3] It would be fascinating to speculate on exactly how much this relatively detailed and very practical exposure to the 'Holy Language' would have influenced Benjamin's thought on language, form and meaning, but such speculation must be deferred to another time and another place. *Post scripta*, we must also speak in defence of a different kind of limitation which we have had to accept. Even though we have aimed to give a broad overview of Benjamin's most important writings, from his *Frühwerk* to his *Spätwerk*, it was unavoidable that at least an equal number of equally important texts could not be discussed in any detail, or indeed at all. As we mentioned in the final chapter, an analysis of Benjamin's doctoral thesis, *Der Begriff der Kunstkritik in der deutschen Romantik*, in the context of his theologically inspired theory of truth would have served to further contextualise the concept of Medium, but it lay outside our present scope. By the same token, one could read Benjamin's essays on Karl Kraus, Franz Kafka or Goethe's *Wahlverwandtschaften* in the context of his preoccupation with the eminently Jewish form that is commentary, which we used and analysed throughout this book, but this intuition must at present also remain an intention, this conclusion therefore *unabgeschlossen*, this epilogue an apology.

This book itself, and the investigation it contains, cannot be concluded in any other than an arbitrary way, but this does not mean that our conclusions, however interim, partial or deferred, are themselves arbitrary or meaningless. What we have sought to do in this volume is to give a new *Ansatz* to the study of Walter Benjamin and his Judaism, in terms of the mainstream Jewish tradition and not just the Kabbalah, with reference to concrete written sources rather than mere speculation, and presenting detailed and critical interpretations of his work in the light of our findings. Others will be the judge of its merits, but if all this book does is to provoke the reader into taking up Benjamin's texts with renewed interest, and perhaps from a slightly different perspective, we would be sincerely gratified.

Notes

Introduction

1 Gershom Scholem, *Tagebücher nebst Aufsätzen und Entwürfen bis 1923*, edited by Karlfried Gründer und Friedrich Niewöhner, 2 vols. (Frankfurt am Main: Jüdischer Verlag, 1995–2000), vol. 2, 297. Hereafter *TB*.

2 Theodor W. Adorno, 'Benjamin, der Briefschreiber', in *Noten zur Literatur* (Frankfurt am Main: Suhrkamp, 1981), 583–590; 583. See also Walter Benjamin, *Briefe*, edited by Gershom Scholem and Theodor W. Adorno, 2 vols. (Frankfurt am Main: Suhrkamp, 1993), 14.

3 Gershom Scholem, *Walter Benjamin: die Geschichte einer Freundschaft* (Frankfurt am Main: Suhrkamp, 1975), 17 (hereafter *GF*).

4 Walter Benjamin, *Gesammelte Schriften*, edited by Rolf Tiedemann, Hermann Schweppenhäuser and others (Frankfurt am Main: Suhrkamp, 1974–1999), VI, 475. We will refer to Benjamin's *Gesammelte Schriften* in the now canonical way, with a Roman numeral referring to the volume and Arabic numerals referring to the pages.

5 Walter Benjamin, *Gesammelte Briefe*, 6 vols., edited by Christoph Gödde and Henri Lonitz (Frankfurt am Main: Suhrkamp, 1995–2000), vol. I, 436. Hereafter *GB*.

6 Theodor W. Adorno, 'Einleitung zu Benjamins "Schriften"', in *Noten zur Literatur*, 567–582; 573.

7 The topic of Benjamin's Judaism has received some scholarly attention by a few formidable authors, but a full and systematic study of the possible Jewish elements in Benjamin's work remains to be written. Irving Wohlfarth touches upon the subject more than once in his essays 'On the Messianic Structure of Walter Benjamin's Last Reflections', *Glyph*, 3 (1978), 148–212; '"Immer radikal, niemals konsequent…": Zur theologisch-politischen Standortsbestimmung Walter Benjamins', in *Antike und Moderne: Zu Walter Benjamins 'Passagen'*, edited by Norbert Bolz and Richard Faber (Würzburg: Königshausen & Neumann, 1986), 116–137; and 'On Some Jewish Motifs in Benjamin', in *The Problems of Modernity: Adorno & Benjamin*, edited by Andrew Benjamin (London: Routledge, 1992), 157–215. The late Gillian Rose's

thoughtful essay 'Walter Benjamin: Out of the Sources of Modern Judaism' is truly and intellectual *tour de force* which discusses amongst other things tradition, language, history, mourning and remembrance, taking a very broad sweep of Benjamin's work in a very densely-packed and rewarding 35 pages (Gillian Rose, *Judaism and Modernity: Philosophical Essays* (Oxford: Blackwell, 1993), 175–210). Gary Smith explores Jewish aspects of Benjamin's early work in '"Das Jüdische versteht sich von selbst': Walter Benjamins frühe Auseinandersetzung mit dem Judentum', *Deutsche Vierteljahresschrift*, 65/4 (1991), 318–334; and Stéphane Mosès discusses the Jewish affinities of Benjamin's concept of history and ethics in *L'Ange de l'Histoire: Rosenzweig, Benjamin, Scholem* (Paris: Seuil, 1992). Eric Jacobson's recent book *Metaphysics of the Profane: The Political Theology of Walter Benjamin and Gershom Scholem* (New York: Columbia University Press, 2003) concentrates on messianism and politics in the work of Benjamin and Scholem, and even though he addresses some of the issues we will cover, such as language and tradition, his book does so in a less systematic and less comprehensive way than the present volume. Jacobson also briefly discusses the possibility of Molitor's influence on Benjamin, but his assessment is relatively superficial, ignoring some of the more recent research on the topic, published before his book came out (see my articles 'The Anxiety of Influence: Walter Benjamin, Gershom Scholem and Franz Joseph Molitor', in *Millenial Essays on Film and other German Studies*, edited by Daniela Berghahn and Alan Bance (Oxford: Peter Lang, 2002), 128–141 and '"This Still Remarkable Book": Franz Joseph Molitor's Judaeo-Christian Synthesis', *Journal for Modern Jewish Studies*, vol. 1 (2), 2002, 167–181).

8   Gershom Scholem, 'Walter Benjamin', in *Judaica 2* (Frankfurt am Main: Suhrkamp, 1995), 193–227; 219.

9   Gershom Scholem, *Briefe*, 3 vols., edited by Itta Shedletzky (München: Beck, 1994–1999), vol. 2, 54–55. Hereafter *SB*.

10   Gershom Scholem, *Von der mystischen Gestalt der Gottheit: Studien zur Grundbegriffen der Kabbala* (Frankfurt am Main: Suhrkamp, 1977), 285.

11   Lieven De Cauter, *De Dwerg in de Schaakautomaat: Benjamins Verborgen Leer* (Nijmegen: SUN, 1999), 52 ff.

12   Lieven De Cauter, *De Dwerg in de Schaakautomaat*, 109n.

Chapter One: The Jewish Tradition

1   On Hasidism, see Gershom Scholem, *Die jüdische Mystik in ihren Hauptströmungen* (Frankfurt am Main: Suhrkamp, 1996), notably chapter 9, 'Der Chassidismus in Polen, die letzte Phase der jüdischen Mystik', 356–385.

2   Letter to Ludwig Strauß of 10 October 1912, *GB* I, 69–70.

3   Gershom Scholem, 'Offenbarung und Tradition als religiöse Kategorien im Judentum', in *Über einige Grundbegriffe des Judentums* (Frankfurt am Main: Suhrkamp, 1970), 90–120; 90.

4   Franz Joseph Molitor, *Philosophie der Geschichte oder über die Tradition in dem alten Bunde und ihre Beziehung zur Kirche des Neuen Bundes. Mit vorzüglicher Rücksicht auf die Kabbalah*, first edition, 4 vols. (Frankfurt am Main/Münster: Hermann/Theissing, 1827–1853), vol. 1, 11. Hereafter, we will refer to this book with the italic capital *M*, a roman numeral for the volume and Arabic numerals for the page.

5   David Stern, 'Midrash and the Language of Exegesis: A Study of Vayikra Rabbah, Chapter 1', in *Midrash and Literature*, edited by Geoffrey Hartman and Sanford Budick (New Haven: Yale University Press, 1986), 105–124; 108.

6   James L. Kugel, 'Torah', in *Contemporary Jewish Religious Thought*, 995–1005, 1000.

7   Baruch J. Schwartz, 'Torah', in *The Oxford Dictionary of the Jewish Religion*, 696–698; 697.

8   David Stern, 'Midrash', in *Contemporary Jewish Religious Thought*, 613–620, 619.

9   Gershom Scholem, 'Walter Benjamin', 199. Interestingly, Scholem rephrases Warburg's dictum ever so slightly, as the original is usually given as 'der liebe Gott *steckt* im Detail'. Scholem's use of the word *wohnen* instead of the more colloquial *stecken* gives the quotation the ring of a true theological *Lehrsatz*.

10 M. *Avot*, V, 22; translation modified. All quotations from the Talmud (and Mishnah) are taken from the Soncino edition (*The Babylonian Talmud: Translated into English with Notes, Glossary and Indices*, edited by Isidore Epstein, 35 vols. (London: Soncino Press, 1935–1952)). As is customary, the name of the individual tractate will be preceded by 'M.' for *Mishnah* or 'B.' for *Bavli*, and followed by Roman numerals and a letter *a* or *b* to indicate the number and side of the folio.

11 Harvey Goldberg, 'Epilogue: Text in Jewish Society and the Challenge of Comparison', in *Judaism Viewed from Within and from Without*, edited by Harvey E. Goldberg (New York: State University of New York Press, 1987), 315–329, 319–320.

12 'Wenn Jemand ein Ding hinter einem Busche versteckt, es eben dort wieder sucht und auch findet, so ist an diesem Suchen und Finden nicht viel zu rühmen.' (Friedrich Nietzsche, 'Über Wahrheit und Lüge im Aussermoralischen Sinne', in *Sämtliche Werke: Kritische Studienausgabe*, edited by Giorgio Colli and Mazzino Montinari, 15 vols. (München: DTV, 1988), vol. I, 883).

13 Gershom Scholem, 'Offenbarung und Tradition als religiöse Kategorien im Judentum', 92.

14 The genealogy of the Jewish tradition is quite an intricate affair, and the usual constraints force us to omit a discussion on yet more additions to the *Mishnah*, such as the *Tosefta* and the *Baraiyta*. For a very thorough scholarly treatment of the documents of the Jewish tradition, we refer the reader to Günter Stemberger's standard work *Introduction to the Talmud and Midrash*, second edition, translated and edited by Markus Bockmuehl (Edinburgh: T&T Clark, 1996). A very good introduction to the basic texts of the Jewish tradition is *Back to the Sources: Reading the Classic Jewish Texts*, edited by Barry W. Holtz (New York: Simon & Schuster, 1992).

15 Robert Goldenberg, 'Talmud', in *Back to The Sources*, 142.

16 Günter Stemberger, *Introduction to the Talmud and Midrash*, 4.

17 Barry W. Holtz, 'Midrash', in *Back to the Sources*, 177–211; 186.

18 For a very lucid and concise overview of the Jewish legal tradition, see David M. Feldman's essay 'The Structure of Jewish Law', in *Jewish Law and Legal Theory*, edited by Martin Golding (New York: New York University Press, 1993), 3–19.

19 See Gershom Scholem, *Judaica 5: Erlösung durch Sünde*, translated by Michael Brock (Frankfurt am Main: Suhrkamp, 1992) and his magnum opus *Sabbatai Sevi: the Mystical Messiah*, translated by R. Zwi Werblowski (Princeton: Princeton University Press, 1973).

20 This image follows a similar logic to the kabbalist concept of the breaking of the vessels, *Shevirat ha-Kelim*, according to which during creation the divine glory of God was poured into vessels which subsequently broke and spread shards or *Klipot* throughout the created world. Sparks of the divine glory still stick to these fragments or shards, and every time a Jew performs a *mitzvah*, these sparks are 'kicked up'. This is the origin of the kabbalist and hasidic idea that when every Jew

on earth would perform a *mitzvah* at the same time, the Messiah would come, as it would completely reconstitute the divine glory lost at creation. The importance of this analogy lies in the very physical and spatial metaphors used in the story, echoing the Mishnaic-Talmudic image of the divinity of the text as something which can almost spill out of the book (see William Scott Green, 'Romancing the Tome', 159–161; see also Martin S. Jaffee, 'A Rabbinic Ontology of the Written and Spoken Word: On Discipleship, Transformative Knowledge and the Living Texts of Oral Torah', *Journal of the American Academy of Religion*, 65:3 (Fall 1997), 525–549; 538–540).

21 David M. Feldman, 'The Structure of Jewish Law', 15.

22 *Ibid.*, 16.

23 Adin Steinsalz, 'Talmud', in *Contemporary Jewish Religious Thought*, 953–957; 957.

24 David M. Feldman, 'The Structure of Jewish Law', 5.

25 Quoted in Geoffrey Hartman, 'Imagination', in *Contemporary Jewish Religious Thought*, 451–472; 461.

26 Talking to Scholem about his essay *Über das Programm der kommenden Philosophie*, Benjamin remarked: 'Eine Philosophie, die nicht die Möglichkeit der Weissagung aus dem Kaffeesatz einbezieht und explizieren kann, kann keine wahre sein.' (quoted in *Anmerkungen der Herausgeber*, II, 938).

27 The significance of this opposition between the traditional and the historicist perspective is made clear by the following quotation from the *Passagen-Werk*, in which Benjamin explains 'wie diese Arbeit – vergleichbar der Methode der Atomzertrümmerung – die ungeheuren Kräfte der Geschichte freimacht, die im "Es war einmal" der klassischen Historie gebunden liegen. Die Geschichte, welche die Sache zeigte, "wie es eigentlich gewesen ist", war das stärkste Narkotikum des Jahrhunderts.' (V, 578).

28 Paul Mendes-Flohr quotes Franz Rosenzweig's *Stern der Erlösung*, saying: 'For Israel "the memory of its history does not form a point fixed in the past, a point which year after year becomes increasingly past. It is a memory which is really not past at all, but eternally present."' (Paul Mendes-Flohr, 'History', in *Contemporary Jewish Religious Thought*, 371–387; 372). It is interesting to see that Rosenzweig, a contemporary author with whose work Benjamin was certainly familiar, also characterises the Jewish concept of history as emphatically opposed to the historicist perspective. But he was certainly not the only one to be drawn to this notion at the time: Ernst Bloch,

Gershom Scholem and Martin Buber are also among the authors who question the epistemological and political claims of historicism by drawing on elements from the Jewish tradition.

29 Quoted in Jacob Neusner, 'The Study of Religion as the Study of Tradition: Judaism', *History of Religions*, 14 (1975), 191–206; 192.

30 The Jewish concept of remembrance or commemoration becomes increasingly important in Benjamin's work towards the end of his life, cumulating in this melancholy parable, the last addition to the *Thesen über den Begriff der Geschichte*. In his book *L'Ange de L'Histoire: Rosenzweig, Benjamin, Scholem* (Paris: Seuil, 1992), Stéphane Mosès summarises the significance of this concept as follows: 'C'est dans cette remise en question de la toute-puissance de la réalité historique au nom d'une exigence éthique qu'il faut chercher le sense "théologique" de la dernière philosophie de l'histoire de Benjamin. Les concepts dérivés de la mystique juive ont précisément pour fonction de subverter la Raison historique en donnant une nouvelle chance à tout ce qui, dans la passé, à été écrasé, oublié ou laissé pour compte. C'est ainsi que la notion benjaminienne de "remémoration" (*Eingedenken*) reprend la catégorie juive du "ressouvenir" (*Zekher*), qui ne désigne pas la conservation dans la mémoire des événements du passé, mais leur réactualisation dans l'expérience présente.' (156).

31 Although he presents an altogether more cursory and selective approach of the Jewish tradition, Stéphane Mosès comes to a similar diagnosis: '*Critique de la continuité temporelle, critique de la causalité historique, critique de l'idéologie du progrès*, tels sont les trois thèmes à travers lesquels le travail du théologico-politique vient miner les fondements mêmes de la vision positiviste de l'histoire.' (*l'Ange de l'Histoire*, 157).

32 Aaron Lichtenstein, 'Study', in *Contemporary Jewish Religious Thought*, 931–937, 931.

33 Janet Aviad, 'Education', in *Contemporary Jewish Religious Thought*, 156.

34 Nathan Rotenstreich, 'Tradition', in *Contemporary Jewish Religious Thought*, 1008. Rotenstreich does not quote Molitor *verbatim*, and the entry in his bibliography rather mystifyingly reads 'Franz Joseph Molitor, *Philosophie der Geschichte oder Über die Tradition* (1851)', which is not a publication date for any of the volumes. This may suggest that Rotenstreich has not actually read the work or that he may be paraphrasing from memory (or lecture notes). This, as we will point out in the next chapter, has often seemed to be the case with Molitor's elusive book. Nevertheless, Molitor does write words to the effect of

Rotenstreich's paraphrase in book one, which we quoted earlier in this chapter (*M* I, 21–22).

35   See Avraham Walfish, 'Masorah', in *The Oxford Dictionary of the Jewish Religion*, 445. These concepts are also explained in the first book of *Philosophie der Geschichte*: 'So werden auch oft viele Worte ganz anders gelesen als geschrieben, oft wird auch im Lesen etwas ergänzt, was nicht im Text stehet, welches unter dem Namen ולא כתיב קרי (K'ri w'lo Ch'thibh, geschrieben und nicht gelesen) bekannt ist.' (*M* I, 55).

36   Lieven De Cauter, *De Dwerg in de Schaakautomaat*, 77. The formula can be found, for example, in B. '*Eduyyoth*, VIII, 7.

37   Robert Gordis, *The Dynamics of Judaism: A Study in Jewish Law* (Bloomington: Indiana University Press, 1990), 80.

38   Paul Mendes-Flohr opposes both conceptions of history in a way that is reminiscent of Benjamin's concepts of the 'empty' time of progress and the pregnant, meaningful *Jetztzeit*, or 'Now-time': 'In fact, chronology, a defining feature of the diachronic conception of history, is hardly of significance to the Jewish historical imagination. Thus the rabbis could claim that "there is no late and early in the Torah." (B. *Pesahim*, 6b). The sacred history (and teachings) of the Torah are eternal and not bound by the sequential or linear progression of profane time.' ('History', in *Contemporary Jewish Religious Thought*, 371–387; 372).

39   Another Talmudic legend can be cited here to indicate that this 'dialogue' between past and present could also go in the opposite direction. In a discussion on a point of law, Rabbi Eliezer ben Hyrcanus found himself in a minority position, and called upon three miracles to prove him right, all of which duly occurred. The majority was unmoved by this, and Eliezer called upon a *Bat Kol*, or a heavenly voice, to support him. A voice indeed thundered out: 'Who are you to differ with Rabbi Eliezer, for the law is with him on every point.' But Rabbi Joshua cited Deuteronomy 30:12, stating 'It is not in heaven', meaning that the Torah was given on Sinai, and the majority position was maintained. Rabbi Nathan later met the prophet Elijah and asked what God did in that hour, and Elijah replied: 'He smiled and said "my children have overcome me!"' (B. *Baba Meziah*, 59b; see also Gershom Scholem, 'Offenbarung und Tradition als religiöse Kategorien im Judentum', 103–104). This is a not only very strong affirmation of the above-mentioned majority rule in rabbinic law, it also serves to emphasise the fact that the past can also be called upon to answer for and in the present.

40   David Stern, 'Midrash and the Language of Exegesis: A Study of Vayikra Rabbah, Chapter 1', in *Midrash and Literature*, edited by Geoffrey Hartman and Sanford Budick (New Haven: Yale University Press, 1986), 105–124; 110.

41   Günter Stemberger paraphrasing Le Déaut in *Introduction to the Talmud and Midrash*, 235.

42   William Scott Green, 'Romancing the Tome', 147.

43   David Stern, 'Midrash and the Language of Exegesis', 105.

44   Stemberger, *Introduction to the Talmud and Midrash*, 237.

45   This is a slightly deceptive way of phrasing it, as orthodoxy would have it that there is nothing accidental about these correspondences, as all is already in it (everything is *déjà-là*, to use a modern, but no less traditional phrase). A very similar methodology underlies Benjamin's *Passagen-Werk*, as it was succinctly formulated in the following quotation: 'Notwendigkeit, während vieler Jahre scharf auf jedes zufällige Zitat, jede flüchtige Erwähnung eines Buchs hinzuhören.' (V, 587). If the indefinite article in this passage were replaced by the definite article, this quotation could be a description of the attentiveness required by midrashic interpretation.

46   Stemberger, *Introduction to the Talmud and Midrash*, 240.

47   *Genesis*, translated by H. Freedman, 2 vols. (London: Soncino Press, 1939), vols. 1 and 2 of *The Midrash*, edited and translated by H. Freedman and Maurice Simon, 10 vols. (London: Soncino Press, 1939).

48   The topos of (divine) breath bestowing life as well as meaning is a very pervasive one in the Jewish tradition, and would merit a study in its own right. It is therefore quite significant that Benjamin should have chosen this very topos to illustrate the immaterial and purely spiritual relationship of human language and objects: 'Dieses symbolisches Faktum spricht die Bibel aus, indem sie sagt, daß Gott dem Menschen den Odem einblies: das ist zugleich Leben und Geist und Sprache. – ' (II, 147).

49   David Stern, 'Midrash and the Language of Exegesis', 108 (our emphasis).

50   A thought-provoking parallel to the interweaving of style and preoccupation in Benjamin's *Arcades Project* can be found in Arthur Cohen's description of the 'classical rabbinic style' with 'its interweaving of various theological motifs and preoccupations, its refusal to separate out high argument from examples drawn from the most mundane events of life, its continuous care for using simple fidelities and loyalty to halakhah as occasions for promising large redemptions.'

('Redemption', in *Contemporary Jewish Religious Thought*, 761–765; 761).

51 James L. Kugel, 'Two Introductions to Midrash', in *Midrash and Literature*, edited by Geoffrey Hartman and Sanford Budick (New Haven: Yale University Press, 1986), 77-103; 79.

52 The original reads 'חי הוא ברמו של עולם' or 'he lives in the heights of the *world*' and not 'חי הוא ברמו של דבר', 'he lives in the heights of the *word*', as the translators of the Soncino edition would have it (I am grateful to Seth Kunin and Edward Ball for drawing my attention to this mistake). Oddly enough, this fairly crucial error of the original translation, published between 1935 and 1952, has been duplicated in the new Hebrew–English edition of the Talmud some fifty years later (tractate *Menahoth* was published in this edition in 1989).

53 David Stern, 'Midrash', in *Contemporary Jewish Religious Thought*, 613–620; 619. This is also the opinion of Jacob Neusner in his rejoinder 'A Rabbinic Theory of Language?' and in a milder form it is also voiced in Howard Eilberg-Schwartz's response to it *ad loc. cit.* The reason we emphasise the theological side so strongly is because Benjamin himself can be seen to struggle with it, trying to yoke together such apparently irreconcilable opposites as a religious concept of tradition and a very thoroughly secularised, demythified materialism, with mixed success, we might add.

54 Shalom Rosenberg, 'Revelation', in *Contemporary Jewish Religious Thought*, 815–825; 817.

Chapter Two: Franz Joseph Molitor

1 For Molitor's biography, see the entry 'Molitor: Joseph Franz [*sic*]' in the *Allgemeine deutsche Bibliographie* of 1885 (vol. 22, 108–110), Carl Frankenstein, *Franz Joseph Molitors metaphysische Geschichtsphilosophie* (Berlin: Reuther und Reichard, 1928), 106–117; Christoph Schulte, '"Die Buchstaben haben... ihre Wurzeln oben." Scholem und Molitor', in *Kabbala und Romantik*, edited by Eveline Goodmann-Thau, Gerd Mattenklott and Christoph Schulte (Tübingen: Max Niemeyer, 1994), 143–164; and Scholem's article on Molitor in the *Encyclopaedia Judaica*, vol. 22, 227–228. A more recent article, incorporating much of the same information as the above is Anja Hallacker, 'Franz Joseph Molitor: Freimaurer – Lehrer – Kabbalist', in *Christliche Kabbala*, edited by W. Schmidt-Biggemann, (Ostfildern: Thorbecke,

2003), 225–246. Save Scholem's entry in the *Encyclopaedia Judaica*, the only articles on Molitor to appear in English are my own 'The Anxiety of Influence: Walter Benjamin, Gershom Scholem and Franz Joseph Molitor', in *Millenial Essays on Film and other German Studies*, edited by Daniela Berghahn and Alan Bance (Oxford: Peter Lang, 2002), 128–141; '"This Still Remarkable Book": Franz Joseph Molitor's Judaeo-Christian Synthesis', *Journal for Modern Jewish Studies*, vol. 1 (2), 2002, 167–181 and '"The True Words of the Mystic": Gershom Scholem and Franz Joseph Molitor', *Australian Journal of Jewish Studies*, vol. 17, 2003, 131–153.

2   Quoted in Hans-Jörg Sandkühler, *Freiheit und Wirklichkeit: Zur Dialektik von Politik und Philosophie bei Schelling* (Frankfurt am Main: Suhrkamp, 1968), 249.

3   In a letter to Schelling accompanying a valedictory copy of his book, Molitor writes: 'Soll das Göttliche nur an eine Zeit – nur an eine einzelne Form gebunden sein? Oder soll nicht vielmehr die Schuld bloß an dem Suchenden liegen, wenn er in manchen Gestalten nichts Höhres findet?' (quoted in Hans-Jörg Sandkühler, *Freiheit und Wirklichkeit*, 249–250). It seems that Schelling, who was sent a copy of the book by Molitor along with Hegel, Goethe and Görres, did not take the criticism too well, and the correspondence between the two subsequently suffered a twenty-year gap.

4   Franz Joseph Molitor, *Ideen zu einer künftigen Dynamik der Geschichte* (Frankfurt am Main: Bernhard Körner, 1805), 5.

5   Bettina von Arnim, *Die Günderode*, in *Werke und Briefe*, 5 vols., edited by Gustav Konrad (Frechen/Köln: Bartmann, 1959), vol. 1, 447.

6   Bettina von Arnim, *Briefwechsel mit Goethe*, in *Werke und Briefe*, vol. 2, 105–106. It is quite remarkable how much Molitor's experience resembles that of Walter Benjamin in this respect. The impression we get from the former's letters to Schelling is of someone who, in spite of his already frugal lifestyle, is endlessly struggling to make ends meet and can count his earthly possessions on the fingers of one hand, which is not unlike Benjamin's experience as a freelance writer living on a shoestring in Paris. In order to be able to carry out their unpopular research, Benjamin and Molitor were constantly trying to find sources of funding and frequently found themselves in the undignified position of having to justify the expenditure of every single penny to their benefactors.

7   Bettina von Arnim, *Briefwechsel mit Goethe*, 104.

8   Franz Joseph Molitor, *Ueber Bürgerliche Erziehung mit Beziehung auf die Organisation des jüdischen Schulwesens in Frankfurt am Main* (Frankfurt am Main: J.C.B. Mohr, 1808), 18.

9   Hirschfeld is a remarkable character in many ways, but most pertinent to our argument here is that he appears to have been the Jewish equivalent (and forerunner) of Molitor in that his thinking was a "Jewish–Christian syncretism based on the Cabalistic [*sic*] system of ideas." (Jacob Katz, *Jews and Freemasons in Europe 1727–1939* (Cambridge, Mass.: Harvard University Press, 1970), 67; see also Scholem's entry on Hirschfeld in the *Encyclopaedia Judaica*, vol. 8, 523–524).

10   See Frankenstein, *Molitors Metaphysische Geschichtsphilosophie*, 114; Katz, *Jews and Freemasons*, 63–69 and Schulte, "'Die Buchstaben haben... ihre Wurzeln oben.'", 146–147.

11   Quoted in Katz, *Jews and Freemasons*, 87–88.

12   Molitor reiterated this conviction without qualification in his lapidary statement to Schelling: 'Das Christentum kann man nicht ohne das Judentum begreifen.' (quoted in Sandkühler, *Freiheit und Wirklichkeit*, 258). His study of Jewish purity laws, contained in volume III of *Philosophie der Geschichte*, is nigh-on 600 pages long and contains a fifteen-page appendix of quotations from various kabbalist texts in Hebrew, with Molitor's own German translation.

13   Quoted in Sandkühler, *Freiheit und Wirklichkeit*, 256.

14   *Ibid.*, 258.

15   *Ibid.*, 255. The controversies surrounding the appearance of *Philosophie der Geschichte* eventually led to the publication of the second edition of the first volume in 1857, which is 300 pages longer than the first edition of 1827, and in which Molitor attempts to answer his many critics. In spite of its expansion, however, the second edition contains very little new material and his chapters on the Jewish tradition and the Hebrew language are virtually dientical with the first edition. After the publication of the first volume, however, Molitor did enjoy a certain degree of popularity, and the *Allgemeine Deutsche Biographie* notes that his house became 'der Sammelpunkt für hoch oder nieder gestellte Dilettanten der Philosophie', adding with some degree of consternation '(auch Frauen)' (vol. 22, 109).

16   Quoted in Sandkühler, *Freiheit und Wirklichkeit*, 255–256.

17   *Philosophie der Geschichte* contains quite a few of these lists, for example of all the major rabbis and rabbinic academies from the destruction of the second temple up to 1723 (*M* I, 283–292), important

mystical writings from the third century CE to the twelfth century CE (*M* I, 76–82), the most important numbers and their mystical connotations (*M* III, 47–58) and the calendar of religious feasts and laws regarding them (*M* III, 58–65).

18 Gershom Scholem, *Von der mystischen Gestalt der Gottheit: Studien zu Grundbegriffen der Kabbalah* (Frankfurt am Main: Suhrkamp, 1995), 285. In his book *Gershom Scholem: politisches, esoterisches und historiographisches Schreiben* (München: Wilhelm Fink, 2003), Daniel Weidner also devotes a few pages to Scholem's reading of Molitor, emphasizing, as we have, that Philosophie der Geschichte is not so much a book on the Kabbalah as it is about '[die] Kommentarliteratur bzw. [das] Phänomen der Tradition als solcher' (180). As such, Scholem's Auseinandersetzung with Molitor gave him the opportunity 'sich die jüdische Tradition nicht nur praktisch anzueignen, sondern auch über diese Aneignung zu reflektieren; dabei übernimmt er Molitors Lösung nicht eindeutig, sondern versucht auf verschiedene Weise, das Problem zu reformulieren' (181).

19 Gershom Scholem, 'Wissenschaft vom Judentum einst und jetzt', in *Judaica* (Frankfurt am Main: Suhrkamp, 1963), 147–164; and *Judaica VI: Die Wissenschaft vom Judentum* edited and translated by Peter Schäfer (Frankfurt am Main: Suhrkamp, 1997). The former is the transcript of a lecture held in German at the Leo Baeck Institute in London in 1959, yet it is essentially a shorter, bowdlerised version of the original Hebrew essay from 1944, translated in *Judaica VI*, which is a far more violent, no-holds-barred attack on the failings of the *Wissenschaft des Judentums*. On the comparison between these two texts and on Scholem's *Auseinandersetzung* with the *Wissenschaft des Judentums*, see Peter Schäfer, 'Gershom Scholem und die "Wissenschaft des Judentums"', in *Gershom Scholem: Zwischen den Disziplinen*, edited by Peter Schäfer and Gary Smith (Frankfurt am Main: Suhrkamp, 1995), 122–156; also Schäfer's *Nachwort* in *Judaica VI*, 71–108; David Biale, *Gershom Scholem: Kabbalah and Counter-History*, second edition (Cambridge, Massachusetts: Harvard University Press, 1982) and Moshe Idel, 'Rabbinism versus Kabbalism: On G. Scholem's Phenomenology of Judaism', *Modern Judaism*, 11:3 (1991), 281–296.

20 On the history and background of the *Wissenschaft des Judentums*, see Michael Meyer, 'The Emergence of Jewish Historiography: Motives and Motifs', *History and Theory*, 27:4 (1988), 160–175; an excellent overview of both early and late *Wissenschaftler* can be found in Michael Brenner, Stefi Jersch-Wenzel and Michael A. Meyer, *Deutsch-*

Jüdische Geschichte in der Neuzeit, 4 vols. (München: C.H. Beck, 2000), vol. 2, 136–145 and 343–348; on Leopold Zunz specifically, see Leon Weiseltier, '*Etwas über die jüdische Historik:* Leopold Zunz and the Inception of Modern Jewish Historiography', History and Theory, Vol. 20, No. 2. (May, 1981), 135–149.

21 There was no love lost between Abraham Geiger and Heinrich Graetz, for instance, partly because they were on opposite sides of the Reform debates, but partly also because Graetz was abhorred by Geiger's apparent tolerance of mysticism, which Graetz considered to be a non-Jewish, hellenic phenomenon (see Michael Brenner, 'Gnosis and History: Polemics of German-Jewish Identity from Graetz to Scholem', *New German Critique*, 77 (1999), 45–60; 47–48).

22 See Michael Brenner, 'Gnosis and History', 45.

23 Gershom Scholem, 'Wissenschaft vom Judentum einst und jetzt', 156. the use of the term 'widerhaarig' is far from accidental, but rather an overt reference to Benjamin's description of the task of the historical materialist 'die Geschichte gegen den Strich zu bürsten.' (I, 697).

24 See Gershom Scholem, *Judaica VI*, 36–38.

25 Heinrich Graetz, *Volkstümliche Geschichte der Juden*, 2 vols. (Köln: Parkland, 2000), vol. 2, 253–254. Graetz's onslaught on the Kabbalah is relentless in these pages, and even if Scholem's overall evaluation of the *Wissenschaft des Judentums* is itself open to discussion, he is not far off the mark when he describes Graetz's work as follows: 'Das klassische Buch der spanischen Kabbala, der "Sohar", heißt bei ihm das Lügenbuch, und es gibt, wenn er auf die Kabbalisten zu sprechen kam, seinem Temperament entsprechend, ein ganzes Lexikon von Schimpfereien.' (*VBJ*, 131).

26 Gershom Scholem, ''Wissenschaft vom Judentum einst und jetzt', 157.

27 Ironically, Zunz, Geiger and Graetz, to varying degrees, all claimed to picture the totality of Judaism in their work, yet all of them shared a pronounced dislike of at least one aspect of it. With Zunz it was Talmudic scholarship, with Geiger it was the accumulation of Tradition and for Graetz it was mysticism (see Meyer, 'The Emergence of Jewish Historiography', 166 ff. and Weiseltier, '*Etwas über die jüdische Historik*', 138 ff.).

28 Gershom Scholem, ''Wissenschaft vom Judentum einst und jetzt', 156.

29 Gershom Scholem, *Judaica VI*, 51.

30 Gershom Scholem, *Die jüdische Mystik in ihren Hauptströmungen* (Frankfurt am Main: Suhrkamp, 1980), 2.

31 Gershom Scholem, 'Die Erforschung der Kabbala von Reuchlin bis zur Gegenwart', in *Judaica III: Studien zur jüdischen Mystik* (Frankfurt am Main: Suhrkamp, 1973), 247–263; 258.

32 Gershom Scholem, *Von der mystischen Gestalt der Gottheit*, 285.

33 Fifty-four years later, in the essay 'Der Name Gottes und die Sprachtheorie der Kabbala', Scholem returns to this topic and again uses *Philosophie der Geschichte* to explain the mystical meaning of language: 'Die Welt der Sprache ist also die eigentliche "geistige Welt". Der Buchstabe ist das Element der Weltschrift. In dem fortdauernden Akt der Schöpfungssprache, die alle Dinge durchzieht, ist die Gottheit der einzige unendliche Redner, aber auch zugleich der urbildliche Schreiber, der sein Wort in seine erschaffenen Werke einsenkt.' A note to this paragraph says simply: 'Nach F.J. Molitor, *Philosophie der Geschichte oder über die Tradition*, 1. Teil, 2. Aufl. 1857, S. 553.' (*Judaica III*, 36).

34 The mystery surrounding Molitor has been perpetuated by the new six-volume edition of the Benjamin's correspondence, as the editors consistently quote the wrong dates and only one of the places of publication: *GB* I, 359 and II, 20 both have 1828 as the date of the first volume, whereas the earlier edition of the correspondence quoted the correct date, 1827 (*Briefe*, 136). It may be a very innocent editorial oversight, but the fact that the first, correct, date has been 'corrected' suggests that the editors did not have direct access to the work themselves. They also quote Münster as the place of publication, whereas the first volume was actually published in Frankfurt (in 1827).

35 Baader's collected works are still available in a facsimile edition of the second imprint of the *Sämtliche Werke* of 1857, which is the one Benjamin would have used (Franz Xaver von Baader, *Sämtliche Werke: Systematisch geordnete, durch reiche Erläuterungen von der Hand des Verfassers bedeutend vermehrte, vollständige Ausgabe der gedruckten Schriften samt Nachlaß, Biografie und Briefwechsel*, 16 vols., edited by Franz Hoffmann, Julius Hamberger, Anton Lutterbeck, Emil August von Schaden, Christoph Schlüter and Friedrich von der Osten, second edition (Aalen: Scientia Verlag, 1987)). The letters from Baader to Molitor can be found in vol. 15, 516, 520 and 548–549.

36 Benjamin refers Scholem to pages 340, 343–349 and 356–357 of the same volume, containing the 'Erste' and 'Zweite Sendschreiben an den Herrn Professor Molitor in Frankfurt' (Baader, *Sämtliche Werke*, vol. 4, 329–362). The texts are mentioned again in a letter dated 23 December

1917 (*GB* I, 408). So it does indeed sound like Benjamin fulfilled his intention 'mit einiger Intensität zu studieren'.

37   Gershom Scholem, *Von Berlin nach Jerusalem: Jugenderinnerungen*, translated by Michael Brocke and Andrea Schatz, second edition (Frankfurt am Main: Suhrkamp, 1997), 132 (hereafter *VBJ*). The year 1916 is confirmed as the year of acquisition on the fly-leaf of Scholem's own copy of Molitor's book, which is currently in the Hebrew Library of Jerusalem, in which he had written (in Hebrew): 'These volumes were already in my collection in 1916, when I bought the book in Berlin.' (quoted in '"Die Buchstaben haben... ihre Wurzeln oben.": Scholem und Molitor', in *Kabbala und Romantik*, edited by Eveline Goodman-Thau, Gerd Mattenklot and Christoph Schulte (Tübingen: Max Niemeyer, 1994), 145–164; 159).

38   In a letter to Harry Heyman dated 12 November 1916, Scholem speaks very highly of Molitor, saying that his book has greatly improved his knowledge of Judaism and that he 'infinitely regrets' not owning it: '[...] die "Philosophie der Geschichte oder über Tradition" [sic] von Molitor, ein großes 4bändiges Werk über jüdische Mystik von einem katholischen Kabbalisten, das mich sehr gefördert hat, und das nicht zu besitzen ich unendlich bedaure. Allein auf 700 Seiten behandelt er im 3. Bande die Lehre vom Unreinheit im Judentum, der wichtigste Teil seiner Darstellung. Über dieses Buch habe ich viele Gedanken, darunter auch richtige.' (*SB* I, 58).

39   Scholem's ambivalent attitude towards the Germans comes to the fore quite clearly in a series of articles he wrote in the early sixties on the historical relationship between Jews and Germans, the first of which is headed by the telling title 'Wider den Mythos vom deutsch-jüdischen "Gespräch"' (*Judaica 2* (Frankfurt am Main: Suhrkamp, 1995), 7–11).

40   *Allgemeine Deutsche Biographie* (1885), vol. 22, 109.

41   Winfried Menninghaus, *Walter Benjamins Theorie der Sprachmagie* (Frankfurt am Main: Suhrkamp, 1995), 189.

42   *Ibid.*, 189.

43   *Ibid.*, 189.

44   It was the teacher's task to teach the pupil how to learn ('*lernen zu lehren*' as Scholem phrases it), an autotelic activity which was in essence multi-dialogical, occurring not only in the dialogue between teachers and pupils and between pupils amongst each other, but also between the students (teachers or pupils) and the text. These characteristics, which we discussed at length in the previous chapter, fascinated both Scholem and Benjamin.

45 'Wann bringen sie den Molitor?' (*GB* II, 19).

46 Letter from Scholem to Benjamin, dated 19 April 1934, in Walter Benjamin and Gershom Scholem, *Briefwechsel* (Frankfurt am Main: Suhrkamp, 1980), 135.

47 In a diary entry dated 8/9 October 1916, more than a month before Benjamin wrote *Über Sprache*, Scholem has copied out two pages from a notebook Benjamin lent to him, which contained '*Notizen zu einer Arbeit über die Kategorie der Gerechtigkeit*' (*TB* I, 401). These notes are about the difference between law and justice, about divine justice and the messianic and about socialism and communism. In other words, four years before he actually wrote *Zur Kritik der Gewalt*, Benjamin was already thinking about these topics at the time when he was beginning to develop a more intimate knowledge of Judaism. In fact, on the same day that Scholem copied out these *Notizen*, Benjamin and himself read *Die Schwankenden* by Achad Ha'am together. The possible influence of this author on Benjamin still remains to be investigated.

48 Originally submitted in 1976, this dissertation was eventually published as a short book in 1987 (Reiner Dieckhoff, *Mythos und Moderne: über die verborgene Mystik in den Schriften Walter Benjamins* (Köln: Janus Presse, 1987).

Chapter Three: Philosophie der Geschichte

1 'Die judische Kirche überläßt vielmehr diese Sache [the study of hidden meanings of the Torah], als etwas rein Innerliches, dem eignen innern Gefühle eines Jeden, und weit entfernt, gewisse allgemein verbindende mystische Lehrsätze aufzustellen, sucht dieselbe sogar die Forschung in der höheren Mystik zu beschränken, um den gefährlichen Folgen vorzubeugen, die für schwache und unvorbereitete Gemüther leicht entspringen können; daher nur die Weisesten im Volke zur Einweihung in die höheren Geheimnisse gelangen konnten.' (*M* I, 12–13). The idea that mainstream Judaism sought to police mystical traditions because of their radical, antinomian, anarchist and apocalyptic potential is also conveyed by several of Scholem's writings, most famously his study of Shabbetai Tsevi, the seventeenth-century false Messiah.

2 Benjamin's *Ideenlehre* or doctrine of ideas is a complicated, almost baroque construction, which can be found at the seams of his work from

its very beginnings. It is drafted in the essay *Über Sprache überhaupt und über die Sprache des Menschen* and elaborated in *Ursprung des deutschen Trauerspiels*, where Leibniz's monad and the concept of allegory are brought into the picture. Later mentions of the monad, the idea, the allegory and the dialectical image in the series of essays on Baudelaire and in the notes for the *Passagen-Werk* make it clear that all of these terms are part of the construction that is this enigmatic *Ideenlehre*, or, as the veil of mystery shrouding this *Ideenlehre* is never removed entirely, it may well be the case that all these terms *are* in fact the *Ideenlehre*, merely seen from a different perspective. Benjamin believed that criticism ought to use those concepts which were most suited to its objects, and these objects might be as different from each other as sixteenth-century emblems are from prostitutes, but that does not necessarily mean that the apparently different concepts he uses are radically different in their deepest essence.

3   Gershom Scholem, *Die jüdische Mystik in ihren Hauptströmungen*, 204 ff.

4   'Wollen mehrere, insonderheit Morinus, behaupten, weil man viele von den Parabeln und mystischen Lehren des Sohars in den Midraschim und der G'mara finde, so mußte dieses Buch nach diesen Schriften verfaßt seyn. Welch ein Schluß! Wie kann man wohl glauben, daß die mystische Erklärungs-Weise erst zur Zeit der G'mara aufgekommen, da man in der Mischnah, die doch ein kurzer Inbegriff der Gesetzes-Tradition ist, die deutlichsten Beweise der allerhöchsten Mystik findet, [...].' (*M* I, 74).

5   'Die sogenannte Civilisation, wodurch der Jude von dem alten Orientalismus abgeführt, und dem europäischen Leben assimilirt wird, darf durchaus nicht gehemmt, und dem Juden die Annäherung zu dem Christen versagt werden; solches wäre nicht nur unmenschlich, sondern den Lehren des Christenthums völlig zuwider; andern Theils darf aber auch keine Regierung die Hand dazu bieten, den Rabbinismus zu zerstören. Denn dieses hieße das Judenthum, welchem eine Dauer bis zum letztem Ende geweissagt ist, selber ausrotten, und in den Plan der Gottheit selber eingreifen. Kein menschlicher Verstand vermag hier aus sich, das Rechte zu treffen.' (*M* I, 291).

6   There is an interesting parallel between this quotation and Molitor's description of Jewish mysticism in the introduction, where he says that the study of higher mysticism in Judaism was also left to the individual rather than being actively encouraged by the 'church' (as he calls both the Jewish religious community and the Christian institution). This, in turn, is entirely in line with the view that Molitor seeks to present a

homogeneous picture of Judaeo-Christian mysticism, both in time and in space, even though such a homogeneity was already disputed by scholars in his day and age.

7 Molitor expresses the substantial importance of Judaism for Christianity in no uncertain terms: 'Weit wichtiger als die bloße Uebereinstimmung der Form ist die auffallende Aehnlichkeit des Inhaltes in der jüdischen Tradition und der christlichen Lehre, die freilich nicht durchgängig, doch aber in den meisten Hauptlehren deutlich hervortritt. So findet man in der jüdischen Mystik, außer dem Geheimniß der heil. Dreifaltigkeit, das Geheimniß der Erlösung, so wie noch viele andere sublime Lehren der christlichen Religion, wenn auch nicht immer ganz theologisch richtig ausgedrückt, doch wenigstens auf eine höchst frappante Weise angedeutet.' (*M* I, 305–306).

8 In § 20, 17–18, Molitor had defined the Megillot Setharim as the concise written versions of the oral Torah, used by teachers as mnemonic aids, which were entirely esoteric, as students had to be taught through the spoken word only. This, as Molitor points out, is of course also the case with Jesus, who can only be seen writing once throughout the Gospels, in John 8:1–11 (where Jesus writes in the sand with his finger, but the reader is not told what). The passage in question cannot be found in the oldest manuscripts and versions of the New Testament, and its literary style does not match that of the rest of John, which has lead some to classify it as apocryphal. This doubtful provenance makes the passage even more fascinating, as it deals with the very questions of tradition and the permanence of writing. As John is by far the most literary and theoretically sophisticated of the four canonic gospels, it is tempting to read these passages as later literary *Überarbeitungen* of the fascinating subject matter of the gospels, exploring possibilities rather than recounting facts.

9 'Einen der stärksten Beweise, daß Christus der Herr allerdings eine hierarchische Ordnung in der neuen Kirche einführte, und den Typus der jüdischen Hierarchie aufs Christenthum übertrug, gehet aus der mystischen Zahl der zwölf Apostel und der siebenzig Jünger deutlich hervor, und erhält in der Offenbarung Johannes noch seine völlige Bestätigung.' (*M* I, 248n). Obviously, the Catholic Molitor is also implicitly attacking the Protestant conviction that the hierarchic structure of the Catholic church has no foundation in Scripture.

10 This is in fact a point made by Molitor himself when he states that the Jews never lost the truth or lapsed into positive error: 'Wie hätte auch der Maschiach bei seinem Erscheinen verstanden werden können,

wären das Gesetz, die Propheten und die Tradition ganz vergessen, verdreht und entstellt gewesen?' (*M* I, 180).

11   The tone of this passage is so apologetic that hardly anything remains to be said even against these alleged 'exaggerations': 'Obwohl der Heiland zwar an verschiedenen Orten, z.B. Matth. 15. 2., ferner 23. 4., wider die Ueberlieferungen und Satzungen der Aeltesten eifert, so auch Paulus an Titus 1. 14., so waren diese Beschuldigungen doch eigentlich nicht gegen die Kirche und ihren wahren Ueberlieferungen gerichtet, sondern nur die großen Uebertreibungen jenes, ursprünglich zwar aus frommer Absicht eingeführten, aber immer drükkender gewordenen Seders gemeint, §. 289., welches aber blos ein menschlicher Mißbegriff, keineswegs aber ein positives Gebrechen der Kirche war.' (*M* I, 231–232).

12   Molitor obviously has a warm affection for the Jews and their tradition, so much so that seems prepared to pay far more attention to their commendable characteristics than to their less palatable sides, as he attributes the kind and broad-minded statements in the Talmud (of which there are indeed many) to Judaism as such, whereas he says that the 'Menge absurder fanatischer Sätze [...], insonderheit rücksichtlich der andern Völker' are the opinions of 'Einzelner, nicht aber der ganzen Kirche [...].' (*M* I, 233).

13   There is a distinct sense in which Molitor occasionally assumes the tone of the subject matter he is addressing, much as, as Irving Wohlfarth pointed out, Benjamin believed that he himself was destined to fulfil the messianic role he attributed to the historical materialist, and much as it can be a scarcely resistible temptation to mimic Benjamin's writing when writing on Benjamin (See Irving Wohlfarth, '"Immer radikal, niemals konsequent...": Zur theologisch-politischen Standortsbestimmung Walter Benjamins', in *Antike und Moderne: Zu Walter Benjamins 'Passagen'*, edited by Norbert Bolz and Richard Faber (Würzburg: Königshausen & Neumann, 1986), 116–137).

14   See for instance the letter he writes to Salman Schocken in 1937, in which he explains why he has undertaken his Kabbalah studies: 'Drei Jahre, die für mein ganzes Leben bestimmend geworden sind, 1916–1918, lagen hinter mir: sehr erregtes Denken hatte mich ebensosehr zur rationalsten Skepsis meiner Studiengegenständen gegenüber wie zur intuitiven Bejahung mystischer Thesen geführt, die haarscharf auf der Grenze zwischen Religion und Nihilismus lagen.' (*Briefe*, vol. I, 471). This is yet another indication of the importance Scholem attached to his formative years, 1916–1918, which, as we have seen, were also the

years of his most frequent and intensive intellectual exchanges with Walter Benjamin.

15 Giorgio Agamben, *Le temps qui reste: un commentaire de L'Épître aux Romains*, translated by Judith Revel (Paris: Rivages, 2004).

16 In this passage, Molitor refers to another paragraph where he repeats the claim he made earlier, this time from the perspective of the Jewish tradition, and even goes so far as to say that Paul's 'presentation and language' shows 'the most striking similarity to the midrashim': 'Denn in den alten jüdischen Schriften erblickt man ganz dieselbe mystische Weise der Parabeln, Allegorien und R'masim, wie sie in den Büchern des neuen Testamentes, besonders in Paulus vorkommen, dessen Darstellung und Sprache überhaupt die frappanteste Aehnlichkeit mit den Midraschim hat, wie dieses Jeder bezeugen wird, der dieselben nur einigermaßen kennt.' (*M* I, 305).

17 Emphasising the similarity of this description with the mediaeval system of crafts and guilds, Molitor adds in a footnote: 'Nach diesen Prinzipien waren einst die Universitäten, die Zünfte und das Ritterwesen eingerichtet.' (*M* I, 7). In his letters to Scholem in 1917–1918, Benjamin would often state his conviction that this was indeed how education ought to be structured.

18 As we will discuss in the next chapter, Benjamin uses the metaphor of an individual wave in infinite sea to convey the same notion of an all-embracing tradition, into which the individual is immersed and subsumed, almost to the extent that he loses his individuality: 'Die Lehre ist wie ein wogendes Meer, für die Welle aber (wenn wir sie als Bild des Menschen nehmen) kommt alles darauf an sich seiner Bewegung so hinzugeben, daß sie bis zum Kamm wächst und herüberstürzt mit Schäumen.' (*GB* I, 381–382)

19 Elsewhere in book I, in a discussion of the Masorah, Molitor stresses the profound importance of the oral component of tradition, much as the art of narration, to Benjamin, is inextricably linked with the physical presence of the narrator: 'Allein da die Lesung der Bibel, wenn sie auch in Punkten verfaßt war, doch immer Traditions-Sache gewesen, so würde die Berufung auf ein punktirtes Heft der Sache keineswegs mehr Autorität gegeben haben; indem es hier nicht darauf ankam, wie die Punktation, sondern wie die Tradition lautete. Die Punkte waren nur Nebensache, und ehe sie förmlich durch die Masorethen aufgezeichnet, blos ein subjektives Vehikel der Ueberlieferung, ohne allen objektiven Charakter, §. 19. und §. 464., Daher das lebendige Zeugniß der Lehrer, was die rechte Leseart sey, weit mehr Autorität hatte, als jede schrift-

liche Versicherung [.] Von einem solchen Glauben an menschliche Treue und Wahrhaftigkeit kann sich freilich unser jetziges philosophisches Zeitalter kaum einen Begriff machen, und doch beruhet die ganze Religion lediglich auf einem solchen Glauben. Denn wenn wir in die mündlichen Ueberlieferungen unserer Vorfahren Zweifel setzen, wie können wir demjenigen vertrauen, was sie uns als schriftliches Wort Gottes hinterlassen haben?' (*M* I, 392). This quotation, *in nuce*, is what Benjamin's (rather complicated) theory of experience ultimately states, namely that the disappearance of 'traditional' forms of communication such as storytelling are symptomatic of a more profound change in human experience. It is this 'devaluation of experience' ('die Erfahrung ist im Kurse gefallen' II, 439) which makes for an empoverishment of human thought, which now excludes previously valuable experiences, such as the religious experience, as Benjamin explains in *Über das Programm der kommenden Philosophie*. Of course, these are only the roughest possible outlines of Benjamin's thoughts on this matter, but it is nevertheless fascinating to see that he and Molitor both think in similar terms about modern times, albeit with a good hundred years between them, and about the inability of the present 'philosophisches Zeitalter' to grasp the fullness of (religious) experience which the past was able to.

20 Gershom Scholem was well aware of this paradox, as he writes in his diary on 24 March 1918: 'Aber das ist es ja: an meiner Arbeit ist das Wesentliche ja gerade die *mündliche Lehre*, das persönliche (!!) Verhältnis der Menschen in der Lehre, und hiervon läßt sich nicht mehr niederschreiben als eigentlich nur die *Methode*. Denn alles andere würde geschrieben eine Paradoxie enthalten wie alle geschriebene Tradition.' (*TB* II, 157). This statement has a counterpart in Benjamin's correspondence, namely in his frequent insistence that there are certain things about which it is better to speak face to face than to write, as he says in a letter dated June 1917: 'Doch von diesen Dingen ist es besser reden als schreiben.' (*GB* I, 363; see also *GB* I, 358, 391, 402–403, 409, 414, 418–419, 428, 436, 441 and 488).

21 Molitor is caught in quite a difficult position, as he finds himself defending an eminently Jewish conception of language, and one to which the standard Christian is in many ways diametrically opposed (particularly the, albeit protestant, concept of *sola fides*, which emphatically puts meaning above form). Apparently loath to pledge allegiances either way, Molitor thus again ends up with a paradox: 'Unläugbar hat die praktische Kabbalah einen tiefen Grund; doch ist nicht

in Abrede zu stellen, daß von Juden und Christen mit derselben viel Aberglauben und Unfug getrieben worden, absonderlich weil die unwissende Menge in dem Wahne befangen war: die geschriebene Worte seyen Alles; da doch diese die bloßen Träger sind, und in der Seele und in dem Glauben allein die lebendigmachende Kraft liegt, wie dieß [sic] von allen ächten Kabbalisten einstimmig gelehrt wird. Doch ist die Grenzlinie zwischen dem wahren Glauben und dem Aberglauben sehr fein und zart, und daher der Irrthum gar zu leicht möglich. Denn die äußern Formen sind keineswegs blos etwas gleichgültig Todtes, wie der flache Unglaube gewöhnlich behauptet, sondern in denselben liegt allerdings eine wirkliche, obwohl blos äußere erregende, und daher keine innere heiligmachende Kraft.' (*M* I, 46–47). It is quite clear that this statement does not sit entirely comfortably with the previous quotation, in which a greater emphasis is put on the very real mystical force of language in the holy name. One way of treating such contradictions, as Benjamin himself was wont to do, is to suspend the contradiction in a constellation, but even though the effect of Molitor's paradoxical statements is such, it is rarely overtly stated as his intention (this, of course, may be due to the fact that Molitor remains a believer, and thus can resolve paradoxes, rather facilely, one might say, with a leap of faith. The fact that Benjamin does not resolve his paradoxes, but cultivated them, is also the strongest argument *against* the hypothesis, or Scholem's wishful thinking perhaps, that Benjamin believed in God).

22   In the tenth of Benjamin's *Protokolle zu Drogenversuchen*, recording his experiment with opium, Benjamin writes: 'Es gibt keine nachhältigere Legitimation des crocks [*Benjamin's name for opium*] als das Bewußtsein, mit seiner Hilfe auf einmal, in jene versteckteste, im allgemeinen unzugänglichste Oberflächenwelt einzudringen, welche das Ornament darstellt. [...] Es handelt sich dabei einmal um die Mehrsinnigkeit des Ornaments. Es gibt keins, das sich nicht mindestens von zwei verschiedenen Seiten ansehen ließe, nämlich als Flachengebilde oder aber als lineare Konfiguration. [...] Es wird an anderer Stelle darauf hinzuweisen sein, daß diese vielfältige Interpretierbarkeit, die ihr Urphänomen im Ornament hat, nur eine andere Seite der eigentümlichen Identitätserfahrung darstellt, die der crock eröffnet.' (VI, 603–604).

23   This automatically leads us to the Saussurean principle of the arbitrariness of the signifier–signified relationship, which, interestingly enough, the mystical view on language would not *automatically* exclude or deny. Admittedly most language mysticism tends to adhere to the belief

in a created language which must thus necessarily be overdetermined, but it is not impossible to insist that the materiality of language can have a real and systematisable meaning (rather than systematised) while maintaining that the relationship between signifier and signified need not be motivated. The prime example of this is probably Mallarmé's vowel-colour poetry, which in fact amounts to subjective mysticism. In the Jewish tradition, too, the non-arbitrary nature of the signifier–signified relationship can never be used *a priori*, but must always follow as an *a posteriori* coda when the case for a certain argument has already been made. In other words, anyone who would want to state the divine origin of a certain word must first find reasons why this should be so, and these reasons invariably come from the text or from language itself, never actually *directly* from God. Or as Laplace once memorably said: 'Sire, je n'avais pas besoin de cette hypothèse.'

24 Molitor's language mysticism is quite reminiscent of Mallarmé's, which we mentioned in the previous note, but its dynamic, or we might even say dialectic – in the Benjaminian sense – is remarkably close to what Benjamin writes on the evolution of the *reine Sprache*, which will eventually become music, in *Aufgabe des Übersetzers*: 'Die Worte sind Ausdrücke von Begriffen. Die Worte werden aus Vokal- und Consonanttönen gebildet, die an sich selber noch keinen gestalteten Begriff oder Gedanken, sondern blos die verschiedenen Arten von Gefühlen und Empfindungen bezeichnen. Das Gefühl verhält sich zu dem Gedanken, wie das Qualitative der innern, zum Quantitativen der Außenwelt. Der Gedanke quillt aus dem Gefühl; das Denken ist der Akt der Gestaltung, wodurch die Innerlichkeit und Unendlichkeit des Fühlens zur Endlichkeit und objektiven Aeußerlichkeit des Begriffs heraus gebildet [sic] wird. So wie überhaupt die Einheit und Innerlichkeit das Ursprüngliche, die Entfaltung in äußeren Gegensätzen, das hervorgegangene Geoffenbarte ist, so verhält es sich auch in der Sprache; wo das Gefühl das Ursprüngliche, der Begriff aber das Secundäre bezeichnet. Es walten also auch in der Sprache zwei Principien ob, das des Denkens und das des Gefühls, oder das logische und musikalische Princip, da letzteres den Grund von ersterem enthält.' (*M* I, 357–358).

25 Benjamin's essays on Kafka have been discussed exhaustively and well, although unfortunately rarely at the same time. Much like Kafka's own work, Benjamin's essays on him are very dense texts and the notes that accompany the essays in the *Gesammelte Schriften* run over many pages, offering a plethora of often well-hidden themes and topics to the unsuspecting critic. This may well be the reason why the definitive

231

study is still waiting to be written. For a good discussion of certain aspects of tradition in Benjamin and Kafka, see Robert Alter, *Necessary Angels: Tradition and Modernity in Kafka, Benjamin and Scholem* (Cambridge, Massachusetts: Harvard University Press, 1991) and for a good overview, see Bernd Müller, *Denn es ist noch nichts geschehen: Walter Benjamins Kafka-Deutung* (Köln: Böhlau, 1999). See also Daniel Weidner's article 'Jüdisches Gedächtnis, mystische Tradition und moderne Literatur: Walter Benjamin und Gershom Scholem deuten Kafka', *Weimarer Beiträge*, 46:2 (2000), 234–249.

26   According to Molitor, however, the promise – or threat, depending on one's perspective – of a small yet fundamental change in the law was always inherent within the law itself: 'Die Aenderung des Gesetzes in den Tagen des Maschiachs wird in den jüdischen Kirche selber gelehrt, wie dieses aus dem Sohar, den Midraschim und dem Thalmud erhellt. Wenn also im Christenthum das alte Gesetz von Sinai modificirt worden, so stehet solches mit der jüdischen Glaubenslehre in gar keinem Widerspruche; die Juden können also mit Recht der christlichen Kirche nicht den Vorwurf machen, daß sie willkürlich ohne Grund verfahren, und blos den Heiden zu gefallen das Gesetz verändert hätte. Was übrigens von Seiten der christlichen Kirche aus dem Judenthum beibehalten und was aufgehoben wurde, beruhet keineswegs auf blos äußeren zufälligen Beweggründen, sondern auf tiefen wesentlichen Principien, die größtentheils alle in der mystischen Theologie des Judenthums selber ihren Grund haben.' (*M* I, 244n).

27   Ernst Bloch, *Spuren* (Frankfurt am Main: Suhrkamp, 1985), 201–202.

28   In a letter dated 9 July 1934, written in response to the Benjamin's manuscript of the abovementioned *Kafka*-essay, Scholem already reminded his friend who the author of the 'remark about the Messiah' was: 'Und eine Frage: von wem stammen nun eigentlich diese vielen Erzählungen: hat Ernst Bloch sie von Dir oder Du von ihm? Der auch bei Bloch erscheinende große Rabbi mit dem tiefen Diktum über das messianische Reich *bin ich selber;* so kommt man noch zu Ehren!! Es war eine meinern ersten Ideen über die Kabbala.' (Gerschom Scholem, *Walter Benjamin und sein Engel: Vierzehn Aufsätze und kleine Beiträge* (Frankfurt am Main: Suhrkamp, 1983), 195; see also *GB* IV, 463). With his characteristic, now slightly cheeky secretiveness, Benjamin replied to Scholem's question as follows: 'Dies für heute. Denn die Herkunft der Geschichten aus dem "Kafka" bleibt mein Geheimnis, das zu lüften Dir nur bei persönlicher Anwesenheit gelingen würde, wo ich Dir dann allerdings noch eine ganze Anzahl gleich schöner versprechen könnte.'

(*GB* IV, 461). In the letter to Landmann quoted above, Scholem denies Bloch's claim, made in the nineteen-sixties, that he acquired all his knowledge of the Kabbalah from conversations with Scholem, conversations which the latter said never took place, adding: 'Aber so war Bloch nun mal.' (173). This also sheds a different light on the plagiarism controversy between Bloch and Benjamin, suggesting that Bloch did actually hear the story of the 'understated apocalypse' from Benjamin, which in turn lends greater credence to the latter's claim that Bloch consistently stole his best ideas.

Chapter Four: Benjamin's Language Theory

1   'Es ist notwendig, den Begriff der Übersetzung in der tiefsten Schicht der Sprachtheorie zu begründen, denn er ist viel zu weittragend und gewaltig, um in irgendeiner Hinsicht nachträglich, wie bisweilen gemeint wird, abgehandelt werden zu können.' (II, 151). In its 'companion essay', *Die Aufgabe des Übersetzers*, Benjamin does indeed ground the concept of translation in the deepest strata of language theory. This essay, unlike *Über Sprache*, was published during Benjamin's lifetime as the preface to his translation of Baudelaire's *Tableaux Parisiens* of 1923. In a curriculum vitae of 1940, Benjamin still referred to the text as 'den ersten Niederschlag meiner sprachtheoretischen Reflexionen' (IV, 891), but this has everything to do with the fact that *Über Sprache* was never published during Benjamin's lifetime and thus always remained an esoteric document. Nevertheless, in *Aufgabe des Übersetzers*, Benjamin elaborates the concepts of the 'reine Sprache' and the unfolding of language according to the messianic triad of paradise, fall and redemption in a way remarkably similar both to his previous language essay of 1916 and to Molitor's *Philosophie der Geschichte*.

2   Gershom Scholem, 'Walter Benjamin', 219. On the same page, Scholem yet again links the Jewish influence on Benjamin's work with Molitor's *Philosophie der Geschichte*: 'Als ich ihm 1916 erzählte, daß das sechzig bis achtzig Jahre vorher erschienene große vierbändige Werk des Baaderschülers Molitor über die Kabbala, *Philosophie der Geschichte oder über die Tradition*, überraschenderweise noch beim Verlag zu haben sei, gehörte es zu den ersten Werken über das Judentum, die er sich anschaffte, und behauptete viele Jahre einen Ehrenplatz in seiner Bibliothek.' (219).

3　This surgical metaphor is not as fanciful as it may seem. In *Einbahn-straße*, Benjamin himself describes the activity of the *homme des lettres* in the same terms in a short piece entitled 'Poliklinik': 'Der Autor legt den Gedanken auf den Marmortisch des Cafés. Lange Betrachtung: denn er benutzt de Zeit, da noch das Glas – die Linse, unter den er den Patienten vornimmt – nicht vor ihm steht. Dann packt er sein Besteck allmählich aus: Füllfederhalter, Bleistift und Pfeife. Die Menge der Gäste macht, amphitheatralisch angeordnet, sein klinisches Publikum. Kaffee, vorsorglich eingefüllt und ebenso genossen, setzt den Gedanken unter Chloroform. Worauf der sinnt, hat mit der Sache selbst nicht mehr zu tun, als der Traum des Narkotisierten mit dem chirurgischen Eingriff. In den behutsamen Lineamenten der Handschrift wird zu-geschnitten, der Operateur verlagert im Innern Akzente, brennt die Wucherungen der Worte heraus und schiebt als silberne Rippe ein Fremdwort ein. Endlich näht ihm mit feinen Stichen Interpunktion das Ganze zusammen und er entlohnt den Kellner, seinen Assistenten, in bar.' (IV, 131). The description of the writer cutting into the lineaments of handwriting, shifting accents and burning out the growths of the words is an excellent illustration of the concept of the materiality of language, as we described it in the first chapter, but more importantly it also links this linguistic perspective with a privileged user, initiated in an esoteric knowledge which enables him to perform these spectacular operations (one of the words for 'operation' in German is *Eingriff*, emphasising yet again the rather radical physical intrusion into the very heart and matter of the words).

4　See the 'Anmerkungen der Herausgeber,' II, 935.

5　See *GB* I, 343–345, 347, 350, 355, 366ff., 374, 380f., 393, 395, 399, 408, 437 and 458.

6　Letter to Scholem, before and on 6 September 1917 (*GB* I, 381).

7　Letter to Scholem, 22 October 1917 (*GB* I, 393). The punctuation in Benjamin's correspondence is often idiosyncratic, and sometimes verges on the ungrammatical or even incomprehensible, but I feel it would be both inappropriate and arbitrary to tacitly correct it, or to insert [sic] after every instance of doubtful grammar or syntax.

8　From the very inception of their friendship, Benjamin sent Scholem copies of practically everything he wrote – on the latter's insistence. True to his philological nature, Scholem meticulously archived every-thing he received, and it is in large part thanks to this *Sammlung Scholem* that present-day editions of Benjamin's collected works and letters are as extensive and well-documented as they are.

9   Benjamin's claim that 'mehreres aufgeschrieben [ist] was aber noch nicht communicabel ist' is quite reminiscent of the messianic–apocalyptic pathos with which Jesus sometimes speaks, and as described by Molitor in book one: '[...] wenn er ferner spricht: Ich hätte euch noch vieles zu sagen, aber ihr könnt es jetzt noch nicht vertragen, – so zeigt dieses an, daß Christus selbst die Arcan-Disciplin beobachtete, und ihnen nur stufenweise die Geheimnisse enthüllte, indem er bei Herannäherung seiner Leiden weit deutlicher als früher zu ihnen redete, nach der Auferstehung sich noch klarer offenbarte, den letzten Ausschluß aber dem Tröster überließ, der sie in aller Wahrheit unterweisen sollte.' (*M* I, 250). Scholem also noted a certain tendency in Benjamin to identify himself at times with a messianic figure, a tendency which seems to have persisted up to *Über den Begriff der Geschichte*. At times, the theses are marked by the same oblique, yet terse and categorical force of diction which characterises the so-called *Jesusworte* (it is also this paradoxical oblique terseness which lends these *Jesusworte*, and, by extension, Benjamin's 'messianic persona' as it appears here and there throughout his work, their particularly 'Jewish' character, as we described in the first chapter).

10   Scholem appears to have recognised the paradoxical, yet potentially productive position of Benjamin, who was neither Jew nor Gentile in the strictest sense of the word, as early as 1915, when he writes in his diary: '[...] eine verzichtende Jugend, die, wie ich es nenne, um die zerbrochenen Schwerter ihrer Helden stehen wird, mit vollem Bewußtsein das Nationaljudentum verwerfen wird, aber nicht, um in ein besseres Deutschtum aufzugehen, sondern um eine ganze neue Menschheit. Eine revolutionäre Edel-Assimilation: Benjamin z.B.' (entry dated 29 December 1915; *TB* I, 222). Note again the semi-messianic tone in the description of Benjamin. The young Scholem's almost religious adoration for Benjamin before the crisis in their friendship of 1918 is quite explicit in a diary entry dated 1 March of that year, when he writes: 'Ich kann nicht beschreiben, ich kann nur im Wort der Feststellung erklären, welch unendliche Größe der Gestalt mich überkommt, wenn ich an meine Freundschaft mit diesem Propheten Gottes denke.' (*TB* II, 146).

11   On the flyleaf of *Ursprung des deutschen Trauerspiels*, Benjamin writes quite simply 'Entworfen 1916 Verfaßt 1925', thereby giving a very strong indication that the core of his book goes back to the very year in which he wrote *Über Sprache*.

12   Andrew Bowie rightly points out that both Benjamin's concept of truth and, consequently, his writing strategy in the *Erkenntniskritische Vorrede* exhibit similarities with Heidegger, whom Benjamin markedly disliked. In spite of this, Benjamin recognised that they had certain things in common, most notably their interest in scholasticism, as he writes to Scholem in 1921: 'Ich bin auch nach meinen bisherigen Studien vorsichtig geworden und bedenklich, ob es richtig ist die Verfolgung der scholastischen Analogien als Leitfaden zu benutzen und nicht vielleicht ein Umweg, da die Schrift von Heidegger [*Die Kategorien und Bedeutungslehre des Duns Scotus*] doch vielleicht das Wesentlichste des scholastischen Denkens für mein Problem – übrigens in ganz undurchleuchteter Weise – wiedergibt.' (*GB* II, 127). Bowie's reading of Benjamin's work in the context of German Romanticism and contemporary philosophy is most impressive, but paints only part of the picture. His conclusion that Benjamin's concept of remembrance is ultimately meaningless, for instance, is in part due to the fact that he does not read it in its Jewish context, and in part to the fact that failure and hopelessness are as much part of Benjamin's theology as its more 'straightforward' messianism (Andrew Bowie, *From Romanticism to Critical Theory: The Philosophy of German Literary Theory* (London: Routledge, 1997), 239f.).

13   Almost in the same breath, Benjamin describes the being of the Name as a Maimonidean first ground of the ideas and of language, which is not merely the act and expression, but also the source of knowing (not knowledge): 'Es bestimmt die Gegebenheit der Ideen. Gegeben aber sind sie nicht sowohl in einer Ursprache, denn in einem Urvernehmen, in welchem die Worte ihren benennenden Adel unverloren an die erkennende Bedeutung besitzen.' (I, 216). This passage not only confirms the continuity which Benjamin said existed between *Über Sprache* and the *Erkenntniskritische Vorrede*, it also anticipates similar statements about the perceptive qualities of language in *Lehre vom Ähnlichen* and *Über das mimetische Vermögen*, as well as the otherwise enigmatic statement from one of the *Protokolle zu Drogenversuchen*: 'Man hört nicht nur mit den Ohren, man hört auch mit der Stimme.' (VI, 595). We shall return to these texts later.

14   In *Einbahnstraße*, the book of aphorisms which also appeared in 1928 alongside *Ursprung des deutschen Trauerspiels*, and which Benjamin himself very much considered to be the latter's companion volume, we find a paragraph entitled 'Innenarchitektur' about the structure of the tractate, which is very tempting to read as a commentary on his *Trauer-*

spiel book: 'Der Traktat ist eine arabische Form. Sein Äußeres ist unabgesetzt und unauffällig, der Fassade arabischer Bauten entsprechend, deren Gliederung erst im Hofe anhebt. So ist auch die gegliederte Struktur des Traktats von außen nicht wahrnehmbar, sondern eröffnet sich nur von innen. Wenn Kapitel ihn bilden, so sind sie nicht verbal überschrieben, sondern ziffernmäßig bezeichnet. Die Fläche seiner Deliberationen ist nicht malerisch belebt, vielmehr mit den Netzen des Ornaments, das sich bruchlos fortschlingt, bedeckt. In der ornamentalen Dichtigkeit dieser Darstellung entfällt der Unterschied von thematischen und exkursiven Ausführungen.' (IV, 111). Clearly, the notion of a text in which the distinction between thematic and excursive passages has become fluid closely mirrors the appearance of the Talmud, with its interweaving of halakhic and aggadic passages. Even more interesting, however, is Benjamin's description of the tractate as an arabic form: whether or not this is coincidental, Maimonides's *Guide for the Perplexed* was in fact originally written in arabic.

15   Moses Maimonides, *The Guide for the Perplexed*, translated and edited by M. Friedländer, second edition (New York: Dover Publications, 1956), 8. Elsewhere in his introduction, Maimonides talks about why he chose to be selective in his topics in terms which are very reminiscent indeed of Benjamin's concept of truth and revelation within the tractate: 'And even these [selections] have not been methodically and systematically arranged in this work, but have been, on the contrary, scattered, and are interspersed with other topics which we shall have occasion to explain. My object in adopting this arrangement is that the truths should at one time be apparent, and at another time concealed' (3).

16   Maimonides, *Guide for the Perplexed*, 79–80. For a clear summary of Maimonides's major writings as well as his theology, see Colette Sirat, *A History of Jewish Philosophy in the Middle Ages* (Cambridge: Cambridge University Press, 1996), especially 166–185.

17   Although it is a truly fascinating and very revealing text, Benjamin's *Theologisch-politisches Fragment* has not received much scholarly attention, and what has been produced is often not particularly enlightening. Eric Jacobson devoted a long article to it in 2001, which is virtually identical to the first chapter of his book *The Metaphysics of the Profane* from 2003. In both texts, Jacobson quite rightly points out that translating the *Fragment* is not an easy task, but unfortunately goes on to prove this point by producing a translation riddled with inaccuracies. (see Eric Jacobson, 'Understanding Walter Benjamin's Theological-

Political Fragment', *Jewish Studies Quarterly*, vol. 8 (2001), 205–247; 206–207 and *Metaphysics of the Profane: The Political Theology of Walter Benjamin and Gershom Scholem* (New York: Columbia University Press, 2003) 20–21). The first phrase, for example, is translated as: 'First the Messiah completes all historical occurrence', which would have been correct had the first word been *zuerst, erstens, am Anfang, zunächst* or something similar. 'Erst' in this context, however, can only mean 'It is *only* the Messiah…'. Another striking example is the phrase 'es kann nicht zum Ziel gesetzt werden', which Jacobson translates as 'it cannot be set toward a goal'. Bypassing the fact that the expression is not correct English usage, it is a mistranslation of the German 'zum Ziel setzen', which should be rendered 'set *as* a goal'. Both of Jacobson's commentaries on Benjamin's essays are peppered with poor translations and even misunderstandings, to the extent that one cannot but become sceptical of his understanding of Benjamin's German.

18 *Die Aufgabe des Übersetzers* is a most fascinating text in its own right, particularly when read in conjunction with the *Erkenntniskritische Vorrede* or the *Theologisch-politisches Fragment*. Benjamin's description of a translation as 'ein Königsmantel in weiten Falten' which surrounds the original, for example, is surprisingly similar to the description in *Ursprung des deutschen Trauerspiels* of the idea as a dark centre surrounded and illuminated by the phenomena (IV, 15). Similarly, the notion that the translator's 'intention' should not be directed towards the original, but towards 'die Sprache als solche, ihre Totalität', closely mirrors the idea of the death of intention portrayed in the *Erkenntniskritische Vorrede* (IV, 16). Unfortunately, in order not to make our own methodical *Umweg* prohibitively long, we cannot go into these similarities in any detail here.

19 It is a particularly intriguing paradox of the concept of human divinity – apart from the fact that the expression is itself an oxymoron – that the proclamation of one's own divinity, or even the admission of the desire to become sanctified, makes it virtually impossible to then be considered as such. Self-proclaimed messiahs such as Shabbetai Tsevi have always been treated with the utmost suspicion in the Jewish tradition, and Jesus himself usually took care never to proclaim himself to be the Son of God, but merely to confirm what others thought of him: 'He asked them, "But who do you say that I am?" Peter answered him, "You are the Messiah." And he sternly ordered not to tell anyone about him.' (Mk 8: 29–30; see also Mt 16: 20; Mt 21: 27; Mk 11: 33; Lk 9: 20).

20 The remarkable longevity of this concept of truth as the death of intention is borne out by some of the notes for the *Passagen-Werk*, written ten years after *Ursprung des deutschen Trauerspiels*: '[...] jedes Jetzt ist das Jetzt einer bestimmten Erkennbarkeit. In ihm ist die Wahrheit mit Zeit bis zum Zerspringen geladen. (Dies Zerspringen, nichts anderes, ist der Tod der Intentio, der also mit der Geburt der echten historischen Zeit, der Zeit der Wahrheit, zusammenfällt.)' (V, 578). Note also the aquatic metaphor of truth as transitive and intransitive *Versenkung* or immersion in Benjamin's description of Schiller's poem (we will come back to this crucial topos towards the end of this chapter).

21 Eric Jacobson also quotes this passage, again woefully mistranslating parts of it. His version of the final sentence bears very little resemblance to the original, and in fact changes the meaning of what Benjamin actually says: 'The Bible, which is itself considered revelation, must necessarily evolve from the fundamental elements of language.' (*Metaphysics of the Profane*, 87). This should of course read: 'Insofar as the Bible sees itself as Revelation, it must necessarily develop the fundamental truths of language.' Jacobson takes the quotation as evidence that Benjamin did not see his entire essay as a 'midrashic companion to Genesis' as he 'would have been rather unequipped for that' (ibid.). I am inclined to agree that Benjamin did not see his *entire* essay as a midrash, but would maintain that Benjamin was perfectly aware that he was using a Jewish-theological form, whether one calls it commentary or midrash, and that this was very much a conscious decision.

22 As Scholem writes in *Die jüdische Mystik in ihren Hauptströmungen*, in words that sound as if they might have been quoted from *Über Sprache*: 'Sprache erreicht Gott, weil sie von Gott ausgegangen ist. In der Sprache der Menschen, die jedenfalls *prima facie* nur erkennenden Charakters ist, spiegelt sich die schöpferische Kraft Gottes wider. Alle Schöpfung – und das ist ein großes Prinzip bei allen Kabbalisten – ist, von Gott her gesehen, nichts als ein Ausdruck seines verborgenen Wesens, das in der aus Gottes Tiefen selbst quellenden Benennung seiner selbst, in dem heiligen Namen Gottes, seine höchste Vollendung findet.' (*Die jüdische Mystik in ihren Hauptströmungen*, sixth edition (Frankfurt am Main: Suhrkamp, 1996) 19). See also 'Offenbarung und Tradition als religiöse Kategorien im Judentum', in *Über einige Grundbegriffe des Judentums* (Frankfurt am Main: Suhrkamp, 1970), 90–119; 107–108).

23   Jacobson's explanation of the relationship between 'sprachliches' and
     'geistiges Wesen' is quite confused at times, partly because he chooses
     to translate the terms as 'linguistic substance' and 'substance of the
     intellect'. This produces such phrases as 'that, which is communicable
     of the substance of the intellect of a given thing' as a translation for the
     phrase 'das, was an einem geistigen Wesen mitteilbar ist', where he has
     obviously translated the word 'Wesen' twice, once as substance and
     once as thing (*Metaphysics of the Profane*, 93). Most perplexing, how-
     ever, is his rendition of his own sentence 'the linguistic substance of a
     thing is its communicable substance, which is of its intellect and
     therefore its language' into the German 'das sprachliche Wesen ist dem
     geistigen Wesen mitteilbar' (267). As the latter simply means 'the
     linguistic essence is communicable to the spiritual/intellectual essence',
     it is hard to see how that is meant to correspond to his original
     statement, let alone clarify it.

24   Ludwig Wittgenstein, *Werkausgabe Band I: Tractatus Logico-philo-
     sophicus* (Frankfurt am Main: Suhrkamp, 1993), 85. In his article 'The
     Genesis of Judgment', Peter Fenves vehemently rejects any connection
     between Wittgenstein's *Schweigegebot* and Benjamin's *Über Sprache*,
     but he does not consider the paradoxical nature of the latter (his vitriol
     seems to be directed at Benjamin's statement of the ideal but futile
     nature of a being which has no relationship to language). Although
     Fenves' knowledge of Wittgenstein probably far exceeds mine, his
     rather frantic attempt to read *Über Sprache* entirely and exclusively in
     the context of Kant, Husserl, Heidegger and Kierkegaard without even
     a cursory mention of (Jewish) theology – in spite of his promising title
     – nevertheless strikes me as rather tenuous, as it is hard to imagine how
     such a reading could be made fruitful in the *Umkreis* of Benjamin's
     work (Peter Fenves, 'The Genesis of Judgment: Spatiality, Analogy,
     and Metaphor in Benjamin's "On Language as Such and on Human
     Language"', in *Walter Benjamin: Theoretical Questions*, edited by
     David S. Ferris (Stanford: Stanford University Press, 1996), 75–93.

25   There are further fascinating parallels between the thought of Maimo-
     nides, Benjamin and Wittgenstein, and the latter in particular can be
     read, as he rarely is, as one of the only philosophers who have truly
     understood the essence of mysticism. The fact that his approach is not
     dissimilar to Benjamin's comes across perfectly in the lapidary thesis
     6.522: 'Es gibt allerdings Unaussprechliches. Dies *zeigt* sich, es ist das
     Mystische.' (Wittgenstein, *Tractatus Logico-philosophicus*, 85).

240

26   This idea is structurally similar to Maimonides's doctrine of the essence
      of God, which he said was necessarily unknowable and could only be
      described with homonyms and metaphors. In other words, the words
      used by humankind to describe God do not actually describe God *as
      such*, but only an imperfect human construct of a perfect being. This is
      essentially what Benjamin means with his distinction between the
      unknowable 'geistiges Wesen' and the communicable 'sprachliches
      Wesen'. Another fascinating parallel between *Über Sprache* and
      Maimonides's philosophy is the latter's concept of the rationality of
      God and the Law, stating that the Law can be followed by mankind as
      God, as a rational being, would never have decreed a Law which would
      be unfulfillable in principle (an argument not unlike Descartes's postu-
      lation and subsequent denial of the *malin génie*). In a similar move-
      ment, Benjamin states that mankind's God-given task to name the
      whole of creation must also be fulfillable in principle, and that therefore
      human language must be fundamentally akin to the language of objects
      in (the language of) God: 'Unlösbar wäre [diese Aufgabe], wäre nicht
      die Namensprache des Menschen und die namenlose der Dinge in Gott
      verwandt, entlassen aus demselben schaffenden Wort, [...]' (II, 151).

27   Eric Jacobson translates the last sentence of this passage as 'but an idea
      bearing no fruit even within that realm of ideas whose circumference
      defines those of God' (*Metaphysics of the Profane*, 91). He points out
      that this passage is grammatically ambiguous, which is true, but then
      conjures up an ambiguity which is not there, namely 'whether the idea
      of an existence without language belongs to a circle of ideas that God
      does not permit to be fruitful, or if this circle determines the proximity
      of certain ideas to God's ideas (those being fruitful ideas)' (ibid.). There
      is no indication at all in Benjamin's text of God not permitting anything
      – 'diese Idee läßt sich nicht fruchtbar machen' simply means 'this idea
      cannot be made fruitful' – nor of the circle determining anything else
      but the idea(s) of God. The (most probably) non-restrictive relative
      clause 'deren Umkreis diejenige Gottes bezeichnet' can only mean 'the
      circumference of which designates that (or those) of God'. The ambi-
      guity in the passage in fact lies in the words 'diejenige Gottes', the first
      of which can be read as either singular or plural and the second of
      which as a possessive, authorial or object genitive, indicating either the
      idea owned or produced by God, or the notion of 'God'. Since Ben-
      jamin does not talk about God having ideas in *Über Sprache*, but does
      talk about the idea or the concept of God, I would be inclined to read

'diejenige' as a singular and 'Gottes' as an object genitive, and the phrase as 'that (the idea) of God'.

28   In his essayistic short story, 'The Library of Babel', which was written in 1941, Jorge Luis Borges develops a similar idea with regard to the (linguistic) essence of God. Borges defines the universe, which some call 'the Library', and which contains an infinite number of hexagonal chambers, as '*a sphere whose exact center is any hexagon and whose circumference is unattainable.*' Characteristically, concepts and possibilities at the limits of thought lead Borges, too, into the realm of theology: 'Mystics claim that their ecstasies reveal to them a circular chamber containing an enormous circular book with a continuous spine that goes completely around the walls. But their testimony is suspect, their words obscure. That cyclical book is God.' ('The Library of Babel', in *Collected Fictions*, 112–118). The idea of God as an (impossible) circular book, mimicking the unattainable (and hence impossible) circumference of the universe is quite similar to Benjamin's notion of God as the circumference of the realm of ideas. The relationship of these ideas to meaning as such is explained by Borges as follows: 'In order for a book to exist, it is sufficient that it be *possible*. Only the impossible is excluded. For example, no book is also a staircase, though there are no doubt books that discuss and deny and prove that possibility, and others whose structure corresponds to that of a staircase.' ('The Library of Babel', 117). Drawing the logical conclusion form these two quotations, we can state that in order for God, who is a book, to exist, it suffices that he should be *possible*. Whether or not the idea of God can be made fruitful is another matter altogether: Borges says that there is a book in the Library that contains an endless sequence of the letters M C V repeated from the first line to the last: 'For every rational line or fortright statement there are leagues of senseless cacophony, verbal nonsense, and incoherency.' ('The Library of Babel', 114). By the same token, Benjamin does not feel the need to confirm or deny the existence of God: this existence is completely irrelevant and entirely unconnected to the *idea* of God, which is the only thing with which theology *pur sang* should concern itself. Although the connection between Benjamin and Borges has been noted in passing, a comprehensive study of such patterns in Benjamin and Borges remains to be written (see David Stern, *Midrash and Theory: Ancient Jewish Exegesis and Contemporary Literary Studies* (Evanston: Northwestern University Press, 1996), 8 *passim*).

29   The 'absolute Verhältnis des Namens zur Erkenntnis', which exists only in God, should probably be read as the precursor to the distinction between *Wahrheit* and *Erkenntnis* discussed in the *Erkenntniskritische Vorrede*. The reason why we suspect this to be so is because Benjamin defines human *Erkenntnis* in postlapsarian terms as the knowledge between good and evil, which degrades language to a *Mittel*, a means to an end, in other words, designed to accomplish an intended task: 'Indem der Mensch aus der reinen Sprache des Namens heraustritt, macht er die Sprache zum Mittel [...]' (II, 153). And as we have seen, intention and truth are diametrically opposed to one another.

30   The fact that this community of human language should be with the *creative* word of God is even more significant in view of the paragraph that follows the passage from Molitor quoted above, in which he too identifies the 'divine speaking and writing' as creative and infinite: 'Denn die Gottheit ist der einzige, unendliche, allmächtige Redner, in dem ewig fortdauernden Akte der Schöpfungs-Sprache, womit sie immer aufs neue die Schöpfung hervorbringt, und alles Leben mit ihrem göttlichen Odem beodmet [sic].' (*M* I, 341).

31   Winfried Menninghaus claims, as we discussed in the previous chapter, that Benjamin had no knowledge whatsoever of the Kabbalah at the time when he wrote *Über Sprache überhaupt und über die Sprache des Menschen*, and that it is therefore not very productive to quote its sources in an attempt to interpret the theory of language propounded in it: 'Ein unvermittelter Rekurs auf den historischen Textbestand der Kabbala widerspricht also erstens Benjamins eigenen, von Scholem bestätigten Aussagen über sein "hilfloses Nichtwissen auf diesem mystischen 'Erdstrich'." Und er läßt zweitens die Dunkelheit von Benjamins Texten, statt sie zu erhellen, vollends ins Ungreifbare und Unsinnige abgleiten.' (*Walter Benjamins Theorie der Sprachmagie*, 190–191). I feel this is too dismissive by far, as we have pointed out not only that Benjamin's knowledge of the Jewish tradition as such, as he would have gained from his intensive conversations with Scholem, far exceeded the norm of what one would call 'embryonic knowledge', but also that these topoi are not really Kabbalist *pur sang*, but rather form part and parcel of the substance of the Jewish tradition. Moreover, as Benjamin himself states quite clearly, he derives these principles partly on his own account from the form of the Bible as revelation and from Jewish traditional thinking on language itself.

32   In an earlier chapter of book one, Molitor uses the same word, *unmittelbar*, to describe how the Bible speaks (or spoke) to mankind (before

the Fall into tradition): 'Allerdings ist es wahr, daß der Geist des Lebens aus der heiligen Schrifte unmittelbar zu uns spricht; allein welche reflexionslose, reine, ungetrübte und heilige Stimmung des Gemüths wird nicht auch erfordert, um diese göttliche Sprache recht zu verstehen [...] Es ist wahrlich eine große Täuschung zu glauben: man könne der Tradition gänzlich entbehren, [...]' (*M* I, 48).

33 Molitor explains the (residual) 'magic' of the *Urschrift* by establishing a continuity between divine language and writing and human language and writing (which he had described as 'eine Nachbildung des göttlichen Redens und Schreibens'). In one paragraph, he brings together all these topoi and connects them to the Kabbalist doctrine which states that he who knows how to combine letters in the correct way, i.e. someone who understands the mystical import of *gematria* and *notarikon*, which we discussed in the first chapter, would be able to perform miracles: 'So wie das Wort die Abbildung des Gedankens und die fünf Sprachwerkzeuge des Mundes die verleiblichte Offenbarung der innern, Gedanken erzeugenden Grundthätigkeit des Geistes sind: so können die Formen und Gestalten der Urschrift nichts anders gewesen seyn, als der leiblich fixirte Abdruck der unterschiedlichen Bewegungen, die der Geist, mittelst seiner fünf leiblichen Sprach-Werkzeuge hervorbringt; so daß also die Gestalten in der Natur die verborgenen Kräfte des denkenden Geistes offenbaren, wie die Gestalten in der Natur die verborgenen Kräfte des allmächtigen Schöpfers verkündigen. Wenn der Mensch als die kleine Welt ein Bild der großen göttlichen Welt, und die fünf Sprachorgane Abdrücke der fünf geistigen Principien sind, so muß auch das kleine menschliche Alphabet mit dem großen göttlichen in Uebereinstimmung stehen. Dadurch erhält jener so unverständlich klingenden Satz der Kabbalisten [...] seine Erklärung: daß die Buchstaben Abdrücke göttlicher Kräfte sind, daß Gott durch die Magie der Buchstaben Himmel und Erde erschaffen, und derjenige, welcher die Versetzung der Buchstaben verstehe, Wunder zu wirken im Stande wäre u.s.w.' (*M* I, 341–342).

34 In the words of Molitor: 'So sagen z.B. die heiligen Ambrosius und Prosper: "die Himmel seyen ein heiliges Buch mit Blättern und wunderbaren Instruktionen." [...] Die Möglichkeit das Buch der Natur richtig zu lesen, hat aber der Mensch, mit der Fähigkeit die innere Sprache Gottes zu verstehen, verloren; [...]' (*M* I, 340).

35 Molitor's version of this idea is quite interesting: 'Dies Ausprägung der innern Idee in der äußern Gestalt, heißt überhaupt Schrift.' (*M* I, 340). If we replace 'der innern Idee' by 'des geistigen Wesens' and 'Schrift'

by 'Sprache', this sentence would not look out of place in an essay such as *Über Sprache*.

36 'Der Mensch teilt sich Gott durch den Namen mit, den er der Natur und seinesgleichen (im Eigennamen) gibt, und der Natur gibt er den Namen nach der Mitteilung, die er von ihr empfängt, denn auch die ganze Natur ist von einer namenlosen stummen Sprache durchzogen, dem Residuum des schaffenden Gotteswortes, welches im Menschen als erkennender Name und über dem Menschen als richtendes Urteil schwebend sich erhalten hat.' (II, 157). This 'schaffende Gotteswort', which maintains itself *in* and suspended *over* mankind, in its turn echoes the hypothesis mentioned at the onset of *Über Sprache*, stating that the 'geistiges Wesen' of an object exists in its 'sprachliches Wesen', which, in the exact same words, is the abyss 'über [dem die Sprachtheorie] sich schwebend zu erhalten [hat]' (II, 141). It is clear by now that this particular paradoxical construction is at the very core of Benjamin's language essay, and it is this construction which would later evolve into his concept of the *Dialektik im Stillstand*.

37 Gershom Scholem, 'Walter Benjamin', 212.

38 See Jacques Derrida's seminal reading of the Saussurean sign and its implications in 'Signature événement contexte', in *Marges de la Philosophie* (Paris: Minuit, 1972), 365–393.

39 See Williston Walker's *A History of the Christian Church*, fourth edition (Edinburgh: T&T Clark, 1997), 173–180 and 300–310; see also Jaroslav Pelikan, *The Christian Tradition: A History of the Development of Doctrine: Volume 1: The Emergence of the Catholic Tradition (100–600)* (Chicago: The University of Chicago Press, 1975), 256–277 and *Volume 3: The Growth of Mediaeval Theology (600–1300)*, 229–242. A shorter introduction is Gill Evans's highly readable *A Brief History of Heresy* (Oxford: Blackwell, 2003), esp. 67ff.

40 The original Greek text of the gospel according to John is marginally but very significantly different from its translation in both the King James Version and the New Revised Standard Version. Whereas the latter two opt for the stylistically pleasing parallellism 'and the Word was with God, and the Word was God', the original is actually the chiastic 'and the Word was with God and God was the Word', thus appearing to give primacy to neither God nor the Word, and even hinting at the linguistic essence of the deity. The third verse is even more significant in this respect, as it is grammatically ambiguous and appears to deepen the equivalence established in the first verse between God and the Word. Whereas both the King James and NRSV specify that it

was 'though *him*' or 'by *him*' that everything came into being, the original is not as precise. As both θεὸς and λόγος are masculine nouns, the δι' αὐτοῦ which designates the agent of creation can refer to either God or the Word. This ambiguity continues into the fourth verse, 'in him/it was life', and it firmly establishes John both as the most theologically sophisticated as well as – arguably – the most Jewish of the synoptic Gospels. What is even more tantalising is that the standard German version of the Gospels, the Luther translation which Benjamin would have known and used, removes the ambiguity in favour of the Word, not of God: 'Im Anfang war das Wort, und das Wort war bei Gott, und Gott war das Wort. Dasselbe war im Anfang bei Gott. Alle Dinge sind durch dasselbe gemacht, und ohne dasselbe ist nichts gemacht, was gemacht ist'.

41 In volume four of *Philosophie der Geschichte*, Molitor reiterates this idea of an objective language translated by human perception: 'Die Ahnung eines innern, verborgenen, qualitativen, magischen Lebens in dem Seyn der Wesen erweckt in uns jenes namenlose wunderbare Gefühl, das wir bei'm Anblick der Natur empfinden. Auf diesem Gefühle beruht eigentlich die ganze Poesie und symbolische Sprache; nie würde der Mensch darauf gekommen seyn, in den äußern Dingen Symbole innerer unsichtbarer Verhältnisse zu erblicken, so er nicht durch ein dunkles, doch aber ganz bestimmtes Gefühl geleitet worden wäre, daß dem äußern quantitativen Seyn ein inneres qualitatives magisches Leben zu Grunde liege, und das objektive Aeußere der theils bewußte, theils bewußtlose Ausdruck einer mehr oder weniger tiefen innerlichen Lebenssubjektivität sey. – Dies dunkle ahnende Gefühl einer allgemeinen Lebenssubjektivität in der Natur, welches der Urwelt in so hohem Grade eigen gewesen, zur größern Klarheit des Begriffes zu erheben, ist der Gegenstand der wissenschaftlichen Mystik, deren Begründung, und damit die höhere Wiedergeburt der gesammten Wissenschaft der kommenden Zeit vorbehalten zu seyn scheint.' (*M* IV, 252). Molitor's 'dunkle ahnende Gefühl' of a continuous qualitative life underlying the quantitative phenomenology of nature, which may be grasped in the 'Klarheit des Begriffes' by the 'Wissenschaft der kommenden Zeit' is echoed extremely closely in Benjamin's essay *Über das Programm der kommenden Philosophie*: 'Für den vertieften Begriff der Erfahrung ist aber, wie schon gesagt, Kontinuität nächst der Einheit unerläßlich und in den Ideen muß der Grund der Einheit und der Kontinuität jener nicht vulgären und nicht nur wissenschaftlichen sondern metaphysischen Erfahrung aufgewiesen werden.' (II, 167). In

this essay, Benjamin seems to have answered Molitor's call to elevate the intuition of unity into the clarity of a concept, and this concept is experience, as summarised in the concluding *Lehrsatz*: 'Erfahrung ist die einheitliche und kontinuierliche Mannichfaltigkeit der Erkenntnis.' (II, 168).

Chapter Five: Medium

1   It is tempting to think that this description foreshadows the concept of integral prose, which Benjamin develops a few years later. His description of Kant's prose in *Über das Programm* is in the context of the *Lehre*, which is essentially an early permutation of integral prose itself. On this idea of integral prose, see particularly Lieven De Cauter, *De Dwerg in de Schaakautomaat*, 354–367.

2   Gershom Scholem, 'Walter Benjamin', 206. In the same essay, Scholem characterises the unmistakable importance of the idea of the *Lehre* to Benjamin as follows: 'Zwei Kategorien sind es vor allem, die in seinen Schriften immer wieder im Zentrum auftauchen, und, wie ich sagte, gerade in ihren jüdischen Fassungen: einmal die Offenbarung, die Idee der Tora, die Vorstellung von der Lehre und von heiligen Texten überhaupt, und zum anderen der Messianismus und die Erlösung. Die Bedeutung, die sie als regulative Ideen seines Denkens besaßen und die einer eigenen Analyse in der Tiefe wert wäre, kann nicht überschätzt werden' (220–221).

3   'Es bestand sicherlich bei Kant eine Tendenz gegen die Zerfällung und Aufteilung der Erfahrung in die einzelnen Wissenschaftsgebiete und wenn ihr auch die spätere Erkenntnistheorie den Rekurs auf die Erfahrung im gewöhnlichen Sinne, wie er bei Kant vorliegt, wird abschneiden müssen, so ist doch andrerseits im Interesse der Kontinuität der Erfahrung ihre Darstellung als das System der Wissenschaften wie sie der Neukantianismus gibt noch mangelhaft und es muß in der Metaphysik die Möglichkeit gefunden werden ein reines systematisches Erfahrungskontinuum zu bilden; ja ihre eigentliche Bedeutung scheint hierin zu suchen zu sein' (II, 164).

4   'Je unabsehbarer und kühner die Entfaltung der kommenden Philosophie sich ankündigt, desto tiefer muß sie nach Gewißheit ringen deren Kriterium die systematische Einheit oder die Wahrheit ist.' (II, 158).

5   As we mentioned in a previous chapter, Molitor uses the exact same metaphor to describe the tense genealogical relationship between Judaism and Christianity: 'Judenthum und Christenthum verhalten sich wie Knospe und Blüthe, was in dem einen noch verschlossen liegt, ist in dem andern durch die Sonne des Lebens in reicher herrlicher Fülle aufgegangen.' (*M* I, 313).

6   Benjamin makes this statement in the context of the object of *Erkenntnis*, of which he writes: 'Ihm bleibt der Besitzcharakter. Diesem Besitztum ist Darstellung sekundär. Es existiert nichts bereits als ein Sich-Darstellendes. Gerade dies aber gilt von der Wahrheit.' (I, 209). The difference between a reward that can be had, a treasure, and a much more valuable reward which eludes possession, experience, is indeed apparent in Benjamin's parable from *Der Erzähler*. But there is a further complication in Benjamin's definition of truth as 'ein Sich-Darstellendes', namely his insistence that it does not exist (already). This leads us to a fairly crucial point in Benjamin's *Lehre*, which we have been unable to discuss in any great detail, and that is the fact that even though Benjamin does provide us with definitions of truth, true experience and the *Lehre*, it does not necessarily mean that they are accessible to us, or that they exist as such. But, as he himself said on a similar topic about Kafka: 'Wer nicht versteht, was Kafka den Gebrauch dieses Namens [Gott] verbietet, versteht von ihm keine Zeile' (II, 1219).

7   This crucial letter, which was written in response to one of Scholem's essays on education and the Jewish youth movement, also contains an indication of the importance Benjamin attached to the concept of tradition, which he sees as far more important than the subordinate concept of 'Beispiel', as he admonishes Scholem: 'Ich wünschte mir daß Sie in der Ausarbeitung Ihres Aufsatzes den Begriff des Beispiels dergestalt eliminierten und zwar in dem der Tradition aufheben möchten.' (*GB* I, 382). We will come back to Benjamin's *Auseinandersetzung* with the concept of tradition later in this chapter.

8   In *Geschichte einer Freundschaft*, Scholem describes the relevance of this Jewish concept of the *Lehre* to Benjamin as follows: 'In diesen Jahren, zwischen 1915 und mindestens 1927, nahm die religiöse Sphäre für Benjamin eine dem grundsätzlichen Zweifel durchaus entrückte zentrale Bedeutung ein, in deren Mittelpunkt der Begriff der "Lehre" stand, die für ihn den philosophischen Bereich zwar einschloß, aber durchaus transzendierte. In seinen Frühschriften kommt er immer wieder auf diesen Begriff zurück, den er im Sinne der ursprünglichen

Bedeutung des hebräischen "Tora" als "Unterweisung" verstand, Unterweisung nicht über den wahren Stand und Weg des Menschen in der Welt, sondern über den transkausalen Zusammenhang der Dinge und ihr Verfaßtsein in Gott verstand. Es hatte mit seinem, immer stärker eine mystische Note annehmenden Begriff von Tradition viel zu tun' (73).

9   Molitor discusses this concept in book one of *Philosophie der Geschichte*, where he explains the term for rabbinical students, *Chabberim*, as 'Gefährten', literally meaning 'companions on a journey' (*M* I, 185 ff.).

10   Scholem enthusiastically acknowledges receipt of this letter in a diary entry dated 19 September 1917: 'Höchst erfreuenden Brief von Walter Benjamin bekommen. Über Unterricht' (*TB* II, 37). This letter seems to have prompted both Scholem and Benjamin to think about the concept of tradition as a medium, and, as we will point out later, the former subsequently devoted himself to a *Quellenstudium* of his and Benjamin's intuitions, finding quotations from the Talmud to back up his arguments.

11   After its initial appearance in *Über Sprache* and *Über das Programm*, *Medium* again becomes a central concept in Benjamin's doctoral thesis *Der Begriff der Kunstkritik in der deutschen Romantik* (1919–1920), in which Benjamin names the early German Romantics as the first to establish the autonomy of the artwork (see *GB* I, 441), which thus becomes a 'Sich-Darstellendes', and in which he uses the concept of *Reflexionsmedium* to link art, criticism and knowledge as such: 'Die Erkenntnis in dem Reflexionsmedium der Kunst ist die Aufgabe der Kunstkritik' (I, 65). The term *Medium – Reflexionsmedium, Denkmedium –* still refers to the sphere in which thought or art as such must necessarily exist, so its meaning does not appear to have shifted to a considerable extent from its original use in the abovementioned essays. Unfortunately, it does not lie within our present scope to reread *Der Begriff der Kunstkritik* in the context of Benjamin's earlier reflections on tradition, education and knowledge, but it seems likely that Benjamin refracted these reflections through the early German Romantics, coming up with a unified theory of their art criticism which was as much inspired by theology as it was by the Romantics' own writings. Equally probable in my view is the hypothesis that these seemingly disparate conceptions actually share the same deep structure. Or in the words of Scholem: 'Benjamin unternahm es zu zeigen, wie ästhetische Ideen mit theologischen Kategorien aufs innigste zusammenhängen'

('Walter Benjamin', 210). One of Benjamin's own subtle hints which may well point in this direction is the description of his thesis in a letter to Ernst Schoen as 'ein Hinweis auf die durchaus in der Literatur unbekannte wahre Natur der Romantik [...]' (*GB* II, 23). As Lieven De Cauter already pointed out, there seems to be a hidden agenda between and under the lines of *Der Begriff der Kunstkritik*, which is eminently summarised in its own description of Schlegel's work: 'Bei Schlegel tritt [...] das Gradnetz seiner Gedanken unter den überdeckenden Zeichnung fast nie hervor' (I, 44). See Lieven De Cauter, *De Dwerg in de Schaakautomaat*, 32 ff.

12 Scholem also mentions writing a letter to Benjamin in which he expresses his amazement at how much he and his friend had learned about the Jewish tradition over the past years: 'An Walter: Ich denke jetzt manchmal mit Staunen daran, was ich in den sechs Jahren getan habe, in denen die vergangene Epoche Ihres Lebens [sich] beschlossen findet. Ich habe gelernt, wobei freilich dieses Wort nicht in der deutschen, sondern in den unübersetzbaren tiefen Bedeutung zu nehmen ist, die es im Hebräischen und Jiddischen hat, wo lernen schlechthin immer nur die Lehre betrifft. Es ist ein reines Wunder, daß Walter nun auch da ist.' (*TB* II, 151).

13 A good example of *hybris* punished in spite of the piety of the subject in question is the story of Moses and the water from the rock: it is the impatience of the great man which leads him to tap the rock a second time, and which elicits the rather cruel punishment that he will not be allowed to see the promised land for himself (Num 20: 9–13).

14 Benjamin's attempt to use this immediacy strategically elicited the following famous criticism from Adorno on *Über einige Motive bei Baudelaire*: '[...] das theologische Motiv, die Dinge beim Namen zu nennen, schlägt tendenziell um in die staunende Darstellung der bloßen Faktizität'. Even though he was not convinced, as Benjamin was, that this strategy could possibly be effective, Adorno did interpret its essence quite correctly, as he writes in the same letter: 'Täusche ich mich nicht, so gebricht es dieser Dialektik am einem: der Vermittlung' (Letter from Adorno to Benjamin, 10 November 1938, in *Theodor W. Adorno – Walter Benjamin: Briefwechsel 1928–1940*, edited by Henri Lonitz, second edition (Frankfurt am Main: Suhrkamp, 1995), 368 and 366 respectively). Benjamin's reply is polite but firm. He refuses to compromise the 'esoteric' doctrine informing his work, and suggests that this particular 'productive interest' has been with him too long to give up now: 'Wenn ich mich [in San Remo] weigerte, im Namen eige-

ner produktiver Interessen mir eine esoterische Gedankenentwicklung zu eigen zu machen und insoweit über die Interessen des dialektischen Materialismus und des Instituts hinweg zur Tagesordnung überzugehen, so war da zuletzt nicht allein Solidarität mit dem Institut noch bloße Treue zum dialektischen Materialismus im Spiel, sondern Solidarität mit den Erfahrungen, die wir alle in den letzten fünfzehn Jahren gemacht haben. Es handelt sich also um eigenste produktive Interessen von mir auch hier; ich will nicht leugnen, da sie den ursprünglichen gelegentlich Gewalt anzutun versuchen können. Es liegt ein Antagonismus vor, dem enthoben zu sein ich nicht einmal im Traum wünschen könnte' (*GB* VI, 184; *Adorno – Benjamin: Briefwechsel*, 379).

15   'So läßt sich also die Aufgabe der kommenden Philosophie fassen als die Auffindung oder Schaffung desjenigen Erkenntnisbegriffes der, indem er zugleich auch den Erfahrungsbegriff *ausschließlich* auf das transzendentale Bewußtsein bezieht, nicht allein mechanische sondern auch religiöse Erfahrung logisch ermöglicht.' (II, 164).

16   As we mentioned before, Benjamin's letter prompted Scholem too to think about the talmudic joke, and he paraphrases Benjamin's words in his 'Kleine Anmerkungen über Judentum', written in Jena late 1917 and early 1918: 'Walter definiert den talmudischen Witz als das Sich-Selbst-Überschlagen der Lehre' (*TB* II, 206). It is hardly a coincidence that Benjamin's definition of the talmudic joke should use almost the same metaphor as the one he used in his letter on tradition and education, which describes the latter as a 'herüberstürzen aus lebendiger Fülle'. The idea that the talmudic joke is the very *locus* where tradition overturns and collapses onto itself is very accurately reflected in the passage from *Baba Meziah* quoted above, as it calls into question divine authority by affirming the profane. This antinomian, even anarchic subordination of the divine to the profane constitutes the messianic paradox, which lies at the very heart of Benjamin's concept of *profane Erleuchtung*.

17   See also VI, 564, 565 and 581. In one of the notes for the *Passagen-Werk*, Benjamin describes a similar authoritative lightheartedness with reference to space and history: 'Ein nur Wachsfiguren bewohnbarer Aufbau. Damit fange ich plastisch so viel an; der ganze Piscator kann einpacken. Habe die Möglichkeit, mit winzigen Hebelchen die ganze Beleuchtung umzustellen. Kann aus dem Goethehaus die londoner Oper machen. Kann die ganze Weltgeschichte daraus ablesen. Mir erscheint im Raum, weshalb ich die Kolportagebilder sammle. Kann alles im Zimmer sehen; die Söhne Karls III. und was sie wollen.' (V, 286).

251

18   Wissing recorded two other thought-provoking statements in the same *Protokoll* in which the fluid, aqueous metaphor is used, this time to elucidate the notions of images and writing: 'Bilder wollen nur ihren Fluß, denen ist alles gleich', and 'Ich möchte schreiben etwas, das so aus Sachen kommt wie der Wein aus Trauben.' (VI, 596). The last image is particularly interesting in the context of the physical conception of the sign in the Jewish tradition, which we discussed in the first chapter, and its full implications remain to be studied.

19   One notable exception is Hermann Schweppenhäuser's essay 'Die Vorschule der profanen Erleuchtung' (in Hermann Schweppenhäuser, *Ein Physiognom der Dinge: Aspekte des Benjaminschen Denkens* (Lüneburg: Dietrich zu Klampen, 1992), 104–123). However, this essay bears the mark of the editor of Benjamin's collected writings – and it is as such that he deserves the highest praise – in that it is more an extended series of quotes than a serious attempt to shed light on the essence of the *Protokolle zu Drogenversuchen*, somewhat like a bad case of a *staunende Darstellung des bloßen Textes*. A similar critique can be levelled against Tillman Rexroth's editor's note to the first publication of some of the *Protokolle*, but then Rexroth's intention was never to elucidate, but merely to introduce (quoted in VI, 819–821).

20   See for instance *Konvolut I: das Interieur, die Spur*, notes I 2, 6 and I 2a, 1 (V, 286), which incorporate material from the second *Haschischversuch*; see also L°, 13 and M°, 6 from the early notes (V, 1020 and V, 1023 respectively).

21   Towards the end of 1927, Benjamin starts announcing the incipient *Passagenwerk* in his correspondence, tentatively and teasingly. At this point, he still seems extremely reluctant to give anything away about its substance before the work is finished, yet at the same time, he already fears, thirteen years before its final failure, that he will not be able to finish the work (this time because he was still planning to go to Jerusalem and teach at the new Hebrew University). As he writes to Alfred Cohn on 16 October 1927: 'Im übrigen aber bin ich mit Angst und Bangen an eine neue Arbeit verloren, die sich mit Paris beschäftigt. Und weil ich meine documentation vor der Abfahrt zusammenbringen will, verwende ich jede verfügbare Stunde an die Bibliothèque Nationale. Bin ich einmal hier fort, so ist die Literatur, die ich brauche für mich nicht mehr zugänglich.' (*GB* III, 292–293). This early sense of urgency where the *Passagen-Werk* is concerned never leaves Benjamin, and it is his unwillingness to leave his sources in the Bibliothèque Nationale behind which ultimately endangers his attempt to escape the

European war zone beyond redemption. As he wrote twelve years before his death, and the very same letter to Scholem: '[...] nie habe ich mit solchem Risiko des Mißlingens geschrieben [...]' (*GB* III, 322). This sense of urgency later becomes part of Benjamin's philosophy of history, as he writes in thesis V of *Über den Begriff der Geschichte*: '"Die Wahrheit wird uns nicht davonlaufen" – dieses Wort, das von Gottfried Keller stammt, bezeichnet im Geschichtsbild des Historismus genau die Stelle, an der es vom historischen Materialismus durchschlagen wird. Denn es ist ein unwiederbringliches Bild der Vergangenheit, das mit jeder Gegenwart zu verschwinden droht, die sich nicht als in ihm gemeint erkannte.' (I, 695; see also V, 579).

22   The editors appear to be in agreement on the importance of the hashish-project to Benjamin's thought as a theoretical rather than an impressionistic study, stating that 'Das *Buch über Haschisch* war demnach eher als philosophische und erkenntniskritische Studie geplant denn als Sammlung aparter Wahrnehmungen im Rauschzustand.' (*GB* IV, 114–115).

23   See for instance the first note of the second *Haschisch-Impression*: 'Die Erinnerung ist weniger reich, trotzdem die Versunkenheit eine geringere als beim vorigen Mal war. Ich war, genau gesagt, weniger versunken, aber tiefer drinnen' (VI, 560).

24   *Konvolut I* contains an edited transcription of this passage: 'Übrigens schließt diese Stimmung eine Abneigung gegen den freien, sozusagen uranischen Luftraum ein, der auf die ausschweifende Tapezierkunst der damaligen Innenräume ein neues Licht wirft.' (V, 286). This passage shows a remarkable similarity to Wittgenstein's statement in his *Philosophische Untersuchungen*: 'Das Ideal, in unseren Gedanken, sitzt unverrückbar fest. Du kannst nicht aus ihm heraustreten. Du mußt immer wieder zurück. Es gibt gar kein Draußen; draußen fehlt die Lebensluft.' (Ludwig Wittgenstein, *Werkausgabe Band I: Philosophische Untersuchungen* (Frankfurt am Main: Suhrkamp, 1993), 296). Both statements share the lapidary nature of the doctrinal *Lehrsatz*, Wittgenstein's even more so than Benjamin's, and both state the semantic and epistemic – but crucially in no way moral – superiority of the sphere of the 'inside' over the 'outside'.

25   The metaphor of weaving is repeated once more in a later *Protokoll*, where Benjamin writes: 'Es bildet sich jetzt ein Gespinst. Alles verbindet sich mit schwarzem Hintergrund wie auf schlechten Stichen.' (VI, 596; see also VI, 567). The concept of the texture, *das Gewebe*, is particularly fascinating in the context of the Jewish tradition: as we

mentioned before, the name for the subdivisions of the *Sedarim* in the Mishnah and Talmud is *Massekhtot*, or textures. It would be interesting to see in how far the metaphor of the texture in Benjamin's work can be linked to theological motifs. In the case of both the *Haschisch-Protokolle* as well as the *Passagen-Werk*, this link might well be found in the revelation of unexpected correspondences, but we have neither time nor space to elaborate this concept in depth.

26 *Adorno – Benjamin: Briefwechsel*, 370. In the same letter, Adorno adds the following sentences to his wife's observation, showing that he understood Benjamin's sensitivities about both the precarious and the esoteric nature of his project: 'Lassen Sie uns Sie dazu ermuntern uns doch Zugang zum Allerheiligsten zu verschaffen. Ich glaube, Sie brauchen weder um die Stabilität des Gehäuses besorgt zu sein noch dessen Profanierung zu fürchten.' (370–371).

27 Adorno – Benjamin: Briefwechsel, 315.

28 See Benjamin's letters to Gretel Adorno of 25 May 1933 and June 1934 (*GB* IV, 216–218 and 440–442 respectively). The first letter is particularly interesting, as Benjamin gives an encrypted, but nevertheless quite elaborate and revealing description of one of his experiments with opium, but does so in a way that suggests Gretel was already familiar with this practice. The language Benjamin uses, however, is instantly recognisable to anyone who has read any of the *Protokolle*. Describing the consolation provided by the drug, Benjamin writes: 'Woher er kommt, ist eigentlich nicht allzu schwer erratbar, wenn Sie sich nur in die Schilderung des Raums versenken, den ich vor Ihnen entstehen lassen werde und dabei einige Listen nicht vergessen, zu denen ich vor Jahren schon bisweilen meine Zuflucht genommen habe, ja, sie gemeinsam mit Ihnen zu nehmen versprochen habe und deren Künste ich Ihnen, wenn ich nicht sehr irre, im Gespräch schon einmal angedeutet habe.' (*GB* IV, 217). The use of the (code)word *versenken* reveals the topic of this letter beyond doubt, and the fact that Benjamin had already spoken to Gretel about it could mean that she was aware of Benjamin's incipient theory of intoxication.

29 In another note, Benjamin develops the metaphor in an elaborate description of the *Passage des Panoramas*: 'Es war im allerersten Augenblick, als beträte man ein Aquarium. An der Wand des großen verdunkelten Saales zog es von schmalen Gelenken durchbrochen wie ein Land hinter Glas erleuchteten Wassers entlang. Das Farbenspiel der Tiefseefauna kann nicht brennender sein. [...].' (V, 1051). This note is included in the collection entitled *Pariser Passagen II*, written in 1928

254

and 1929, which happens to be around the same time that Benjamin made the following note for one of his *Protokolle* describing perception under the influence of hashish: 'Das ist doch ganz klar, es ist die Welt durch Glas gesehen' (VI, 567 and 569).

30 See also the reference to Maurice Renard's novel *Le Péril Bleu*, which describes people on earth from the perspective of 'Bewohner eines fremden Sterns' as 'Geschöpfe vom Grunde eines Meeresbodens' (V, 994).

31 See also the amended version of this note in *Konvolut H: Der Sammler* (V, 272), which we quoted above.

32 Benjamin quotes a letter from Engels to Mehring to this effect: 'Es ist dieser Schein einer selbständigen Geschichte der Staatsverfassungen, der Rechtssysteme, der ideologischen Vorstellungen auf jedem Sondergebiete, der die meisten Leute vor allem blendet. [...] seitdem die bürgerliche Illusion von der Ewigkeit und Letztinstanzlichkeit der kapitalistischen Produktion dazugekommen ist, gilt ja sogar die Überwindung der Merkantilisten durch die Physiokraten und Adam Smith als ein bloßer Sieg des Gedankens, nicht als der Gedankenreflex veränderter ökonomischer Tatsachen, sondern als die endlich errungene Einsicht in stets und überall bestehende tatsächliche Bedingungen' (V, 585–586).

33 It seems that Benjamin was fully aware of the difficulties his project would face from the onset. In one of the earliest notes, he writes: 'Architektur als wichtigstes Zeugnis der latenten "Mythologie". Und die wichtigste Architektur des 19ten Jahrhunderts ist die Passage. – Versuch, aus einem Traum zu erwachen als bestes Beispiel des dialektischen Umschlagens. Schwierigkeit dieser dialektischen Technik.' (V, 1002).

34 In the 'final' version of the *Über den Begriff der Geschichte*, this passage was cut considerably: the entire explanation of why the image of the past is so fragile has been left out, possibly because, as a revelation itself, it was too explicit (see I, 695). So even in the latest stages of his work, we again have an esoteric, *verschollener* text underlying Benjamin's writings.

35 Susan Buck-Morss's otherwise insightful book on the *Passagen-Werk*, *The Dialectics of Seeing: Walter Benjamin and the Arcades Project* (Cambridge, Massachussetts: The MIT Press, 1989), is conspicuously silent on this matter, and even Lieven De Cauter, whose book *De Dwerg in de Schaakautomaat* incorporates two extremely revealing

chapters about the *Passagen-Werk*, professed to be quite bemused by it in conversation.

36 See also VI, 581 and notes G°, 5 (V, 1009) and c°, 3 of the *Passagen-Werk*, the latter of which opens with the highly significant line: 'Zweideutigkeit der Passagen als eine Zweideutigkeit des *Raumes*' (V, 1050).

37 David Stern, 'Midrash and the Language of Exegesis', 108 (our emphasis).

38 Benjamin situates the optical on the side of the dream and the haptic or tactile firmly on the side of awakening, this is why he saw a revolutionary potential in the figure of the collector, for whom the touch of an object is of the utmost importance: 'Besitz und Haben sind dem Taktischen zugeordnet und stehen in einem gewissen Gegensatz zum Optischen. Sammler sind Menschen mit taktischem Instinkt. Übrigens hat neuerdings mit der Abkehr vom Naturalismus der Primat des Optischen aufgehört, der das vorige Jahrhundert beherrscht' (V, 274).

39 As he was crossing the Pyrenées, trying to reach Spain, Benjamin was carrying a large black briefcase, in all probability containing *Über den Begriff der Geschichte*, about which he said to his guide, Lisa Fittko: 'You must understand that this briefcase is the most important thing to me, […] I cannot risk losing it. It is the manuscript that *must* be saved. It is more important than I am.' (Lisa Fittko, 'The Story of Old Benjamin', quoted in 'Anmerkungen der Herausgeber', V, 1187).

40 The version which eventually made it into *Über den Begriff der Geschichte*, a text with an extremely complex redaction, has been condensed into a more concentrated image, yet it still contains the highly significant *Lehrsatz*, hidden in a grammatical ambiguity, stating that the dwarf of theology sits 'in Wahrheit': 'Bekanntlich soll es einen Automaten gegeben haben, der so konstruiert gewesen sei, daß er jeden Zug eines Schachspielers mit einem Gegenzuge erwidert habe, der ihm den Gewinn der Partie sicherte. Eine Puppe in türkischer Tracht, eine Wasserpfeife im Munde, saß vor dem Brett, das auf einem geräumigen Tisch aufruhte. Durch ein System von Spiegeln wurde die Illusion erweckt, dieser Tisch sei von allen Seiten durchsichtig. In Wahrheit saß ein buckliger Zwerg darin, der ein Meister im Schachspiel war und die Hand der Puppe an Schnüren lenkte. Zu dieser Apparatur kann man sich ein Gegenstück in der Philosophie vorstellen. Gewinnen soll immer die Puppe, die man "historischen Materialismus" nennt. Sie kann es ohne weiteres mit jedem aufnehmen, wenn sie die Theologie in ihrem Dienst nimmt, die heute bekanntlich klein und häßlich ist und sich ohnehin nicht darf blicken lassen.' (I, 693).

41 'Diese Übung hat sich allen Epochen, denen die unumschreibliche Wesenheit des Wahren vor Augen stand, in einer Propaedeutik aufgenötigt, die man mit dem scholastischen Terminus des Traktats darum ansprechen darf, weil er jenen wenn auch latenten Hinweis auf die Gegenstände der Theologie enthält, ohne welche der Wahrheit nicht gedacht werden kann.' (I, 208). Benjamin uses the term *Propaedeutik* to refer to the exercise of the form, which is the *Traktat*, meant to prepare philosophy to become a 'Darstellung der Wahrheit', speaking with the 'didaktische Autorität der Lehre' (I, 207–208). It is quite interesting that he later chooses to use the same term, in its German version *Vorschule*, to describe the relationship of intoxication to *profane Erleuchtung*, and it may serve as yet a further indication of the structural and conceptual parallels which continue to inform Benjamin's work.

42 The implication that the *kommende Philosophie* could thus well be, quite simply, theology, is anticipated by Benjamin himself at the end of his essay: 'Eine solche Philosophie wäre entweder in ihrem allgemeinen Teile selbst als Theologie zu bezeichnen oder wäre dieser sofern sie etwa historisch philosophische Elemente einschließt übergeordnet.' (II, 168).

43 In the *Nachtrag* to *Über das Programm*, Benjamin insists on the same distinction between theology and religion: 'Zunächst ist es klar daß es sich im Grunde nicht um die Frage nach dem Verhältnis zwischen Philosophie und Religion, sondern nach dem zwischen Philosophie und Lehre von der Religion handeln muß; mit andren Worten um die Frage nach dem Verhältnis der Erkenntnis überhaupt zur Erkenntnis von der Religion.' (II, 169–170). In a short text from around 1917, with the ambitious title *Über die Ordnung der Dinge*, Scholem, perhaps quite surprisingly, says he feels it is 'augenblicklich ganz gleichgültig, ob das Zentrum der Dinge nun "existiert" oder "nicht existiert". (Dies ist die mir also höchst uninteressante Fragestellung der Atheisten).' (*TB* II, 107). Scholem's attitude towards religious belief, not least his own, is quite ambiguous and often even contradictory, as Daniel Weidner points out (see *Gershom Scholem*, 67 and 242). In diary entries between 1914 and 1918, he confesses to having profoundly atheist thoughts and at one point even goes so far as to say that he can no longer believe in a personal God (*TB* I, 79). Yet towards the end of his life, when he writes *Geschichte einer Freundschaft*, Scholem claims that both his and Benjamin's belief in God was always unproblematic and unquestionable (*GF*, 73), denying the deeply-felt scepticism of his youth. For this

reason alone, Scholem's judgement of Benjamin's religious beliefs should probably not be taken as gospel truth.

44   The essay reads: 'Die Bibel, indem sie sich selbst als Offenbarung betrachtet, muß notwendig die sprachlichen Grundtatsachen entwickeln' (II, 147), which means that because the Bible sees itself as revelation, it has to develop the basic facts of language, and not, as Eric Jacobson would have it: 'The Bible, which is itself considered revelation, must necessarily evolve from the fundamental elements of language.' (*Metaphysics of the Profane*, 87). In this one sentence, Jacobson has reversed the word order of both main clause and subclause, turning what Benjamin says completely on its head.

45   In the Septuagint, this becomes ἐγώ εἰμι ὁ ὤν, which translates as '*I* [emphatically] am who [is] being', with the last form being a present participle. This expresses even more clearly the radical immediacy of existence described in the passage, and could even be said to mimic the construct state in the original Hebrew.

46   From this perspective, Benjamin does remain faithful to the heterodoxy we have described above, which conceives of God as a linguistic entity, when he quotes Hamann in *Über Sprache*: "'*Sprache, die Mutter* der Vernunft und *Offenbarung*, ihr A und Ω'" (II, 147).

47   Note that Benjamin uses the same construction to define God as he does in *Über Sprache*, where God is not addressed directly, but described through his penumbra: '[...] im Bezirk der Ideen, deren Umkreis diejenige Gottes bezeichnet, [...]' (II, 141). It is tempting to interpret this cautious circumnavigation as a strategy dictated by the theological nature of the concept, as we have explained above.

48   Thesis 27 is no less remarkable, as it basically repeats what Benjamin had written to Scholem in 1917: 'Die Lehre ist das Medium, in dem sich der Lernende in den Lehrer verwandelt. Die Gelehrten sind die Schüler der Weisen' (*TB* II, 302).

Epilogue

1   *Walter Benjamin – Gershom Scholem: Briefwechsel 1933–1940*, edited by Gershom Scholem, first edition (Frankfurt am Main: Suhrkamp, 1980), 137.

2   The ethics of Benjamin's philosophy of history and their roots in Jewish theology are discussed in Michael Löwy, *Rédemption et Utopie: Le*

Judaïsme Libertaire en Europe Centrale: Une Étude d'Affinité Élective (Paris: Presses Universitaires de France, 1988) and in Stéphane Mosès, *L'Ange de l'Histoire: Rosenzweig, Benjamin, Scholem* (Paris: Seuil, 1992).

3   Hans Puttnies and Gary Smith, *Benjaminiana: eine biographische Recherche* (Giessen: Anabas, 1991), 67.

Bibliography

Theodor W. Adorno, *Noten zur Literatur*, edited by Rolf Tiedemann (Frankfurt am Main: Suhrkamp, 1981).

—— *Minima Moralia: Reflexionen aus dem beschädigten Leben* (Frankfurt am Main: Suhrkamp, 1997).

Giorgio Agamben, 'Langue et Histoire: Catégories Historiques et Catégories Linguistiques dans la Pensée de Walter Benjamin' in *Passages: Walter Benjamin at Paris*, edited by Heinz Wismann (Paris: Cerf, 1986), 781–807.

—— *Le temps qui reste: un commentaire de L'Épître aux Romains*, translated by Judith Revel (Paris: Rivages, 2004).

Robert Alter, *Necessary Angels: Tradition and Modernity in Kafka, Benjamin and Scholem* (Cambridge, Massachusetts: Harvard University Press, 1991).

Bettina von Arnim, *Werke und Briefe*, 5 vols., edited by Gustav Konrad (Frechen/Köln: Bartmann, 1959).

Steven Aschheim, *Scholem, Arendt, Klemperer: Intimate Chronicles in Turbulent Times* (Bloomington: Indiana University Press, 2001).

Franz Xaver von Baader, *Sämtliche Werke: Systematisch geordnete, durch reiche Erläuterungen von der Hand des Verfassers bedeutend vermehrte, vollständige Ausgabe der gedruckten Schriften samt Nachlaß, Biografie und Briefwechsel*, 16 vols., edited by Franz Hoffmann, Julius Hamberger, Anton Lutterbeck, Emil August von Schaden, Christoph Schlüter and Friedrich von der Osten, second edition (Aalen: Scientia Verlag, 1987).

Ian Balfour, 'Reversal, Quotation (Benjamin's History)', *Modern Language Notes*, 106 (1991), 622–647.

James Barr, *The Semantics of Biblical Language* (London: SCM Press, 1983).

Walter Benjamin, *Gesammelte Schriften*, 7 vols. and 3 suppl., edited by Rolf Tiedemann, Herman Schweppenhäuser and others (Frankfurt am Main: Suhrkamp, 1974–1999).

—— *Briefe*, 2 vols., edited by Gershom Scholem and Theodor W. Adorno, second edition (Frankfurt am Main: Suhrkamp, 1973).

—— *Gesammelte Briefe*, 6 vols., edited by Christoph Gödde and Henri Lonitz, (Frankfurt am Main: Suhrkamp, 1995– 2000).

—— *Walter Benjamin – Gershom Scholem: Briefwechsel 1933–1940*, edited by Gershom Scholem, first edition (Frankfurt am Main: Suhrkamp, 1980).

—— *Theodor W. Adorno – Walter Benjamin: Briefwechsel 1928–1940*, edited by Henri Lonitz, second edition (Frankfurt am Main: Suhrkamp, 1995).

—— *One-Way Street and Other Writings*, translated by Edmund Jephcott and Kingsley Shorter (London: Verso, 1997).

Yosef Ben-Shlomo, 'The Spiritual Universe of Gershom Scholem', *Modern Judaism*, 5:1 (1985), 21–38.

David Biale, *Gershom Scholem: Kabbalah and Counter-History*, second edition (Cambridge, Massachusetts: Harvard University Press, 1982).

—— 'Gershom Scholem's Ten Unhistorical Aphorisms on Kabbalah: Text and Commentary' *Modern Judaism*, 5:1 (1985), 67–93.

Ernst Bloch, *Werkausgabe*, 19 vols. (Frankfurt am Main: Suhrkamp, 1985).

Norbert W. Bolz and Richard Faber (eds.), *Antike und Moderne: Zu Walter Benjamin's 'Passagen'* (Würzburg: Königshausen & Neumann, 1986).

Thorleif Boman, *Hebrew Thought Compared with Greek*, translated by Jules L. Moreau (London: SCM Press, 1960).

Joseph Bonsirven, *Exégèse Rabbinique et Exégèse Paulinienne* (Paris: Beauchesne, 1939).

Jorge Luis Borges, *Collected Fictions*, translated by Andrew Hurley (London: Penguin, 2000).

Andrew Bowie, *From Romanticism to Critical Theory: The Philosophy of German Literary Theory* (London: Routledge, 1997).

Michael Brenner, *The Renaissance of Jewish Culture in Weimar Germany* (New Haven: Yale University Press, 1996).

—— 'Gnosis and History: Polemics of German-Jewish Identity from Graetz to Scholem', *New German Critique*, 77 (1999), 45–60.

Michael Brenner, Stefi Jersch-Wenzel and Michael A. Meyer (eds.), *Deutsch-Jüdische Geschichte in der Neuzeit*, 4 vols. (München: C.H. Beck, 2000).

David Instone Brewer, *Techniques and Assumptions in Jewish Exegesis before 70 CE* (Tübingen: J.C.B Mohr, 1992).

Gerald Bruns, 'Midrash and Allegory: The Beginnings of Scriptural Interpretation', in *The Literary Guide to the Bible*, edited by Robert Alter and Frank Kermode (London: Collins, 1987), 625–646.

—— 'The Hermeneutics of Midrash', in *The Book and the Text: The Bible and Literary Theory*, edited by Regina Schwartz (Oxford: Blackwell, 1990), 189–213.

Susan Buck-Morss, 'Walter Benjamin – Revolutionary Writer (I)', *New Left Review*, 128 (1981), 50–75.

—— 'Walter Benjamin – Revolutionary Writer (II)', *New Left Review*, 129 (1981), 76–97.

—— *The Dialectics of Seeing: Walter Benjamin and the Arcades Project* (Cambridge, Massachussetts: The MIT Press, 1989).

Rudolf Bultmann, 'Boman, Hebräisches und Griechisches Denken', *Gnomon*, 27 (1955), 551–558.

George Bradford Caird, *The Language and Imagery of the Bible* (London: Duckworth, 1980).

Arthur A. Cohen and Paul Mendes-Flohr (eds.), *Contemporary Jewish Religious Thought: Original Essays on Critical Concepts, Movements and Beliefs* (New York: The Free Press, 1987).

F.L. Cross and E.A. Livingstone, *The Oxford Dictionary of the Christian Church*, third edition (Oxford: Oxford University Press, 1997).

Joseph Dan, 'Gershom Scholem's Reconstruction of Early Kabbalah', *Modern Judaism*, 5:1 (1985), 39–66.

—— 'Scholem's view of Messianism', *Modern Judaism*, 12:2 (1992), 117–128.

Jean Daniélou, *The Theology of Jewish Christianity*, translated by John A. Baker (London: Darton, Longman & Todd, 1964).

Lieven De Cauter, *Archeologie van de Kick: Verhalen over Moderniteit en Ervaring* (Amsterdam/Leuven: De Balie/Van Halewijck, 1995).

—— *De Dwerg in de Schaakautomaat: Benjamins Verborgen Leer* (Nijmegen: SUN, 1999).

Jacques Derrida, *Marges de la Philosophie* (Paris: Minuit, 1972).

—— 'Des tours de Babel', in *Psyché: Inventions de l'Autre* (Paris: Galilée, 1987), 203–235.

—— 'Prénom de Benjamin', in *Force de Loi: Le Fondement Mystique de l'Autorité* (Paris: Galilée, 1994), 67–146.

Astrid Deuber-Mankowsky, *Der frühe Walter Benjamin und Hermann Cohen: jüdische Werte, kritische Philosophie, vergängliche Erfahrung* (Berlin: Verlag Vorwerk 8, 2000).

Nicholas de Lange, *Judaism*, second edition (Oxford: Oxford University Press, 2003).

Hent de Vries, 'Theologie als Allegorie: Over de Status van de Joodse Gedachtenmotieven in het Werk van Walter Benjamin', in *Vier Joodse*

Denkers in de Twintigste Eeuw: Rosenzweig – Levinas – Benjamin – Fackenheim, edited by H.J. Heering a.o. (Kampen: Kok Agora, 1987), 23–51.

—— 'Anti-Babel: the "Mystical Postulate" in Benjamin, de Certeau and Derrida', *Modern Language Notes*, 107 (1992), 441–477.

Reiner Dieckhoff, *Mythos und Moderne: über die verborgene Mystik in den Schriften Walter Benjamins* (Köln: Janus Presse, 1987).

Michael N. Dobkowski, 'Judaism and Marxism: On the Necessity of Dialogue', in *Approaches to Modern Judaism*, vol. 1, edited by Marc Lee Raphael (Chico, California: Scholars Press, 1983), 31–62.

Jürgen Ebach, 'Agesilaus Santander und Benedix Schönflies: Die verwandelten Namen Walter Benjamins', in *Antike und Moderne: Zu Walter Benjamins 'Passagen'*, edited by Norbert Bolz and Richard Faber (Würzburg: Königshausen & Neumann, 1986), 148–153.

Howard Eilberg-Schwartz, 'Who's Kidding Whom?: A Serious Reading of Rabbinic Word Plays', *Journal of the American Academy of Religion*, 55 (1987), 765–788.

Hans Erler and Ernst Ludwig Ehrlich (eds.), *Judentum verstehen: Die Aktualität jüdischen Denkens von Maimonides bis Hannah Arendt* (Frankfurt: Campus, 2002).

Gillian Evans, *A Brief History of Heresy* (Oxford: Blackwell, 2003).

David M. Feldman, 'The Structure of Jewish Law', in *Jewish Law and Legal Theory*, edited by Martin P. Golding (New York: State University of New York Press, 1993), 4–19.

David S. Ferris (ed.), *Walter Benjamin: Theoretical Questions* (Stanford: Stanford University Press, 1996).

Aris Fioretos, 'Contraction (Benjamin, Reading, History)', *Modern Language Notes*, 110 (1995), 540–564.

Adolphe Franck, *Die Kabbala oder die Religions-Philosophie der Hebräer*, translated by Adolf Jelinek (Leipzig: Heinrich Hunger, 1844).

Carl Frankenstein, *Franz Joseph Molitors metaphysische Geschichtsphilosophie* (Berlin: Reuther und Reichard, 1928).

H. Freedman and Maurice Simon (eds.), *The Midrash*, 10 vols., translated and edited by H. Freedman and Maurice Simon, (London: Soncino Press, 1939).

Heinrich Graetz, *Volkstümliche Geschichte der Juden*, 2 vols. (Köln: Parkland, 2000).

Klaus Garber, *Zum Bilde Walter Benjamins: Studien, Porträts, Kritiken* (München: Wilhelm Fink, 1992).

Lloyd P. Gartner, *History of the Jews in Modern Times* (Oxford: Oxford University Press, 2001).

Birger Gerhardsson, *Memory and Manuscript: Oral Tradition and Written Transmission in Rabbinic Judaism and Early Christianity*, translated by Eric J. Sharpe (Lund/ Copenhagen: Gleerup/ Munksgaard, 1961)

Arthur Gibson, *Biblical Semantic Logic: A Preliminary Analysis* (Oxford: Blackwell, 1981).

Sander L. Gilman and Jack Zipes (eds.), *The Yale Companion to Jewish Writing and Thought in German Culture 1096–1996* (New Haven: Yale University Press, 1997).

Eveline Goodman-Thau, Gerd Mattenklott and Christoph Schulte (eds.), *Kabbala und Romantik* (Tübingen: Max Niemeyer, 1994).

Harvey E. Goldberg, 'Epilogue: Text in Jewish Society and the Challenge of Comparison', in *Judaism Viewed from Within and from Without*, edited by Harvey E. Goldberg (New York: State University of New York Press, 1987), 315–329.

Robert Gordis, *The Dynamics of Judaism: A Study in Jewish Law* (Bloomington: Indiana University Press, 1990).

William Scott Green, 'Scripture in Rabbinic Judaism', *Horizons in Biblical Theology*, 9 (1987), 27–40.

—— 'Romancing The Tome: Rabbinic Hermeneutics and the Theory of Literature', in *Semeia 40: Text and Textuality*, edited by Charles E. Winquist (Decatur, Georgia: Scholars Press, 1987), 147–168.

Susan A. Handelman, *The Slayers of Moses: The Emergence of Rabbinic Interpretation in Modern Literary Theory* (Albany: State University of New York Press, 1982).

—— *Fragments of Redemption: Jewish Thought and Literary Theory in Benjamin, Scholem and Levinas* (Bloomington: Indiana University Press, 1991).

N.S. Hecht, B.S. Jackson, S.M. Passamaneck, D. Piatelli, and A.M. Rabello (eds.), *An Introduction to the History and Sources of Jewish Law* (Oxford: Clarendon Press, 1996).

Moses Hess, *Rome and Jerusalem*, translated and edited by Rabbi Maurice J. Bloom (New York: Philosophical Library, 1958).

Johannes Hessen, *Platonismus und Prophetismus: Die antike und die biblische Geisteswelt in strukturvergleichender Betrachtung* (Munich: Ernst Reinhardt, 1939).

Hans Heinz Holz, 'Kontinuität und Bruch im Denken Walter Benjamins', in *Bruch und Kontinuität: Jüdisches Denken in der europäischen*

Geistesgeschichte, edited by Eveline Goodman-Thau and Michael Daxner (Berlin: Akademie Verlag, 1995), 129–139.

K. Hruby, 'Exégèse Rabbinique et Exégèse Patristique', in *Exégèse Biblique et Judaisme*, edited by Jacques-E. Menard (Strasbourg: Faculté de Théologie Catholique, 1973), 187–218.

Moshe Idel, *Kabbalah: New Perspectives* (New Haven: Yale University Press, 1988).

—— 'Rabbinism versus Kabbalism: On G. Scholem's Phenomenology of Judaism', *Modern Judaism*, 11:3 (1991), 281–296.

Carol Jacobs, *In the Language of Walter Benjamin* (Baltimore: Johns Hopkins University Press, 1999).

Irving Jacobs, *The Midrashic Process: Tradition and Interpretation in Rabbinic Judaism* (Cambridge: Cambridge Univerity Press, 1995).

Louis Jacobs, *A Jewish Theology* (London: Darton, Longman & Todd, 1973).

Eric Jacobson, 'Understanding Walter Benjamin's Theological-Political Fragment', *Jewish Studies Quarterly*, vol. 8 (2001), 205–247.

—— *Metaphysics of the Profane: The Political Theology of Walter Benjamin and Gershom Scholem* (New York: Columbia University Press, 2003).

Martin S. Jaffee, 'A Rabbinic Ontology of the Written and Spoken Word: On Discipleship, Transformative Knowledge and the Living Texts of Oral Torah', *Journal of the American Academy of Religion*, 65:3 (1997), 525–549.

Christoph Jamme and Otto Pöggeler (eds.), *Homburg vor der Höhe in der deutschen Geistesgeschichte: Studien zum Freundeskreis um Hegel und Hölderlin* (Stuttgart: Klett-Cotta, 1981).

Werner G. Jeanrond, Theological Hermeneutics: Development and Significance (London: SCM Press, 1994).

Immanuel Kant, *Kritik der reinen Vernunft*, 2 vols., edited by Wilhelm Weischedel (Frankfurt am Main: Suhrkamp, 1974).

Jacob Katz, *Jews and Freemasons in Europe 1727–1939*, translated by Leonard Oschry (Cambridge, Mass.: Harvard University Press, 1970).

Heinrich Kaulen, 'Leben im Labyrinth: Walter Benjamins letzte Lebensjahre', *Neue Rundschau*, 1 (1982), 34–59.

Andreas Kilcher, 'Franz Joseph Molitors Kabbala-Projekt vor dem Hintergrund seiner intellektuellen Biographie', *Zeitschrift für Religions- und Geistesgeschichte*, vol. 55:2 (2003), 137–166.

H.D. Kittsteiner, Jonathan Monroe and Irving Wohlfarth, 'Walter Benjamin's Historicism', *New German Critique*, 39 (1986), 179–215.

Leonard Knothe, 'Zur Frage des Hebräischen Denkens', *Zeitschrift für die Alttestamentliche Wissenschaft*, 70 (1958), 175–181.

Ralf Konersmann, *Erstarrte Unruhe: Walter Benjamins Begriff der Geschichte* (Frankfurt am Main: Fischer, 1991).

—— 'Walter Benjamins "Kritische Historie"', *Neue Rundschau*, 103:3 (1992), 140–158.

Peter Koslowski (ed.), *Die Philosophie, Theologie und Gnosis Franz von Baaders: Spekulatives Denken zwischen Aufklärung, Restauration und Romantik* (Wien: Passagen, 1993).

Jakob Z. Lauterbach (ed.), *Mekilta de-Rabbi Ishmael: A Critical Edition On the Basis Of the Manuscripts and Early Editions with an English Translation, Introduction and Notes*, 3 vols., edited and translated by Jacob Z. Lauterbach (Philadelphia: The Jewish Publication Society of America, 1976).

Michael Löwy, *Rédemption et Utopie: Le Judaïsme Libertaire en Europe Centrale: Une Étude d'Affinité Élective* (Paris: Presses Universitaires de France, 1988).

—— 'Messianism in the Early Work of Gershom Scholem', *New German Critique*, 83 (2001), 177–191.

Geret Luhr (ed.), *'Was noch begraben lag': Zu Walter Benjamins Exil. Briefe und Dokumente* (Berlin: Bostelmann & Siebenhaar, 2000).

Ludger Lütkehaus, 'Der Philologe als Mystiker inkognito: Gershom Scholems Tagebücher 1917–1923', in *Neue Zürcher Zeitung*, 10 April 2001.

Moses Maimonides, *The Guide for the Perplexed*, translated and edited by M. Friedländer, second edition (New York: Dover Publications, 1956).

Shulamith S. Magnus, 'German Jewish History', *Modern Judaism*, 11 (1991), 125–146.

Hans Mayer, *Der Widerruf: Über Deutsche und Juden* (Frankfurt am Main: Suhrkamp, 1994).

John McCole, *Walter Benjamin and the Antinomies of Tradition* (Ithaca: Cornell University Press, 1993).

Paul Mendes-Flohr (ed.), *Gershom Scholem: The Man and His Work* (New York: SUNY Press, 1994).

Bettine Menke, *Sprachfiguren: Name – Allegorie – Bild nach Walter Benjamin* (München: Wilhelm Fink, 1991).

Winfried Menninghaus, *Walter Benjamins Theorie der Sprachmagie* (Frankfurt am Main: Suhrkamp, 1980).

Bram Mertens, 'The Anxiety of Influence: Walter Benjamin, Gershom Scholem and Franz Joseph Molitor', in *Millenial Essays on Film and other German Studies*, edited by Daniela Berghahn and Alan Bance (Oxford: Peter Lang, 2002), 128–141.

267

—— '"This Still Remarkable Book": Franz Joseph Molitor's Judaeo-Christian Synthesis', *Journal for Modern Jewish Studies*, vol. 1 (2), 2002, 167–181.

—— '"The True Words of the Mystic": Gershom Scholem and Franz Joseph Molitor', *Australian Journal of Jewish Studies*, vol. 17, 2003, 131–153.

—— 'The Arcades Project: A Talmud for our Times?', *New Formations*, vol. 54, 2005, 60–73.

—— '"Hope, yes, but not for us": Messianism and Redemption in the Work of Walter Benjamin', in *Messianism, Apocalypse and Redemption in Twentieth-century German Thought*, edited by Wayne Cristaudo and Wendy Baker (Adelaide: ATF Press, 2006), 63–77.

Henri Meschonnic, 'L'Allégorie chez Walter Benjamin, une Aventure Juive', in Passages: Walter Benjamin et Paris, edited by Heinz Wismann (Paris: Cerf, 1986), 705–741.

Michael Meyer, 'The Emergence of Jewish Historiography: Motives and Motifs', *History and Theory*, 27:4 (1988), 160–175.

—— (ed.), *Deutsch-jüdische Geschichte in der Neuzeit* (München: Beck, 2000).

Franz Joseph Molitor, *Ideen zu einer künftigen Dynamik der Geschichte* (Frankfurt am Main: Bernhard Körner, 1805).

—— *Der Wendepunkt des Antiken und Modernen oder Versuch den Realismus mit dem Idealismus zu Versöhnen* (Frankfurt am Main: J.C.B. Mohr, 1805).

—— *Ueber Bürgerliche Erziehung mit Beziehung auf die Organisation des jüdischen Schulwesens in Frankfurt am Main* (Frankfurt am Main: J.C.B. Mohr, 1808).

—— *Philosophie der Geschichte oder über die Tradition in dem alten Bunde und ihre Beziehung zur Kirche des Neuen Bundes. Mit vorzüglicher Rücksicht auf die Kabbalah*, first edition, 4 vols. (Frankfurt am Main/Münster: Hermann/Theissing, 1827–1853).

—— *Philosophie der Geschichte oder über die Tradition in dem alten Bunde und ihre Beziehung zur Kirche des Neuen Bundes: Erster Theil, Zweite, neu bearbeitete und vermehrte Auflage*, second edition (Münster: Theissing, 1857).

Stéphane Mosès, 'L'Idée d'Origine chez Walter Benjamin', in *Passages: Walter Benjamin et Paris*, edited by Heinz Wismann (Paris: Cerf, 1986), 809–826.

—— 'Brecht und Benjamin als Kafka-Interpreten', in *Juden in der deutschen Literatur: ein deutsch-israelisches Symposion*, edited by Stéphane

Mosès and Albrecht Schöne (Frankfurt am Main: Suhrkamp, 1986), 237–256.

—— *L'Ange de l'Histoire: Rosenzweig, Benjamin, Scholem* (Paris: Seuil, 1992).

Stéphane Mosès and Sigrid Weigel (eds.), *Gershom Scholem: Literatur und Rhetorik* (Köln: Böhlau, 2000).

George Mosse, 'Gershom Scholem as a German Jew', *Modern Judaism*, 10:2 (1990), 117–133.

Bernd Müller, *Denn es ist noch nichts geschehen. Walter Benjamins Kafka-Deutung* (Köln: Böhlau, 1999).

Rainer Nägele, 'Benjamin's Ground', in *Benjamin's Ground: New Readings of Walter Benjamin*, edited by Rainer Nägele (Detroit: Wayne State University Press, 1988), 19–37.

—— 'Das Beben der Barock in der Moderne: Walter Benjamins Monadologie', *Modern Language Notes*, 106 (1991), 501–527.

Jacob Neusner, 'The Study of Religion as the Study of Tradition: Judaism', *History of Religions*, 14 (1975), 191–206.

—— 'A Rabbinic Theory of Language?', *Journal of the American Academy of Religion*, 56 (1988), 762–763.

—— (ed.), *The Christian and Judaic Invention of History*, AAR Studies in Religion, vol. 55 (Atlanta, Georgia: Scholars Press, 1990).

—— *Rabbinic Judaism: Structure and System* (Minneapolis: Fortress Press, 1995).

Jürgen Nieraad, 'Walter Benjamins Glück im Untergang: Zum Verhältnis von Messianischem und Profanem', *The German Quarterly* 63:2 (1990), 222–232.

Friedrich Nietzsche, *Kritische Studienausgabe*, 15 vols., edited by Giorgio Colli and Mazzino Montinari (Berlin/ München: de Gruyter/Deutscher Taschenbuch-verlag, 1988).

William O.E. Oesterley and George H. Box, *A Short Survey of the Literature of Rabbinical and Medieval Judaism* (London: Society for Promoting Christian Knowledge, 1920).

Michael Opitz and Erdmut Wizisla (eds.), *Aber ein Sturm Weht vom Paradiese Her: Texte zu Walter Benjamin* (Leipzig: Reclam, 1992).

—— (eds.) *Benjamins Begriffe,* 2 vols. (Frankfurt am Main: Suhrkamp, 2000).

Johannes Pedersen, *Israel: Its Life and Culture*, 2 vols., translated by Aslaug Møller (London: Oxford University Press, 1926–1940).

Jaroslav Pelikan, *The Christian Tradition: A History of the Development of Doctrine*, 5 vols. (Chicago: The University of Chicago Press, 1975–1991)

John Pizer, *Toward a Theory of Radical Origin: Essays on Modern German Thought* (Lincoln: University of Nebraska Press, 1995).

Andreas Polterman and Emil Sander, 'Rede im Exil: Theologische Momente im Werk Walter Benjamins', in *'Kritische Theorie' zwischen Theologie und Evolutionslehre*, edited by Wilfried Kunstmann and Emil Sander (München: Wilhelm Fink, 1981), 23–85.

Hans Puttnies and Gary Smith, *Benjaminiana: eine biographische Recherche* (Giessen: Anabas, 1991)

Anson Rabinbach, 'Critique and Commentary / Alchemy and Chemistry: Some Remarks on Walter Benjamin and this Special Issue', *New German Critique*, 17 (1979), 3–14.

—— 'Between Enlightenment and Apocalypse: Benjamin, Bloch and Modern German Jewish Messianism', *New German Critique*, 34 (1985), 78–124.

—— *In the Shadow of Catastrophe: German Intellectuals between Apocalypse and Enlightenment* (Berkeley: University of California Press, 1997).

Rainer Rochlitz, *The Disenchantment of Art: the Philosophy of Walter Benjamin*, translated by Jane Marie Todd (New York: the Guilford Press, 1996).

Gillian Rose, *Judaism and Modernity: Philosophical Essays* (Oxford: Blackwell, 1993).

Franz Rosenzweig, *Der Stern der Erlösung* (Frankfurt am Main: Suhrkamp, 1995).

Peter Ruch, 'Biblische Texte als Erzählungen: Von Walter Benjamin Theologisch Lernen', in *Schweizer Monatshefte*, 71.12 (1991), 979–983.

Norbert M. Samuelson, 'Tradition from a Jewish Perspective', *Toronto Journal of Theology*, 9.1 (1993), 27–50.

Hans-Jörg Sandkühler, *Freiheit und Wirklichkeit: Zur Dialektik von Politik und Philosophie bei Schelling* (Frankfurt am Main: Suhrkamp, 1968).

John F.A. Sawyer, 'Root-Meanings in Hebrew', *Journal of Semitic Studies*, 12 (1967), 37–51.

Peter Schäfer and Gary Smith (eds.), *Gershom Scholem: Zwischen den Disziplinen* (Frankfurt am Main: Suhrkamp, 1989).

Christoph Schmidt, 'Zum Fall Benjamin: Benjamin als jüdischer Theologe?', *Revue de Métaphysique et de Morale*, 90/3 (1985), 405–415.

Gershom Scholem, *Ursprung und Anfänge der Kabbala* (Berlin: Walter de Gruyter, 1962).

—— *Judaica I* (Frankfurt am Main: Suhrkamp, 1963).

—— *Judaica II* (Frankfurt am Main: Suhrkamp, 1970).

—— *Über einige Grundbegriffe des Judentums* (Frankfurt am Main: Suhrkamp, 1970).

—— *Judaica III: Studien zur jüdischen Mystik* (Frankfurt am Main: Suhrkamp, 1973).

—— *Sabbatai Sevi: the Mystical Messiah*, translated by R. Zwi Werblowski (Princeton: Princeton University Press, 1973).

—— *Walter Benjamin: Die Geschichte einer Freundschaft* (Frankfurt am Main; Suhrkamp, 1975).

—— Die jüdische Mystik in ihren Hauptströmungen (Frankfurt am Main: Suhrkamp, 1980).

—— *Walter Benjamin und sein Engel: Vierzehn Aufsätze und kleine Beiträge* (Frankfurt am Main: Suhrkamp, 1983).

—— *Judaica IV*, edited by Rolf Tiedemann (Frankfurt am Main: Suhrkamp, 1984).

—— *Judaica V: Erlösung durch Sünde*, edited and translated by Michael Brocke (Frankfurt am Main: Suhrkamp, 1992).

—— Von der mystischen Gestalt der Gottheit: Studien zu Grundbegriffen der Kabbalah (Frankfurt am Main: Suhrkamp, 1995).

—— *Judaica IV: Die Wissenschaft vom Judentum*, edited and translated by Peter Schäfer (Frankfurt am Main: Suhrkamp, 1997).

—— *Von Berlin nach Jerusalem: Jugenderinnerungen*, translated by Michael Brocke and Andrea Schatz (Frankfurt am Main: Suhrkamp, 1997).

—— *Zur Kabbala und ihrer Symbolik* (Frankfurt am Main: Suhrkamp, 1998).

—— *Briefe*, 3 vols., edited by Itta Shedletzky (München: Beck, 1994–1999).

—— *Tagebücher nebst Aufsätzen und Entwürfen bis 1923*, 2 vols., edited by Karlfried Gründer und Friedrich Niewöhner (Frankfurt am Main: Jüdischer Verlag, 1995–2000).

—— *"Es gibt ein Geheimnis in der Welt": Tradition und Säkularisation*, edited by Itta Shedletzky (Frankfurt am Main: Jüdischer Verlag, 2002).

Gershom Scholem and Betty Scholem, *Mutter und Sohn im Briefwechsel 1917–1946*, edited by Itta Shedletzky and Thomas Sparr (München: Beck, 1989).

Albrecht Schöne, "'Diese nach jüdischem Vorbild erbaute Arche": Walter Benjamins Deutsche Menschen', in *Juden in der deutschen Literatur: ein deutsch-israelisches Symposion*, edited by Stéphane Mosès and Albrecht Schöne (Frankfurt am Main: Suhrkamp, 1986), 350–365.

Christoph Schulte, "'Die Buchstaben haben… ihre Wurzeln oben." Scholem und Molitor', in *Kabbala und Romantik*, edited by Eveline Goodmann-Thau, Gerd Mattenklott and Christoph Schulte (Tübingen: Max Niemeyer, 1994), 143–164.

—— 'Franz Joseph Molitors Philosophie des Judentums', *Menora: Jahrbuch für deutsch-jüdische Geschichte*, 6 (1995), 47–64.

—— 'La philosophie du judaïsme de Franz Joseph Molitor', in *La Philosophie Allemande dans la Pensée Juive*, edited by Gérard Bensussan (Paris: Presses Universitaires de France, 1997), 83–94.

Hermann Schweppenhäuser, *Ein Physiognom der Dinge: Aspekte des Benjaminschen Denkens* (Lüneburg: Dietrich zu Klampen, 1992).

Phillip Sigal, *Judaism: the Evolution of a Faith*, edited by Lillian Sigal (Grand Rapids: William B. Eerdmans, 1988).

Colette Sirat, *A History of Jewish Philosophy in the Middle Ages* (Cambridge: Cambridge University Press, 1996).

Lev Shestov, *Athens and Jerusalem*, translated by Bernard Martin (Athens: Ohio University Press, 1966).

Gary Smith, "'Das Jüdische versteht sich von selbst": Walter Benjamins frühe Auseinandersetzung mit dem Judentum', *Deutsche Vierteljahresschrift*, 65/4 (1991), 318–334.

Günter Stemberger, *Introduction to the Talmud and Midrash*, translated and edited by Markus Bockmuehl (Edinburgh: T. & T. Clark, 1996).

David Stern, 'Midrash and Indeterminacy', *Critical Inquiry*, 15/1 (1988), 132–161.

—— *Midrash and Theory: Ancient Jewish Exegesis and Contemporary Literary Studies* (Evanston: Northwestern University Press, 1996).

Jacob Taubes, 'Walter Benjamin: ein moderner Marcionit?: Scholems Benjamin-Interpretation religionsgeschichtlich überprüft', in *Antike und Moderne: Zu Walter Benjamins 'Passagen'*, edited by Norbert Bolz and Richard Faber (Würzburg: Königshausen & Neumann, 1986), 138–147.

Claude Tresmontant, *A Study of Hebrew Thought*, translated by Michael Francis Gibbon (New York – Tournai – Paris – Rome: Desclee, 1960).

Horst Turk, 'Politische Theologie?: Zur "Intention auf die Sprache" bei Benjamin und Celan', in *Juden in der deutschen Literatur: ein deutsch-israelisches Symposion,* edited by Stéphane Mosès and Albrecht Schöne (Frankfurt am Main: Suhrkamp, 1986), 330–349.

John W.M. Verhaar (ed.), *The Verb 'Be' and Its Synonyms: Philosophical and Grammatical Studies, Foundations of Language: Supplementary Series, vol. 16: The Verb 'Be' in Ancient Greek,* by Charles H. Kahn (Dordrecht: Reidel, 1973).

Williston Walker, *A History of the Christian Church,* fourth edition, edited by Richard A. Norris, David W. Lotz and Robert T. Hardy (Edinburgh: T. & T. Clark, 1997).

Steven Wasserstrom, *Religion after Religion: Gershom Scholem, Mircea Eliade and Henry Corbin at Eranos* (Princeton: Princeton University Press, 1999).

Samuel Weber, 'Lecture de Benjamin', *Critique,* 267–268 (1969), 699–712.

Daniel Weidner, 'Jüdisches Gedächtnis, mystische Tradition und moderne Literatur: Walter Benjamin und Gershom Scholem deuten Kafka', *Weimarer Beiträge,* 46:2 (2000), 234–249.

—— *Gershom Scholem: politisches, esoterisches und historiographisches Schreiben* (München: Wilhelm Fink, 2003).

Leon Weiseltier, '*Etwas über die jüdische Historik:* Leopold Zunz and the Inception of Modern Jewish Historiography', *History and Theory,* Vol. 20, No. 2. (May, 1981), 135–149.

R.J. Zwi Werblowsky and Geoffrey Wigoder (eds.), *The Oxford Dictionary of the Jewish Religion* (Oxford: Oxford University Press, 1997).

Bernd Witte, *Walter Benjamin – Der Intellektuelle als Kritiker: Untersuchungen zu seinem Frühwerk* (Stuttgart: Metzler, 1976).

—— '"Die Welt allseitiger und integraler Aktualität": die Säkularisierung jüdischer Motive in Walter Benjamins Denken', in *Der Deutschunterricht,* 37:3 (1985), 26–37.

—— 'Allegorien des Schreibens: eine Lektüre von Walter Benjamins Trauerspielbuch', in *Merkur,* 46:2 (1992), 125–136.

Ludwig Wittgenstein, *Werkausgabe Band I: Tractatus Logico-philosophicus, Tagebücher 1914–1916, Philosophische Untersuchungen,* edited by Joachim Schulte (Frankfurt am Main: Suhrkamp, 1993).

Irving Wohlfarth, 'On the Messianic Structure of Walter Benjamin's Last Reflections', *Glyph,* 3 (1978), 148–212.

—— 'No-Man's-Land: On Walter Benjamin's "Destructive Character"', *Diacritics,* June (1978), 47–65.

—— 'Walter Benjamin's Image of Interpretation', *New German Critique,* 17 (1979), 70–98.

—— 'History, Literature and the Text: the Case of Walter Benjamin', *Modern Language Notes*, 96:5 (1981), 1002–1014.

—— 'Re-fusing Theology: Some First Responses to Walter Benjamin's Arcades Project', *New German Critique*, 39 (1986), 3–24.

—— '"Immer radikal, niemals konsequent...": Zur theologisch-politischen Standortsbestimmung Walter Benjamins', in *Antike und Moderne: Zu Walter Benjamins 'Passagen'*, edited by Norbert Bolz and Richard Faber (Würzburg: Königshausen & Neumann, 1986), 116–137.

—— 'On Some Jewish Motifs in Benjamin', in *The Problems of Modernity: Adorno & Benjamin*, edited by Andrew Benjamin (London: Routledge, 1992), 157–215.

—— '"Männer aus der Fremde": Walter Benjamin and the German-Jewish Parnassus', *New German Critique*, 70 (1997), 3–85.

Bernhard Wunder, *Konstruktion und Rezeption der Theologie Walter Benjamins: These I und das 'Theologisch-politische Fragment'* (Würzburg: Königshausen & Neumann, 1997).

Leopold Zunz, *Die gottesdienstlichen Vorträge der Juden historisch entwickelt*, second edition (Hildesheim: Georg Holms Verlagsbuchhandlung, 1966).

Index

Studies in German Jewish History

Peter D. G. Brown, SUNY New Paltz
General Editor